THE CURTAIN RISES

****

The
Curtain
Rises

By QUENTIN REYNOLDS

****

RANDOM HOUSE · NEW YORK

Second Printing

THIS IS A RANDOM HOUSE WARTIME BOOK

THE TEXT IS COMPLETE AND UNABRIDGED, BUT EVERY
EFFORT HAS BEEN MADE TO COMPLY WITH THE GOV-
ERNMENT'S REQUEST TO CONSERVE ESSENTIAL MATERIALS

Published simultaneously in Canada by
The Macmillan Company of Canada Limited

DESIGNED BY WARREN CHAPPELL

MANUFACTURED IN THE UNITED STATES OF AMERICA
BY THE HADDON CRAFTSMEN, INC., SCRANTON, PA.

*

———

TO THE WAR CORRESPONDENTS OF AMERICA,

LIVING AND DEAD,

WHO HAVE PROVEN TO THE WORLD THAT YOU CAN

BELIEVE WHAT YOU READ IN THE NEWSPAPERS—

GREAT REPORTERS, GREAT AMERICANS,

GREAT FRIENDS

———

*

TABLE OF CONTENTS

*
———

THE CURTAIN RISES

———
*

✳✳✳✳✳✳✳✳✳✳✳✳✳✳✳✳✳✳✳✳✳✳✳✳

Chapter 1

COME ON ALONG

IT WAS NICE drifting along on the slow waves that only broke when they hit the hard white sand. The sun splashed golden tints on the white buildings that lined the beach. It was easy to shut your eyes and close your ears and live for the moment in a dream world in which there were no guns, no malaria, no long dreary plane trips—no need ever to leave home. But of course you can remain under the spell of a dream only so long.

There were nearly 100,000 air force boys in training at Miami Beach and when they marched along Collins Avenue just behind the beach they sang. Their young voices raised in the Air Force Song insinuated themselves into your consciousness and you couldn't shut them out. And when they finished by shouting the last line:

And nothing'll stop the Army Air Corps
(Except the women)
Nothing'll stop the Army Air Corps . . .

[3]

you realized that there was no use hiding in the blue water any more; no use dreaming dreams that belonged to another world that had come to an end.

The first time you leave for the war zone it is exciting. You are anxious to get going. You chafe at delay and think that the war will be over before you ever get off. You are eager and impatient and you have plans for writing dozens of wonderful stories. It's like that the first time. When you go back for the fourth time it's quite different. You hate to answer the phone, fearing that a cheerful voice will say, "You leave tomorrow." You don't look forward to it. You've known the misery of malaria and dysentery, and you've known the sickening fear that hits your stomach when the air is cleaved by a heavy bomb or when a shell screams over your head. You've known the horrible boredom of war and the dull ache of homesickness and the dreary arguments with censors.

We'd been at Miami a week, and it was a good week to remember. We'd danced and sipped beautiful drinks and played roulette. If there was a war going on somewhere, the only reminders of it were the uniforms on the streets and the singing of clear young voices.

I'd been waiting for a plane bound toward Russia. "I don't believe I'll ever go," I said lazily, from out of the depths of a beach chair. "I can't believe there's a war on anywhere. I've been over there three times. . . . I don't have to go again. . . . What can I accomplish by going over again?"

There was no answer. I leaned back in the chair, feeling sorry for myself. A boy came up and said that there was a phone call for me. I went to the phone on the terrace of the hotel. A cheerful voice said, "This is Captain Blackman at the airport. I've got good news for you. You're off tonight in a lovely C-54. I'll send a car for you at six. Have you had your yellow fever shots?"

"Yeah," I said without enthusiasm, "and also smallpox vac-

"I think they misspelled 'hereon' in that accreditization card," I told him.

"It's spelled h-e-r-e-o-n," he said, puzzled. "That's right, isn't it?"

"It doesn't look right to me. Maybe it is right. I can't spell very well. It looks like there's one too many e's in the word. But I just spell by ear, so forget it."

"It doesn't look right at that," he said thoughtfully.

"Well, let's not bother the War Department with it now," I told him.

"I'm sorry we can't let visitors in here," he said suddenly. "You know how it is—army rules."

Sure I knew. I've been living under army rules ever since the war began. French Army rules, then British Army rules, then Russian Army rules—now American Army rules.

"I'm afraid your baggage is fifteen pounds overweight," he said.

"I always figure my typewriter as hand baggage," I told him, as I'd told airport officials for nearly four years. "I carry that with me. And this brief case—there's nothing in it but copy paper and carbons and extra typewriter ribbons and pencils. I figure that's hand baggage, see? Still, if I'm wrong, open my bag and toss out the top fifteen pounds. I don't care—honestly."

"It's a big plane," he smiled, and I felt a louse because I'd been surly and mean with him.

Then Captain Blackman came up and said, "I can see why you weren't in any hurry to leave. Look, let me take care of this baggage and sign you in and all that nonsense. The ship leaves in ten minutes. You got time to say good-bye."

I said, "Thanks, Captain." There was an understanding right guy. I went outside and we said good-bye casually, and I said, "I'll be back in three months—maybe sooner." I knew that I was lying in my teeth, and she knew it too but made be-

[7]

lieve that she didn't, and suddenly I thought of the thousands of Americans who were saying good-bye as I was and it was a lot tougher on them because if I got fed up or sick or hurt I could tell *Collier's* I wanted to come home and *Collier's* was always good about things like that. I felt a little ashamed because those others couldn't go to their officers and say, "How about home? I've had enough." They couldn't do that and I could. So what was I putting on such an act for anyhow? I wasn't Horatio going off to defend a bridge. I wasn't Tony Basilone or Mickey Maguire or Joe Smith off to God-knows-where for God-knows-how-long with God-knows-what-chance of ever getting back alive. I might never even hear a gun fired in anger. I was a correspondent, a well-paid correspondent, off to write some stories in Russia and Iran and maybe China and India or North Africa. I wasn't Sergeant York, for God's sake. Me? I had the best job in the world. I'd always thought that until this night.

I belong to a good profession, a profession begun by a few very excellent reporters named Matthew, Mark, Luke and John. Some great reporter in Genesis told the story of the creation of the world in 400 words and there are only 297 words in the Ten Commandments. That is great reporting. The Gospels are still the best reporting jobs ever done. The world would never have known much about Christ if it hadn't been for those reporters. Today each Sunday we read the stories they wrote 1,900 years ago and those stories will be read 19,000 years from now. Christ never left a written line. We only know him through the eyes of the reporters of his time.

I thought of this as the engines roared and the wheels of our big C-54 dug into the black moonlit concrete of the runway. The engines weren't loud; some kind of sound-proofing had been done to the interior of this plane. I decided we must have a distinguished passenger aboard to be given one of these lovely ships. I looked around and saw a general across the aisle. I'd met him before, General Edgar Glenn. We had about thirty men in uniform with us, technicians, I learned later, bound for various jobs in Africa and China and India.

"Are we off the ground yet?" one of the less air-minded lads in uniform asked.

"If we aren't," General Glenn said dryly, peering out of the small window, "they've played a dirty trick on us. Our wheels are up."

The lights of Miami twinkled beneath us and then we passed over the coast line, and below us the breakers curled lazily over each other against the beach and then the lights of the city faded and we were free from the land. The enormous plane hummed evenly through the night. The engines really seemed to be purring. Most of the others slept, but I can never sleep in a plane. I read a detective story and watched the Caribbean night change color until its dark shades lightened and a huge, fiery sun arose from the sea and it was dawn. I hadn't bothered to ask where we were headed or in what direction. I just didn't care much.

We found land, a jungle-like land, and hummed smoothly over evil-looking swamps and then there was a huge clearing fringed with long brown huts and we alighted in a place called Trinidad. In peace days Trinidad was a pleasant place to break the monotony of the long cruise to Rio. Trinidad as a steady diet for American lads from Brooklyn, Chicago, or Atlanta is something else again. The airport where we stopped to refuel is far from the town of Port-of-Spain. and the men stationed there have to fashion a life for themselves. The weather ahead wasn't good and the Air Transport Command crew, meticulous in their observance of safety factors, said we wouldn't leave. We wouldn't leave until the next morning. I found an old friend, Captain Mahlon Meier, at the airfield. He showed me around the camp. The hospital interested me especially. I had gotten a terrible sunburn in Miami and the doctor made me take off my shirt and take some treatment. He smeared some evil-smelling ointment on the burn and immediately the sting went out of it. "Irishmen are allergic to sun, I guess," he said sadly.

"Mally" Meier and I had gone to college together and we had a lot to talk about. He told how the army did its best to relieve the monotony of the jungle existence.

Occasionally, there was a break in the rather dull routine of from ten to eighteen working hours a day. This break was usually furnished by much-maligned Hollywood. Three times a week there were motion pictures, and each picture was preceded by the announcement on the screen: "This film donated to the War Department without cost by the Motion Picture Industry of America."

These were not tired old pictures of another day; they were the films you see in first-run picture houses. And very occasionally some unit of movie stars came to Trinidad to give the men some "live entertainment."

The day I arrived, the station was agog with excitement. Pat O'Brien was in Trinidad. I went to see him perform that night. O'Brien stayed on the stage for two hours. He told every gag and sang every song he knew, and when sheer exhaustion forced him to stop, the men arose and cheered for eight minutes. O'Brien stumbled into the wings of the theater and collapsed. His face was drawn; he had lost twenty pounds since I'd seen him three weeks before in New York. He had been giving three and four shows a day and flying anywhere the Air Transport Command had asked him to go. I told him he'd better take a rest, and the Irishman laughed.

"These guys here don't get much rest," he said wearily. "Those guys at Guadalcanal don't get much chance to rest, do they? What right have we civilians to rest? I'll give a show anywhere, any time, as long as two kids in uniform ask for me."

"Do you know what day this is, Pat?" I asked him, and when he shook his head tiredly, I reminded him that it was March 17th.

"St. Patrick's Day!" he yelled. "Glory be! What are we waiting for? If only that Jim Cagney were with us now!"

And so we found a few soldiers who were Irish and we did what Irishmen have done on St. Patrick's Day for hundreds of years—we celebrated. The night out did Pat a lot of good. The next day he took off on a 1,000-mile flight somewhere else, full of energy and with the worn look gone from his eyes.

There was a beach not far away, and in the afternoon there were always a thousand or so very scantily clad pilots, mechanics and ground men riding the surf on blown-up rubber mattresses, the local substitute for surfboards.

We stayed at Trinidad the night and then we hopped off on the next lap, an 1,800-mile jaunt, which the beautiful Douglas took in her stride like the thoroughbred she is.

Natal in Brazil was our destination. Natal is the jumping-off place, and it is one of the few bases which one can name. It is not vulnerable to enemy attack. At Natal, celebrities are as common as mangoes, and mangoes adorn every table of every mess.

Generals and presidents and the wives of generalissimos all pass through Natal on their way to China or India, Casablanca or Russia. All cargo sent abroad sifts through Natal, and thousands of American youngsters load and service the departing planes as casually as they filled up your car with gasoline in peacetime.

Thousands and thousands of pounds of cargo leave each day from Natal, bound for wherever Americans fight. The promises we heard a year ago were fulfilled here at Natal.

Converted transport planes, which were built to carry 20,000 pounds and now carry 30,000 pounds, fly in a steady and increasing stream from Natal across the South Atlantic, bringing American war material into battle.

There are no hangars at Natal, although you'll usually find more than 200 aircraft on the ground. Planes don't stay long enough at Natal to use hangars. Even major repairs, such as changing an engine, are done in the open by men who have had years of training with Pan American, Eastern, TWA or other American lines. These are the best mechanics in the world. They will strip an engine and put it together again as quickly as you would a vacuum cleaner.

From Natal, you take the big jump across the pond. Again, this is a routine flight but it is not without hazard. There are submarines in the South Atlantic; submarines with anti-air-craft guns mounted on their decks. More than one plane has fallen victim to their fire. But we fly high over the South Atlantic.

If you are a passenger and not a pilot who has made the trip fifty times, such a flight can never be routine. You fly at night, and the heat of South America recedes, and the cool breezes that come from far, far south of the equator infiltrate the cabin. The moon is high and the night is studded with stars and, far below, the sea is a velvet carpet, calm and serene. The beauty of the night prevents you from sleeping.

Finally the night goes to sleep, star by star, and a golden dawn emerges from the horizon, bringing another day to you. Suddenly the airplane banks sharply to the right and circles and, with visions of submarines, you wonder what it is all about. We circle and come down, and a co-pilot comes back to point out a swirling mass of bubbling water below us. "Thought it might be a plane in trouble or a submarine," he explains laughingly, "but it's only a school of flying fish." Millions of them leap above the surface, and the water boils and then, caught by the shafts of the sun, cascades in shimmering golden masses. Then there is land ahead. Henceforth, home security enters the picture, and we can neither write nor mention the names of the various bases operated by the Air Transport Command in Central Africa. We land at a large base which the men call Bushtown. We land, feeling a little as Balboa must have felt when he first sighted the Pacific. We feel self-important and adventurous as we step from the big plane and set foot on African soil. But our exultation is short-lived.

A sergeant and his crew take over the ship and we hear him call to his men, "Get this crate serviced in a hurry. We got a million planes coming in here today."

He had exaggerated a little. I stood on the airport nearly an hour, and planes were constantly circling, waiting their turn to land; planes which had also performed this casual miracle of crossing the South Atlantic without incident.

The colonel in charge assigns us to barracks. "You will find four or five houseboys there," he told us. "Give them your laundry and have them press your clothes, if you wish. And we have no locks on our doors here. These boys are honest. No one here has ever missed so much as a toothbrush."

The smiling, ebony-skinned lads who receive us are immaculately clean, and so are the quarters we are given. We sleep three in a room under mosquito netting. American Army doctors unquestionably lead the world in the field of preventive medicine. Actually, mosquitoes aren't very common in this particular part of Central Africa, but those which are here are the nasty malaria-carrying type. And so every man must sleep under mosquito netting, and there are signs warning the men not to attend the evening picture show without wearing mosquito boots. For some reason, these local mosquitoes have a weakness for ankles, and shin-high boots frustrate them completely.

Americans, even American soldiers, are tourists at heart, and every Sunday hundreds of our men climb into trucks and go far into the "bush" to see native life. They are startled by the wild, lush beauty of the interior. Bananas, mangoes, alligator pears (a penny apiece) and plantains hang from trees. Occasionally, the jungle colors its drabness with the violent red and purple of bougainvillaea, roses and strange local flowers.

The Central African is a smiling, friendly, trusting person, and he frankly loves the robust humor and good nature of the American soldier or pilot who will give him a penny just to pose for a picture. In the jungle, natives wear clothes only to attend church on Sunday, and today the mails bound for home are laden with pictures of undraped local belles, which may cause consternation among the men's parents and wives who receive them. The consternation, if any, may be dismissed.

Men and pilots at these African bases do not work by the clock. Whenever planes come in, men are ready to unload or service them. Each base has gasoline (buried underground) ready for the tremendous stream of air traffic that flows through here. Because most of the bases are far removed from cities, the men have to carve a life out of the jungle for themselves. American ingenuity has been equal to the task.

In one jungle base, almost every officer owns a saddle horse. Natives bring them in, and much bargaining takes place before a horse and saddle change hands. The average price is about twenty dollars. Men don't have much else to spend money on.

The post exchange gives them cigarettes for fifty cents a carton. They get American canned beer at many bases for half what we pay at home. They spend a good deal of time souvenir hunting, buying native cloth and juju charms which, the natives insist, ward off everything from malaria to the evil eye.

The route across Africa was originally pioneered by three brilliant Pan American pilots. George Kraigher, John Yeomans and Henry Kristofferson (all colonels now) were responsible. Then a shotgun wedding took place between the commercial lines and our army. The marriage was more successful than most such unions. Army discipline complemented Pan American efficiency beautifully, and today there is no doubt that this combination has resulted in the greatest transport organization ever put together. ATC personnel gave most of the credit to Brigadier General C. R. Smith.

The three flying pioneers and many of their colleagues in other commercial companies were taken over by the army and they immediately went to work. They commandeered airports, operation buildings and barracks. The limited Pan American personnel in Africa had to be enormously enlarged. New bases had to be carved out of the jungle. A thousand problems not directly concerned with flying cropped up.

One fine airport, for instance, which Pan American operated, was excellent in every respect except that the only available water had to be pumped from 300 feet below ground. In the jungle you make your own power, and it couldn't be spared to pump up the amount of water which would be needed by hundreds and hundreds of men every day.

The three trail blazers found a spot six miles from the airport, where clear, pure water lay only thirty feet below the surface. In no time at all, roads had been built, barracks, messrooms, offices and storehouses had sprung up. The jungle receded reluctantly but inevitably, and today hundreds of your sons are living well, eating as well as you do at home and, within the admitted limitations of rigid army existence, thoroughly enjoying life. Sure, they'd rather be home, but you don't hear many complaints from them. They're doing a tough and important job; they are conscious of this and they go about it gravely and conscientiously.

This particular base was unique in that it boasted a miniature zoo. The boys bought two leopard cubs from some natives. The leopards, eight months old, had grown so large that they were no longer allowed to wander about the mess halls or barracks. They were kept in a wooden cage, but they were still friendly and eagerly ate bananas or bits of meat salvaged from the dinner table and fed to them by hand.

The base also had a pet giraffe about nine feet high, three tame gazelles raised since fawnhood, and an ostrich which turned out to be a bit of a sissy. The ostrich was afraid of the jungle and insisted upon spending all its time in the barracks. No one yet has found a way to teach the ostrich the lessons which puppies usually learn in a few weeks, and this complicated matters no end.

Even at this secluded airport, the men had three movies a week. Anyone who thinks that the picture industry is non-essential should hear the shrieks of delight with which our men greet the tri-weekly showing.

There was a radio here, too, and the entertainment programs were listened to avidly. Bob Hope, Jack Benny and Bing Crosby were the favorites. Although the boys get no newspapers, they are strangely apathetic toward our American news commentators, and shouts of "Take him off" usually greet the pontifical tones of some man to whom millions of you at home listen avidly. The boys seem to prefer the BBC, which merely broadcasts the communiques without comment.

Native black troops, British-trained, have been assigned

to our commanding officers to serve as guards. At night they stand watch at the airports. They are instructed to challenge anyone who approaches the airport or the planes. If the answer is not satisfactory they have orders to shoot. Our men found out very quickly that these natives obeyed orders very literally. To escape the terrific heat of the jungle or desert, planes often take off before dawn. It is not especially reassuring to approach the airport and be greeted by the sight of tall, black, sinister-looking men who point bayonets at you and cry "Halt!" The young pilots will yell, "Abokina"—which means "I am your friend"—even before the challenge is given. This is the first word our boys learn in Central Africa.

Most of Central Africa is run by the British. Our men invite the British soldiers and airmen to their films, and the British reciprocate by having our men in to tea or to shows they put on themselves.

One morning I was in the office of Colonel Frank Collins, Chief of Staff at a large installation in Africa. Lord Swinton, Minister to the British Mandated Territories in Africa, was on the phone. He was having some important guests to dinner and he wondered if the commanding officer couldn't spare three pounds of that good American butter.

"Of course I can," the American colonel said. "And by the way, Lord Swinton, I'm a little short of cement and need some to finish a new runway. Could you perhaps spare about three tons of your excellent British cement?"

"Of course I can," Lord Swinton agreed. "I'll exchange a ton of cement for a pound of butter any day!"

The two young pilots who flew our big Douglas across Africa were named Pat and Mike. Captain Pat Passage and Lieutenant Mike Fada seemed to know every tree in the jungle, every grain of sand in the desert. Pat became famous in air-force circles a year ago when he crowded seventy-three Burmese refugees into his DC-3 and flew them to safety. The load of a DC-3 is 27,000 pounds. On that occasion, Pat had to lift 34,000 pounds off the short runway. He did it easily.

"Those Burmese are very small," he says, dismissing the incident. "So I just piled them on top of one another."

What would have been a miracle of transportation two years ago is now something which the Air Transport Command accomplishes dozens of times a day with monotonous regularity.

During the past three years, I have been with every allied navy, army and air force. But never have I seen displayed the efficiency, the high morale of personnel, the technical perfection which characterized the work of our Air Transport Command. One expects it at the established airports of Miami, or Natal in South America. But one finds it, too, in the jungles and deserts of Central Africa where engines are changed and cracked cylinders are replaced just as quickly as such major repair jobs are done at LaGuardia Field. And the thousands of pilots and ground men, who stretch from Miami through Trinidad down the coast of South America, who span the South Atlantic and now billet in large and small airports across Africa, are all Americans.

Cairo is a welcome sight after the long trip. Today, the town is filled with American uniforms. It has become a sort of Air Transport Command junction. From here, planes wing their way north to Teheran and thence to Karachi, New Delhi and Chungking.

Often the planes are filled with mail from home. Our military leaders know how important mail is to the troops. Mail from home gets the highest priority after food, and men in North Africa or Cairo or Teheran are often reading letters which you wrote only ten or twelve days before. Thank the Air Transport Command for that. In fact, thank

[18]

the Air Transport Command for the cigarettes your sons smoke, for the candy bars they munch, for the occasional can of beer (virtually a medical necessity when the climate hits 120 and there is no water) they get.

It is, of course, the American prerogative to criticize. But even the most avid armchair strategist can find no fault with this magnificent organization, headed by General Arnold and run for the most part by former transport company executives. As proof of the efficiency of the Air Transport Command, I only submit that less than a week after I was swimming in the surf at Miami I had lunch in a houseboat on the Nile.

And before I could settle down to sleep in Shepheard's Hotel in Cairo a phone rang and I was on my way to Teheran in Iran. The Air Transport Command (and I had only ordinary press priority as all correspondents have) had brought me more than 10,000 miles in a hot minute. I would have to stay in Teheran a few days they told me (maybe a few weeks) until I could get on a plane to Moscow. I tried to stifle the memory of Miami Beach; I tried to remember that I had the best job in the world.... It didn't help any. I was homesick already, a fine state of mind for a man who was just starting on a long trip.

Teheran, March, 1943

✳✳✳✳✳✳✳✳✳✳✳✳✳✳✳✳✳✳✳✳✳✳✳✳✳

Chapter II

YANKS IN IRAN

Six days after leaving Miami the big transport plane glided serenely over the snow-capped mountains that surround Teheran and then dropped into the heat of Iran's capital. Seen from the air, Teheran gleams whitely in the sun and it seems clean. Actually, like any city in the Near or Middle East, Teheran should be admired from afar. As we circled the huge airport I noticed that it was fringed with fighter aircraft.

There were about 150 P-40s and about forty Airacobras, all en route to Russia. Many of these would be at the front within forty-eight hours. Their guns were cleared, their war paint was on, and they lacked only good weather ahead. Most of the fighting on Russian fronts has been at low altitudes, and the Airacobra, with its great fire power, is an especial favorite of the Red Air Force.

A car was waiting for Colonel Edward Brown of General Connolly's staff and we rolled into the city some six miles away. The first impression you get of Iran's capital is one of filth and poverty. Beggars dressed in ragged, quilted clothing fill the streets. The gutters in the streets are wide and deep and filled with slowly flowing water. This is the Teheran water supply. It comes from the mountains, and when it starts its long trip to the city it is clear and fresh. But it is neither clear nor fresh by the time it flows through the open gutters. We stopped once, and Colonel Brown pointed out a sight which is common in Teheran streets. A small boy was using the gutter as a bathroom. Fifty yards down the block a woman was washing clothing in the water and, beyond that, a beggar was drinking from a rusty can. No one can understand why these open gutters, which are often little more than open sewers, do not spread plague over the city. But it has been like that for 3,000 years and by now the citizens of Iran are quite immune to diseases which Europeans or Americans contract easily.

Virtually every American and British visitor gets dysentery immediately. The troops call the Iranian version of this Middle East disease the Teheran Trots. General Donald Connolly, in charge of the Persian Gulf Service Command, has forbidden his men to eat or drink local products. Our army medical men have inspected slaughterhouses and butcher shops in Iran and have turned thumbs down on the meat which comes from them. Usually the meat is brought from the slaughterhouses in open wagons. The dust and germs it collects en route to butcher shops and hotels can be imagined. Our army serves excellent chlorinated water which, because of a secondary purification process, does not even have the slightly sickening taste of chlorine in it. For the most part, our army in Iran lives on the excellent army C rations. These are virtually all canned goods, but there is nothing wrong with American canned goods.

I would undoubtedly have to wait a few days for my Moscow-bound plane, Colonel Brown said, and he added that he knew that General Connolly would be glad to put me up. The General and his staff occupied a lovely villa that had once belonged to an Iranian bandit chief. In fact, it still belonged to him, but he found it expedient to rent it and have the rent collected by an agent who then delivered it to whatever obscure hiding place the Iranian bandit had found. I went along to the villa and found that Colonel Brown had been correct. General Connolly did ask me to stay at the villa with him.

General Donald Connolly is a very big, stern-looking man with an outthrust chin. When you first meet Connolly, you say to yourself, "Don't get into any trouble with this guy or you will get your ears knocked off." The General is in charge of one of the most important military operations in the world. He has the Persian Gulf Command—which means delivering the goods to Russia. It is one of the toughest of all jobs, too. His men often have to work in temperature well over boiling point, and Connolly has to watch out lest the hard work plus the murderous heat cause mental and physical crackups among the men. Connolly is a tough-looking bloke, but he is devoted to his men and if he gets you in a corner he'll talk for hours about their loyalty and their willingness to work.

"Every man on my staff," he said at breakfast the next morning, "knows more about his particular job than I do, and I'm proud of that. I worry about my men working in the Persian Gulf ports. That's the hottest part of the world, you know, but you never hear any complaints from the boys."

He was interrupted at this point by his aide, Major Ben Wyatt of Texas, who dropped two telegrams on the table. Connolly opened them and then, without a word, handed them to me. They had both come from the same Persian Gulf port. The first merely said: "Temperature today 129 degrees." The second was from his man in charge at the same port. It read: "Because unexpected size latest convoy to arrive, men afraid we may fall behind schedule. They suggest until cargo disposed of their eight-hour day be increased to twelve."

I looked at Connolly, and he didn't look stern or tough now at all. The corners of his mouth twitched as though he were trying to keep from smiling with pride, and he said, "That's what I mean about my men never complaining. Twelve hours' work in that kind of heat would kill a native. Yet these boys ask for it. Do you wonder I'm proud of them?"

I didn't wonder at all. There is nothing glamorous in the job done by the Persian Gulf Command. Their job is transportation. Ships arrive in the ports, loaded to the gunwales with war material for Russia. They unload it, put it on trains and trucks, transport it north, deliver it to the Russians and then go back to do it all over again. At the height of its traffic the Burma Road delivered 18,000 tons of material a month to China. Today more than ten times that amount of war material flows through the Persian Corridor to the Soviet front.

"The Russian front is an extension of the American front," Connolly cries again and again to his staff and to his men. "Every weapon we can put into the hands of a Russian may mean an American life saved."

That is his philosophy, and it has permeated down through the staff to the lowest ranks. It is that philosophy that keeps men at work when their senses are reeling and dull pains in the back of the head warn that the sun is taking its toll.

The food at General Connolly's villa was excellent. He had a cook who could do strangely beautiful things with army rations. My first dinner there featured meatballs and spaghetti, and very good they were too. General Connolly complimented the cook on the dish and then asked him where on earth he had gotten the meatballs.

The cook proudly claimed that the meatballs were nothing but Spam which he had managed to disguise. For months he had been attempting to fool the General, but this was the first time he had been successful.

The respect which Russians, British and Iranians show for General Connolly is an indication of how well he has done his job. Iran has small cause to love any of us. Actually, Iran hates the British, fears the Russians and tolerates us. Connolly's job, therefore, is not only military but diplomatic. He has to play the role of mediator between Iran on the one hand, and Russia and Britain on the other, as well as intervene between the Allies themselves in straightening out difficulties. We, the Allies, are not in Iran by invitation. It is an embarrassing but necessary situation. If we hadn't arrived there first, the Germans would be in occupation and then the material which now flows smoothly through the Persian Corridor from the Gulf, through Teheran and north to Kazvin and Pahlevi and thence to the Russian fighting forces would not be possible.

Iran's peculiar and rather tragic position is caused entirely by an accident of geography. Iran was born to be the gateway to India and, to use the other cliché, the back door to the Caucasus. Any time anyone wanted to conquer India the obvious and only real highway was through Iran (Persia until 1935). Let anyone's covetous eyes glance at the oil fields of Baku and the refineries of the Caucasus and again they sought to open the Persian door. Much as she desired it, Persia was just not allowed to remain neutral. Although larger than France in square miles, she was never strong enough to enforce neutrality. British, Russian and German interests have always conflicted in Iran, and there was nothing much which the tired old country could do about it. She tried to remain neutral in World War I, but circumstances prevented her.

[24]

There was a strong Turkish-German threat at that time, and Britain and Russia "occupied" the country as allies.

The war over, Reza Shah Pahlevi, former Persian Cossack leader and a very tough citizen, tried to streamline his country. He built a magnificent railroad station at Teheran, part of which was his private domain. This private royal station cost about three million dollars. The Shah didn't have that much change in his pocket, so he allowed the Germans to build it for him. They brought the magnificent marble and onyx, the modern plumbing and rest rooms. The Shah added hundreds of priceless Persian rugs. Naturally the Germans expected payment for their help. It was a simple matter for the Shah. He merely sent his agents through the country to announce an arbitrary and absurd price on wheat. In effect, he confiscated the wheat from his peasants. Everybody was happy—except the peasants. There has never been much incentive for any individual effort in Iran. As soon as you managed to put aside a surplus in either produce or money, it somehow found its way very quickly to the pockets of the Shah or his representatives—or to bandits or grafting soldiers from whom protection had to be bought. In addition to his royal railroad station (the Russians, unimpressed, compare it with the Moscow subway), Reza Shah did build many modern government buildings. He even began construction on an opera house but abandoned it when it was brought to his attention that there was no opera company in Iran nor any likelihood of attracting itinerant opera troupes to perform in Teheran. He liberated women from wearing the veil. The power of the priests was broken by edict and decree. He built some factories, hoping to make Iran less dependent upon outside countries for staple commodities. It is true that the Shah owned a great many of these factories, and no one could say that he paid union wages. Iran began to have the framework, at least, of a modern state.

[25]

The Shah was not exactly dreamy-eyed or visionary when it came to feathering his own nest, but until about 1930 there is no doubt that he did a fine job of modernizing his country. At about that time his avarice and his cruelty began to dominate his actions. They tell a thousand stories in Teheran about his eccentricities and his excesses, none of which shows the Shah in a favorable light. He was something less than a Dream Prince to his subjects. Once he ordered that a road be built from Teheran to his palace in the Shimran foothills. He drove to inspect it. The road was a bit bumpy and he hit the royal noggin once or twice when ruts in the road jolted the car. This annoyed him no end. When he arrived at the palace he asked for the engineer who had built the road. The pleased engineer came forward, all set to take a few bows.

"Lie down on this road you have built," His Majesty said. The bewildered engineer did so, and then the Shah calmly gave orders to his chauffeur to drive over the poor wretch. The engineer was hardy; most of his bones were broken, but he did not die.

The Shah liked to own hotels, but it distressed him to have ordinary plebeians stay in his hostelries. He owned one particularly fine hotel on the shores of the Caspian. He went to inspect it one autumn day and, according to custom, orders were given for the paying guests to absent themselves during the royal visit. The wife of a British oil official protested to the management. She had a young child and it was a cold rainy day. There was no place for her to go during the royal visit. The manager insisted and then told of a citizen who had refused to leave on the occasion of the Shah's last visit of inspection. He stayed in his room but curiosity got the better of him. He poked his head out of his door to get a look at the Shah. Unfortunately His Highness saw him. He merely gave one simple order, "Take him to the courtyard and shoot him." The order was carried out immediately.

"But I am a British citizen, not a Persian," the oil man's wife protested.

"Yes, madame, and my former guest was a Swiss citizen, not a Persian," the manager said sadly. The woman and her child spent the afternoon sitting in the back seat of an automobile. It was the only refuge she could find.

Meanwhile, during these innovations, the Germans gave the Shah more and more help. The British and the Russians despised the Iranians and made no secret of their dislike. The Germans flattered them, co-operated with them, and gave them machinery. They helped Iran build its 870-mile Trans-Iranian Railway which stretches from the Persian Gulf to the Caspian Sea. Today it is being used almost exclusively to transport American goods to the Russians. When the war came, there is no doubt that Iran was pro-German. German agents were powerful in Teheran. They had led an unsuccessful revolt against the British in Iraq and both Britain and Russia were convinced they might try to do better in Iran. For once Britain and Russia co-operated nicely in putting the heat on Reza Shah. They had investigated carefully and they gave His Highness names of German agents who had obtained important posts in the Iranian Army. They named Germans in key spots in the communications system. They identified German agents who had spread anti-British and anti-Russian propaganda. Reza Shah quibbled and talked but did nothing. In August, 1941, Russia and Britain stopped sending diplomatic notes and moved in. Reza Shah abdicated a month later in favor of his twenty-four-year-old son, Mohammed Shah Pahlevi. There was virtually no resistance to the occupation. A treaty was drawn up which gave Iran a chance to save face and she broke relations with all countries which were at war with Britain and Russia. Britain and Russia agreed to get out of Iran six months after the war ended and promised to give Iran a vote at the peace table.

Then came the business of America's getting material to Russia under the Lend-Lease agreements. Convoys were having difficulties in the North Sea, the Barents Sea and the White Sea. Thousands of tanks and aircraft were being sunk; obviously other routes would have to be established. The Persian Gulf ports were the only answer. And so we moved in, by tacit agreement, and no one objected. By now young Mohammed Shah Pahlevi had shown that if he had ever held pro-German sympathies he would suppress them for the duration of the war. We agreed to deliver Lend-Lease goods not to the gulf ports alone but to the Russians at Kazvin, some hundred miles north of Teheran. General Connolly and a brilliant staff were sent to supervise the complex job.

It is not a simple matter to help the Russians. They suggested to General Connolly that they would appreciate it if he would send the material even farther north to Pahlevi. This would involve a long haul, requiring trucks. General Connolly said that he'd be glad to comply with their request. He sent his men out to survey the route. Roads were bad, and there was no food, no lodgings and no sanitary arrangements of any kind on the way. He said that he would build installations along the route where his men could be barracked and fed. The Russians, for some strange reason, refused to allow this. This was too close to Russian territory and the Russians regretfully told Connolly that Moscow had not yet given permission for large groups of Americans to enter the region. Connolly shrugged his shoulders and said, "I'm sorry, but that's how it will have to be."

It was an unfortunate impasse, and neither Connolly nor his opposite number in the Russian Army, big, hulking General Alexander Korolev, liked it very much. Actually, our flow of materials was so great that the Russians were unable to move them along fast enough to keep up with Connolly's men. Hundreds of crates filled with ammunition, food, guns, leather, etc., were piled high at Teheran and at Kazvin, waiting to be shipped to Pahlevi. General Korolev pleaded with Connolly to send the loaded trucks north and then have them return immediately to the ports. Connolly, an uncompromising American Army officer, whose first obligation is the health and care of his troops, refused bluntly. He insisted once more that adequate rest camps, maintenance bases and canteens be established along the route before he'd risk his men.

"That's how it will have to be, General," Connolly repeated. "My first duty is to guard the health of my men. By the way, General," he added casually, "why don't you and I run up to Pahlevi and look the road over ourselves?"

Korolev agreed. Canny Connolly knew that Korolev loved hunting. There were plenty of wild boar in the Elburz Mountains through which the road ran. He got four Garand rifles, plenty of ammunition and loaded a truck with good army C rations. He took along Colonel Edward Brown, his advisor on all non-military matters, while Korolev brought his aide, Colonel Makaroff. High in the mountains, Connolly suggested that they might try their luck and perhaps General Korolev would like to use a Garand. Korolev's eyes glittered as he handled the beautiful rifle. Their luck was in. Just before nightfall they got a boar. There was a Red Army outpost on top of the mountain and they headed for it. Inside the hut some twenty Red Army soldiers were huddled in the cold, eating their evening meal of herring, salami and tea.

They blinked when they saw the gold epaulets that Korolev wore and the stars on Connolly's shoulders. Korolev waved them at ease and then he and Connolly squatted with them and shared their fish and tea. Meanwhile two sergeants Connolly had brought along as drivers had dragged the dead boar to the hut. The soldiers who hadn't tasted meat for some time were popeyed at the sight of the huge animal. They built a fire outside the hut. They sliced the boar and soon all of them, generals, sergeants and Red Army privates were roasting the boar in the time-honored Russian way by sticking slices of the meat on swords and holding the swords over the fire. They ate their fill and then sat around the fire and the Russians sang folk songs. It was democracy at its best and a side of it which these Russians had never seen. They didn't realize that American generals ever sat around eating with sergeants, joking with them, laughing with them. They had three days and three nights of roaming about the mountain passes, killing boar, living in the open when there was no shelter and when the taste of boar paled there were those excellent American Army rations. Korolev and Connolly returned to Teheran firm friends. The friendship was cemented when Connolly sent to Cairo for two Garand rifles which he presented to the Red Army General.

A few days later Korolev told Connolly that Moscow had given permission for American soldiers to build barracks in the Pahlevi district. Today American soldiers are driving through those tortuous mountain passes, but they don't mind. They know there are maintenance stations, mess halls and quarters all along the way.

Connolly's diplomatic methods may be unorthodox, but they work. Last April 14th was Army Day even in Teheran. Our troops held a celebration at the big Iran airport. Connolly and Brown had arranged a surprise for the Russian staff which was all present. At the conclusion of the ceremonies forty officers stepped forward, the band struck up the Russian national anthem and the forty American officers sang it—in Russian.

The State Department would have shuddered, had it known.

On May Day last spring, Connolly was asked to review the Russian troops. At the conclusion of the review a group of Red Army men came forward, the band played "The Star-Spangled Banner" and the Russians sang it—in English. That is typical of the way Connolly gets along with the Russians. This Iowa-born Presbyterian understands the Russians better than do the diplomats who made long studies of them. For one thing, Connolly likes them. Russians may be hard to understand, but they're very easy to like.

Connolly has a brilliant staff, all hand-picked. General Stanley L. Scott is his Chief of Staff, and his three assistants are Colonel Roy Graham, Colonel Theodore Osborne and Colonel Peter Purvis, all specialists in transportation and engineering problems. Thirty-four-year-old Colonel Paul Yount is the director of the railroad service, while Brigadier General Don Shingler directs the motor transport service. They are the hardest-working group of men I have ever encountered in any army. Connolly occasionally has to call a halt because the human body can stand only so much punishment in Iranian heat. At one time last spring fifty percent of the staff was in the hospital from overwork. These men have virtually lifted the face of Iran. When they arrived, they found a very worn-out railroad, incapable of carrying large loads. Today, modern Diesels pull tremendous loads over the strengthened roadbed. They found 2,000-year-old camel roads winding through the mountains. Today these are modern roads over which travel heavily laden mechanized convoys.

While I was in Teheran a rather historic event occurred. General Connolly and his whole staff gathered at the Teheran railroad station with General Korolev and his staff. Sergeyev, the genial, smiling Russian consul, was there to represent the political Soviet. A train puffed into the station. It was a long train with about forty-five freight cars loaded with goods from America. This had happened often enough, but this train was different. It was one hundred percent American-manned. The grimy faces of two unmistakable Americans grinned down from the locomotive. One belonged to Sergeant Howard Blair of Breckinridge, Minnesota, while the other belonged to Corporal Chester Clark of Muscatine, Iowa. Blair had once worked on the Great Northern while Clark had worked for the Muscatine line. The American and Russian generals greeted them effusively. Until then Iranian crews had run the railroad. It was exciting to stand there and realize that these cars were filled with goods made by American labor; that the two locomotives which pulled the train were made in America; that the crew which immediately went to work to service the engine were all Americans. It was aid to Russia par excellence, and it was one hundred percent American aid.

British, American and Russian troops in Iran get along very well together. Hundreds of our troops were former railroad men. They come into close contact with Russian troops who have had the same background. The Russian transportation troops wear small insignia on their caps, a crossed hammer and a wrench. These are much prized by our own railroad troops and most of them have managed to persuade Russian pals to give. Railroad men all over the world are a race apart. They love to talk shop, even if it is broken Russian or through an interpreter. Our men and the Russians have this common bond: they sit around the freight yard at Teheran swapping stories and cigarettes and food, and it is seldom you see one of our men who doesn't proudly wear the crossed hammer and wrench on his own cap.

For the most part, our troops came to Iran with greatly mistaken, preconceived ideas about their Russian allies. Fed for years on our well-organized anti-Soviet propaganda at home, they were slightly suspicious at first. Then they were impressed by the discipline in the Red Army and finally they wound up liking these big, healthy-looking almost perpetually smiling troops in the gray-green uniforms and red tabs of the Red Army. They found amazingly good discipline and esprit de corps among the Russians.

Two incidents happened while I was in Teheran which emphasized the behavior and discipline of the Red Army. When the Russians marched into Iran, their commanders told them that any looting would be punished by death. An Iranian merchant was driving along on his donkey one day when two Russian sentries stopped him. This was correct, because he was in occupied territory near Pahlevi where special passes are necessary. They asked for his credentials. He displayed them. Then they asked for the time and, looking at his wrist watch, he told them. They took the wrist watch away from him and ordered him to move on. Instead of moving on, the Iranian merchant went to the nearest Red Army commander and told his story. The commander had the sentries in for questioning. They denied having taken the watch. They were searched and the watch was found on one of them. Both were immediately shot for looting.

It is very seldom one finds Red Army officers in the restaurants or night clubs of Teheran. For one thing, there is a ten o'clock curfew in Teheran and everything is tightly closed up by then. But their quarters are, for the most part, some distance from the center of the city and they keep to themselves at night with rigid orders to behave should they find themselves out late. Teheran is policed by British and American M.P.'s who divide the duty. One night some British M.P.'s found a hideaway evading the curfew hour. They also found a very drunken Russian officer waving a gun and threatening dire things to the assembly. It was a tough spot for a couple of British M.P.'s. They had never arrested an officer before and yet they did have orders to keep the peace. They finally decided to take the Red Army man to the local Russian headquarters. He went under protest. They turned him over to the Russian commander and forgot the incident. But it did not end there. The next morning at nine o'clock Iranian, British and American authorities received identical notes from General Korolev apologizing for the bad behavior of the officer. He added that he had intended to take strong disciplinary measures against him, but that he was unable to do this as unfortunately the officer "had died during the night." That is Red Army discipline.

We have a great many American troops in Iran, far more, perhaps, than the enemy realizes. Chiefly, of course, their job is to transport material from the Persian Gulf to the Russians; but they are ready for combat too. They frankly do not like Iran, but they realize they are doing a difficult and necessary job. They don't have much fun, these exiles from home. Their post exchanges are excellent and that makes life easier. They can get American cigarettes, and a special effort is made to give those of them stationed in the Persian Gulf territory extra rations. Last summer the temperature hit 135 degrees in the gulf ports. This has been called the hottest spot in the world and American troops stationed there will not argue the point.

Our army has done its best for the men. Canned beer has been sent to them and that helps them stave off the horrible heat. Our medical men believe that it helps both their health and morale. They are absolutely right. Some of the men told me that they couldn't have stuck it without the beer. As far as our troops everywhere are concerned, beer is the aristocrat of all drinks. The staple drink in Iran is a concoction called V and V. It is half Persian vodka and half Persian vermouth, and it tastes like liquid soap. Our boys don't go for it at all. Occasionally an officer manages to get a bottle of Scotch. The standard price in Teheran is eighteen dollars a bottle.

Inflation is no obscure academic problem in Iran: it is a fact. The Iranians have little in the way of goods and when their merchandise is gone they can't get any more. A great deal of their wares came from Germany. They are reluctant to sell and when they do they can name their own prices. A small electric-light bulb costs $7.50, toilet paper is $1.80 a roll, American cigarettes outside of the post exchange are eighty cents a package, a pair of shoes costs thirty-five dollars and a second-hand portable typewriter will bring $400. This is Iran. When the war is over our boys are unanimously in favor of giving it back to the Iranians. But as long as the war continues they'll work their heads off and echo General Connolly's creed: "The Russian front is merely an extension of the American front."

Teheran, March, 1943

✳✳✳✳✳✳✳✳✳✳✳✳✳✳✳✳✳✳✳✳✳✳✳✳

Chapter III

MOSCOW GOSSIP

IT IS IMPOSSIBLE to arrive in Moscow and immediately plunge into writing about the place and the people. You can do that in London, and once you could do it in Paris or Berlin or even Teheran, but Moscow is a complexity that cannot so easily be solved. You must get the feel of Moscow before you try to write about the city.

For example, it takes a long time to understand the Russian form of government because it follows no familiar pattern. It is not a democracy as we know democracy; and certainly it is not the communism I have read about in the speeches of Lenin or in the writings of British and American communists. The present form of government in Russia is undoubtedly in a transitional stage. At the moment when her life is threatened she must necessarily follow the doctrine of expediency. Stalin improvises as the conditions demand. He has to. The story of Russian government during the war will make an interesting study for the political economists after it is all over. But it would be presumptuous for a correspondent who spends a few months in Russia to attempt any serious discussion of Soviet politics, just as it would be presumptuous for any Russian writer to think he could fully understand our own form of government in the short space of five months.

And so in the following pages I write of the people of Russia rather than the State. People are much more interesting than governments to me. I kept a diary while I was in Moscow. Perhaps a dozen or so excerpts from it might serve to guide us around Moscow, might bring us a little closer to the Russian people.

Most of what I wrote in the diary is nothing but gossip. Still, I suppose if a thousand years from now someone were to dig up the Winchell columns of the 1920's, he would get a pretty clear picture of life here during those hectic days. You cannot dismiss gossip columns by saying they discuss only trivial things. To a great extent, they reflect the age in which we live.

After we're through gossiping in the following few pages, we'll go to the front and into the factories and hospitals and to cities that have been destroyed. The trivial gossip may give us a better understanding of what makes Russia click.

April 9, 1943:

Walking into the hotel last night I bumped into a tall, good-looking young Russian officer I had met a few days before. He was a war correspondent and an ardent party member. Russian correspondents are given rank and they spend a great deal more time at the front than we are permitted. The disadvantage, of course, in having rank is that you are under military discipline. We sat and had a drink and wound up in the inevitable discussion—capitalism vs. communism.

"How goes the Communist Party in America?" he asked me.

"It is rather small and unimportant," I told him. "At its

[37]

very height it could poll only 100,000 votes out of some 55,000,000."

"That is a pity," he said thoughtfully. "But of course we here had an idiot of a czar ruling us and it was easy to crystallize opposition. You had a Lincoln and have a Roosevelt."

"Communism hasn't got far in America because the majority of workers themselves don't want it," I said, quite truthfully, I think. "We think we have something better than your kind of dictatorship."

He smiled contemptuously. "In czarist days we had a dictatorship of a single man. Now we have collective dictatorship —dictatorship of the people."

"I believe that Stalin has as much power and is as supreme a dictator as Hitler is," I said.

"Thank God we have Stalin." He was emphatic. "Suppose that Trotsky had succeeded Lenin. The war would have been lost long ago. Trotsky was too much under foreign influence. He believed in inviting foreign capital into the country. Foreign capital would have exploited our natural resources; would have taken these from us in exchange, perhaps, for consumers' goods. It would have been nice to have had consumers' goods, but not at that price. Trotsky was not enough of a Russian. Stalin is. Stalin has respect for foreign countries but believes in Russia for the Russians. He insisted that we develop our own resources. If he hadn't done that we wouldn't be turning out tanks, aircraft and guns today. We are grateful for the help given us by America; but you must realize that, in the main, we have fought the war with our own war materials, manufactured here in our own factories, only because Stalin was far-sighted enough to know that we would have to stand alone." Switching the subject, he added, "It is a pity that America stands still and does not progress."

"We're satisfied," I reminded him, "with the framework of

[38]

government we have. If we make changes, and Roosevelt has made many, we make them within that framework."

"But," he interrupted, "capitalism still rules your country. You can't deny it."

I admitted that quite cheerfully.

"Take Roosevelt's proposal to limit net income to $25,000 a year. The capitalists beat that, all right."

I protested that statement. "I honestly believe that the country at large would have rejected that proposal in a nation-wide vote. Every worker in a factory hopes some day to invent some gadget or to work himself up to be the boss so that he can make $25,000 a year. Every office boy dreams of being president or of making a fortune. We believe that any-one who can honestly earn luxury for himself and his family is entitled to it—that is, if he can earn it without detriment to his neighbors."

He laughed cynically. "Roosevelt wouldn't last ten minutes if tomorrow he decided to confiscate great private fortunes to help the war effort. Suppose he confiscated the Morgan, Rockefeller, Ford wealth. He wouldn't last."

"To begin with, we don't have to resort to confiscation to help the war effort. Heavy taxation forces the wealthy to pay up to 95 per cent on what they earn, and bond sales finance the war. Incidentally, money never won a war. Germany is fighting a war and fighting it well with virtually no money."

"I hate to think of the confusion that will follow the war in America," he said moodily.

"Don't think about it, then. Have another drink instead. Let us worry about that."

We talked about Hemingway, whom he admired a lot, and he confessed that in many ways he imitated Hemingway. I hesitate to mention the name of the Russian. To begin with, he had no right to be in my room talking so freely. It is much safer for even party members to remain anonymous in their

relations with foreign correspondents. When we finished talking of Hemingway as a great writer, he had to temper his
admiration with a criticism.

"In his books one sees no hope," he said. "He knows men
and he knows women, but he gives them no hope of a better
world. His books end in the cul-de-sac of democracy. In
America your democracy has attained its apotheosis. It is now
a static thing; it does not progress. You see that in Hemingway. It is a pity that he is so American."

"He lived a long while in France, a long while in Spain,"
I reminded him.

"The same," he said contemptuously. "How great Hemingway would have been had he been a communist! With
his great technique and with a communist background he
would be the modern Tolstoy."

"Tolstoy? You mean that nobleman, that Prince?" I hoped
to get a rise out of him with that.

"Lenin called Tolstoy the Revolutionary Prince," he
smiled. "You Americans seem to think that we communists
completely reject everything that went before us. That isn't
true. We admire Peter the Great enormously. He was a great
revolutionary. Russia was asleep until he came along. He introduced industry and shipbuilding to the country. He woke
the people up. Because he introduced industry you might
say he was the father of capitalism in Russia. If it hadn't been
for capitalism, Lenin couldn't have introduced socialism. Now
we will keep much of the old Russia. Peter the Great's statue
still stands in the square at Leningrad. Tolstoy is still our
literary giant. We have merely added communism to Russia,
retaining the best of the old Russia. The ignorance in your
country about Russia," he added with good nature, "is amazing."

I admitted that indictment, but reminded him that the censorship was such that we were unable to present the real picture of his country.

"Some of the American correspondents tell me that their papers at home actually do not believe that Stalin really dissolved the Comintern last week."

"That's true enough," I told him. "Our American communists don't believe it either, according to reports from home."

"Look back over every speech Stalin ever made—you will not find one paragraph in any of them which would give support to the charges made in your country that he wishes to make the world communistic. He is interested only in Russia. Anyone who had read Roy Howard's interviews with him eight years ago would know that."

Voks, the organization interested in fostering cultural relations with foreign countries, had issued a booklet containing the authorized translation of the Howard interview which took place March 2, 1936. I had a copy. The questions and answers my war correspondent friend had in mind were:

Howard: Does that mean that the Soviet Union has to any degree abandoned its plans and intentions for bringing about the world revolution?

Stalin: We have never had any such plan or intention.

Howard: You appreciate no doubt, Mr. Stalin, that much of the world has long entertained a different impression.

Stalin: Well, Mr. Howard, that is the product of a misunderstanding.

Howard: A tragic misunderstanding?

Stalin: No, comic—well, tragi-comic.

We Marxists believe that revolution will occur in other countries, but only at the time when it will be considered possible or necessary by the revolutionists in each specific country. To attempt to export revolution is nonsense. Without the desire within a country, there will be no revolution.

The Russian people desired revolution and brought it about. Now we are engaged in building up a classless society. But to presume that we want to bring about revolution in other countries by interference in their national life, is unwarranted.

"Assuming that we win the war," I said, "what then? People at home think that Russia may want to impose communism on the rest of Europe. What do you think?"

"I don't think," the Russian correspondent said scornfully. "I know. Why should we want France and Germany and the other countries to be communistic? To become communistic each country would have to have a revolution. A revolution would leave each country weaker than it will be when the war ends. We don't want weak countries torn by internal strife after the war. We want unified countries which will be stable, so that we can deal with them and when we deal with them know that we are dealing with the government the people support. Only then can order come out of the chaos. As for Europe going communistic," he continued, "can you think of one country in Europe that is physically able to make the sacrifices necessary to establish communism within its borders? We sacrificed everything and put ourselves under rigid discipline for twenty years. Then we began to see security and happiness ahead. We felt that those hard twenty years had been worthwhile. Then the war came and our progress had to be interrupted of necessity. No, no country in Europe has the will or desire required to build a communist state. And, if you'll forgive me," he said with disarming charm, "neither has your country. You haven't the capacity for sacrifice."

"That's nonsense," I told him. "Our ancestors made sacrifices for two hundred years before they achieved our present form of government, before they built a foundation that would endure. As a matter of fact, our forefathers began with communism and evolved to a much higher state—democracy."

"What?" he exploded. "Are you going to tell me the Puritan fathers were communists?"

"Sure, they were." I poured him another glass of vodka to steady him after that shock. "William Bradford landed in the *Mayflower* at Plymouth. He was elected governor and, by the will of the people, became a dictator. Just as Stalin is a dictator. Those who were good farmers farmed, and their produce was divided among the community. Just like your collective farms. Those who were good hunters hunted, and threw their bag into the common pot. When a man's family increased and he needed a larger house the community helped him build the house. Plymouth was, in fact, a classless society. Read Bradford's *History of the Plymouth Plantation* if you don't believe me. It was pure, unadulterated communism. The time came when communism was no longer needed. So we went on to something which opened wider horizons to the individual without hurting the state. Something we call democracy and you call capitalism."

"Do you actually think capitalism to be the best of all systems?" he asked incredulously.

"I do," I said complacently. "If only for one reason—it works. I will also bet you a hundred rubles that within ten years you here will have a system or be on your way to developing a system comparable to ours."

"Do you think Stalin would stand for that?" he asked.

"I do," I told him, "because I think he's one of the world's smartest men. He is a great realist, and, when he gets a chance to look the world over, he'll find that on the whole Britain and America are very happy countries. I realize that Stalin is the spiritual successor to Lenin and in a sense is committed to his principles, but," I added casually, "I am sure that Stalin has the courage to revise his principles."

He laughed. "We could argue all night and get nowhere.

But it's good to argue, isn't it? It brings things out into the open."

And so we talked on. Neither of us had opinions—each had convictions. But we argued without heat, parting in friendship, but with virtually no understanding of each other.

April 10:

I have been in Moscow a week now learning all over again the ten words of Russian I learned when I was here in 1941. In a sense, it was like coming home. Most of the correspondents with whom I lived and worked and played in 1941 are still here, with the notable exception of Henry Cassidy of the AP, who is home on leave. The American correspondents here are Henry Shapiro and Meyer Handler of the UP; banjo-playing, Georgia-bred Eddy Gilmore and Bill McGaffin of the AP; Ralph Parker and my old friend Cyrus Sulzberger of the *New York Times*; Edgar Snow of the *Saturday Evening Post*; blond Walter Kerr of the *Herald Tribune*; Bill Downs of *Newsweek* and Columbia Broadcasting; David Nichol of the *Chicago Daily News*, every bit as alert as his brilliant predecessors, Leland Stowe and Arch Steele; Robert Magidoff of NBC and lovable Janet Weaver of the *New York Daily Worker*. The British correspondents, too, are old friends; brilliant Paul Holt of the *Daily Express*; Alfred Cholerton of the *Daily Telegraph*, still plucking at his dark beard, and still, after sixteen years in Russia, talking abominable Russian; John Gibbons, the cheerful Scotsman, representing the *London Daily Worker*; Harold King of Reuter's, the hardest-working correspondent I've ever met; Ronald Matthews of the *Daily Herald*; Marjorie Shaw of the *Sketch*, the only British woman correspondent in Moscow, a charming girl who acts as hostess for all of us when we have parties; Alexander Werth of the *Sunday Times*, one of the soundest and best-informed men on Russia I know; and Jean

Champenois of the Free French Agency. No one could ask for a better crowd to work with or live with or play cards with. With the exception of Janet Weaver, Cholerton, Champenois and Gibbons, we all live at the Metropole, a huge barn-like hotel on the Square of the Revolution. It was once the de-luxe hotel in Moscow, but now, alas, nothing is de-luxe in Russia. But we have hot water every morning for an hour or so. Each room has only one electric-light bulb which makes writing a bit difficult.

They were all news-hungry when I arrived. Any scrap, any tidbit of information about home was important to these homesick, temporary exiles. Eddy Gilmore had to know whether Leo Durocher would play shortstop for the Dodgers or whether he had found anyone to take the place of young Reese. Did Hubbell have another good year in his honest left arm? Who was this Beau Jack who had won the light-weight championship? Was Harry James as hot on the trumpet as reports said he was? Could he play as sweet as Ziggy Elman? Marjorie Shaw and Janet Weaver wanted to know what girls were wearing in New York now. What were the hats like this spring? Were Nylon stockings still available? I had to answer a thousand questions. We talked shop for a week. Where was Knickerbocker? Bill Stoneman? What was Eisenhower like? And Mountbatten? Would Beaverbrook make his peace with Churchill? Was it true that Herbert Morrison was getting bigger every day and was it true that Anthony Eden had grown up? How about Willkie?

I, in turn, had to get acclimated to Moscow through the local gossip. I was horrified to learn that Nikolai Palgunov was still in charge of the press section of the Foreign Office— a very difficult man to deal with. Had things loosened up any? I had thought they had, because I had seen Henry Shapiro's magnificent United Press stories from the front. No, they said sadly; they'd had a few good trips during the winter to

Stalingrad and a few cities which had been recaptured by the Russians, but that was all. I was happy to know that General Joseph A. Michela was still our Military Attaché and that Eddie Page and Tommy Thompson were still at the embassy. I was happier to know that I could have the services of the best secretary-interpreter in Russia, Tania Sofiano, who had worked with me in 1941. She had been working for Paul Winterton of the *News Chronicle* (London). He had returned to London for a vacation and Tania was holding the fort for the *News Chronicle*. But she only had to send one story each morning and she would work with me the rest of the day. The jealousy of my colleagues was beautiful to see.

Tania speaks any language you can think of, and she can write well. Writing cablese was second nature to her. She is a good and loyal citizen of the Soviet Union and a typical Russian woman, willing to make any sacrifice for her country. Her husband, of course, is in the army and her seven-year-old child had been evacuated to the country a year before with Tania's elderly mother. Tania is honest, loyal, intelligent; she has a great knowledge of the drama, ballet, music and literature. Working promises to be a pleasure with Tania Sofiano as assistant.

We sat in Alex Werth's big room while I caught up on local gossip. I had to hear about how the boys had withstood the tough weather. Cholerton had lived in his big double bed most of the winter. There was no heat in his apartment, but there were electric-light plugs. Cholerton got several small electric heaters, plugged them in, placed them at strategic points under the covers and just hibernated. The cold was so intense that the plumbing in the apartment overhead burst, and water dripped from his ceiling all winter. They could never find the leak, but no such mishap would get Chol out of his bed. Our intrepid colleague had borrowed two big umbrellas from the British Embassy and had arranged them over his bed. What if the floor was ankle deep in water? Chol didn't care. He had fixed a stand so that he could type in bed, and he spent a comparatively comfortable winter there.

Ralph Parker of the *Times* (London), who also doubled in brass for the *New York Times,* arrived just before winter had set in. He had brought no warm underwear with him.

"Don't need it," he said smugly. "Don't you know the Russians always overheat their homes? When you visit their homes it would be unbearable to sit there in woolen underwear."

Parker didn't know that even such a starry-eyed admirer of all things Russian as himself was not asked very often to Russian homes. So he shivered through the winter in his Metropole room.

Eddy Gilmore, a born raconteur, told of Ronnie Matthews and his coat, an enormous yellow-leather sheepskin affair, decorated with painted golden designs, undoubtedly the work of some drunken sheep-tender. On front-line trips Matthews always wore the coat despite protests from his colleagues, who insisted that the coat could be seen by Germans twenty miles away.

"Ronnie was in the Royal Navy once—for a hot minute," Gilmore explained, "but they threw him out because he was a pacifist."

"Not exactly," Matthews explained seriously. "They didn't throw me out—they merely gave me the opportunity of resigning. And it wasn't because I was a pacifist. It was because I talked so persuasively that I was making pacifists of the other men on the ship."

"Anyhow," Gilmore went on, "when we were at Kotel-nikovo, they gave us one of those Red Army parties. Ronnie finally disappeared. We went out looking for him and we found him all alone, knee-deep in snow, singing Royal Navy

[47]

songs at the top of his voice underneath a brilliant Kalmuk moon."

"How did Henry Shapiro beat all you guys to the front?" I asked.

"Sheer genius," Shapiro admitted modestly.

"Last year Henry Cassidy got away with that great Stalin story—the answers to questions he sent Stalin," Gilmore explained.

"Well, we AP guys don't want to hog all the best stories. We like to see UP get one now and then, so we told Stalin it would be all right if he allowed a UP man to go to the front. That's how Shapiro got there."

Alex Werth was playing plaintive Chopin on the old piano he had in his room and playing it well, for Werth is a fine pianist. Marjorie Shaw kept passing the vodka bottle and we were all smoking American cigarettes. General Connolly had given me a dozen cartons in Teheran.

"Tell about Bill Downs and the way he disciplined his secretary," Dave Nichol suggested.

"Well," Gilmore explained, "when Downs first arrived he inherited the secretary that Larry Lesueur had when he worked here for CBS. Larry was a friendly soul. No one called him anything but Larry, even Lilly Israelevich, his secretary. Mr. Downs thought he'd have a little dignity in his office. He didn't go for that first-name business. One night we were in Walter Kerr's room, all of us. Downs was boasting how well he had Lilly trained. Just then the phone rang. It was Lilly. Walter answered the phone. Lilly shouted so we could all hear her, 'Hello, Walter, I'm looking for Downs. If he's down there tell him to hurry right up to the office.' Yeah, Downs had her trained fine."

"But I got her working hard," Downs said defensively.

The boys had high praise for the way Marjorie Shaw and Janet Weaver had behaved on the various front trips. The fact that women correspondents might visit the front is never taken into consideration when sanitary and sleeping arrangements are made. One could hardly expect that. But the boys said Marjorie and Janet were two real troupers.

"Our real heroes on those trips," Marjorie said, "were Walter and Eddy. They drank the toasts for us."

"Long years of fraternity-house training helped," Gilmore said modestly.

"I had my early training at Bleeck's near the *Herald Tribune* building in New York," Kerr added, "so it was easy."

It is an astounding truth that Red Army officers do not handle vodka nearly as well as do Americans. Yet they insist upon drinking toasts to every war leader of every allied country. Someone always has to respond. Kerr would do the honors one day and then retire in favor of Gilmore the next. They made a good team and never once did either fail to walk steadily away from the dinner table after one of these endurance contests, even though their walk was made more difficult by such hazards as somnolent Red Army generals.

New York seems a long way off tonight.

April 15:

Yesterday Henry Shapiro had a luncheon party in his room for Luis Quintanilla, the Mexican Ambassador. In two weeks Luis has become one of the most popular diplomats in Moscow. His intelligence, his affable charm and the fact that he trusts us completely all combine to make him popular. Henry also had his assistant, Meyer Handler, Alex Werth and brilliant Jean Champenois for luncheon. Jean and I arrived first. We had a glass of vodka and then, looking idly out of the window, I saw something that startled me. Shapiro's room is an inside room facing on the court. A few of the rooms have balconies and there one flight up and across the court was a very good-looking girl sunning herself on her balcony. She wore what appeared to be a bathing suit, and she was sitting in a reclining chair quite unconscious of our scrutiny. She was slim and blonde, a very rare combination in Moscow. Jean and I eyed her approvingly.

Shapiro arrived with Quintanilla and, after the Ambassador had his first glass, I led him to the window. He, like ourselves, was deeply appreciative of the beauty of the blonde, who was still blissfully ignorant of the fact that she was being very carefully observed by correspondents and diplomats. None of us had ever seen her around the hotel.

"Why isn't she working in a factory?" I asked. It is very rare to see a Muscovite maiden who has any leisure time at one in the afternoon.

"She may be a ballerina," Shapiro volunteered.

"More likely some commissar's girl," Champenois suggested.

"My God," Quintanilla said in a shocked voice, "I think she only has one leg."

We peered more carefully. It was true that only one leg could be seen, but we laughed at Luis and said she was undoubtedly sitting on her other leg. Quintanilla insisted. Suddenly she stood up. She reached for the rail of the balcony to steady herself. It was true—she did have but one leg. We were silent for a moment and a little ashamed of our previous ribald remarks and speculations. How had she lost it? At the front, perhaps. Maybe in a bombing. We all needed another vodka quickly after that shock.

It was a good lunch. Quintanilla had been received by Stalin the evening before, and he was full of praise for the silent man in the Kremlin.

"I knew that he was a great leader," Quintanilla said. "But I never knew that he was a great statesman. He has a profound knowledge even about Mexico and Central America."

I have never met anyone who has been received by Stalin

who says anything else. Averell Harriman, Lord Beaverbrook, Harry Hopkins, Wendell Willkie, Sir Archibald Clarke-Kerr —all agree on Stalin's intelligence and all agree that he is one of the best-informed men any of them had ever met. Quintanilla was impressed, too, with his strength, his affability, his humor. The world has an impression that Stalin is dour, forbidding. In his pictures he looks surly. When I met him eighteen months ago I, like Quintanilla, was surprised to find him smiling, affable and, most amazing of all, very small.

"I wish," Quintanilla said thoughtfully, "Henry Wallace could come over and meet Stalin. I can imagine the two of them sitting down and talking about crops and arguing as to when certain things should be planted. In his broad outlook Stalin reminds me of Wallace. Like Wallace, Stalin is intensely patriotic and, like him, he has a great love of the land."

It is true that Stalin's hobby is growing his own plants. He has a *dacha* (villa) somewhere along the Minsk Road, and there he does his own sowing, planting and takes care of his own garden. It is a great pity, we all feel, that Stalin never allows us an opportunity of really presenting him as he is. If he held occasional press conferences, we could get to know him a little and humanize him and perhaps he would cease being the bogey man which so many millions think him. Even to his countrymen he is little known. He is not a personality but a figure. He isn't loved as Lenin was loved and now is venerated. He is admired universally in Russia, and he is given complete credit for the organization and the great fighting done by the Red Army. Stalin's son, Major Jacob Djugashvili—Stalin's family name—had been with the Red Army since the German invasion. The fact that he was Stalin's son did not make him news in the sense that the son of any famous American would be news to us.

One day there was an article in *Red Star*, the official army newspaper. It was by a Russian colonel whose unit had been surrounded near Smolensk. The unit was completely wiped out or captured. Later, the colonel escaped from his German captors, and in this article he told the story of the battle. He told of the bravery of his men and he ended by writing: "Major Jacob Djugashvili fired his gun until the very last. He died fighting."

That is how Russia learned that Stalin's son had been killed in action. Neither Stalin nor any member of his government ever mentioned the tragedy. No paper ever carried an editorial or a comment upon the death of the young major. The death of one man was not important enough in the long run to affect the destiny of Russia. Stalin? Who knows what he thought? Probably, when informed of it, he merely said, "*Nichevo*," and went on with his work.

In strange contrast was the attitude of Mussolini when his son Bruno was killed while testing a new plane. This was in August, 1941. Three weeks after Bruno's death, Mussolini published a hysterical, emotional book about his son called *I Talk with Bruno*. In his many speeches urging that his people display fortitude Mussolini had gone so far as to forbid women to wear mourning for their loved ones who were killed in action. In the book Il Duce indicated that he was enjoying spiritualistic conversations with the soul of his dead son. His publicized grief and his avowed spiritualism both so at variance with the materialistic concept of life and death exemplified by fascism must indeed have given the people of Italy a hint that their leader was just a little bit nuts.

Stalin is given great credit for pulling the wool over the eyes of the Germans when he made the Soviet-German Pact on August 23, 1939. This gave him two more years to prepare for the war with Germany he knew to be inevitable. This, the good citizens of Russia say, saved Moscow and Leningrad. The good citizens may be 100 percent right. Perhaps Stalin did negotiate that Pact and sign it, knowing it to be a mere scrap of paper. Being a great realist, he knew what any agreement with Hitler was worth. In any case, it was Hitler who broke the Pact—not Stalin. Everyone who has talked to Stalin gets the impression that he has little direct interest in any country but his own and, of course, the Baltic states. There is no ground at all to believe that he would welcome some such thing as a post-war Union of European Soviet Republics. And American communists who would like to see the red star atop our capitol have (as far as I can discover) never received even verbal encouragement from the gentleman who was born Djugashvili. It will take Stalin at least ten years after the war to clean up his own country: to repair the ravaged cities of the South and the West. People in America who are still distrustful and afraid of the Soviet Union lose sight of the fact that this war is going to leave Russia in a horribly weakened condition. I have heard Poles say (very privately), "After the war we could take six Polish divisions and conquer Russia." This is a bit far-fetched, but it is a reflection of what most military observers believe. For a long time Russia is going to be a giant on crutches.

Indicative of the Russian way of thinking is the impatience of every Russian to whom I've spoken about the great amount of speculation in America and Britain as to our "post-war plans." Every time you pick up a magazine of opinion or read the speeches of our statesmen we hear about the "better world" we hope for when the war is done. The Beveridge Report is typical of such reasoning and, no doubt, such speculation and planning will in the long run give us a better America, a better Britain. The Russians want only the status quo they enjoyed when war came to them. They worked hard and suffered intensely for that world and they want to go back to it. They always think of Russia as being in a state of transition. Before the war they were beginning to make consumers' goods, beginning to relax slightly the truly Spartan character of their hitherto miserable existence. In 1935 there came a great day when food and clothing ration cards were withdrawn. It was then Stalin tossed them a phrase which has become a Russian proverb.

"*Zhit stalo luche, Tovarishchi, zhit stalo veselye,*" Stalin cried. "Life is better, comrades, life is gayer." It was too. They were, they felt, on their way somewhere. That is all they want now—to go back and pick up where the war forced them to lay off. All of this is not only the opinion of every foreigner who has had any contact with Stalin but is the opinion without exception of every British, American and French correspondent here in Moscow. We have as much to fear from Soviet Russia as we have to fear from the Eskimos. And, as a threat to our liberty and our established way of living, the Dies Committee offers a far greater danger.

Three of the correspondents have radios. We listen to German stations mostly. The reception is excellent and the musical programs are first rate. The Germans woo you with symphony music or with recordings of good American swing bands and then, of course, there comes the propaganda. Some of it is amazingly clever. Two women with unmistakable American accents carry on a question-and-answer program. Yesterday Betty said to Jane sadly, "Oh, I do hope the Americans will wake up before it is too late." They emphasize the deadly terror of Bolshevism and talk of how Soviet propaganda has influenced America. That is always good for a howl from us. We know, to our sorrow, that the Soviet propaganda is the worst in the world. There are fourteen of us here (British and American correspondents) all wanting to be useful. Without exception, we are all friendly to Russia, although not one of us is a communist. All of us have been captivated by the decency, the honesty and the courage of the Russian people. Apart from government officials, I never met a Russian whom I didn't like. My colleagues all say the same thing. America, unfortunately, still thinks of Russia in terms of communism—not in terms of people. Over here we think of the Red Army men; of the civilians who work and give without stint to further the war effort; of the pitiful creatures who have lived in villages and cities occupied by the Germans. If you think of Russia in those terms you have to come to the conclusion that it is a very wonderful country. And we'd like to explain or interpret this country to America, but the regulations governing our work and our daily life are such that we not only find it hard to get close to the people but find it virtually impossible to send the kind of stories we know would help America to understand and sympathize with these magnificent people.

Instead of being subjected to any intensive propaganda the very reverse is true. We are left severely alone, and it takes weeks to get permission to visit the front or to inspect ruined cities left devastated by the Germans. Stalin, Molotov and Vyshinsky are sacred cows and we are never allowed near them. We do not get even the conventional hand-outs issued by the information or press services of other countries. Virtually our only news sources are the daily newspapers. Moscow has a very friendly British and American press here, but Moscow refuses to accept the fact.

April 20:

I have been trying hard to arrange a visit to the five American Tokyo fliers, who have been interned since April 18, 1942. They began to run out of gasoline after dropping their bombs on Tokyo (and destroying a factory) and they headed for Russia. They landed at Khabarovsk and, in compliance with international law, the Soviet government had no alternative but to intern them. Russia was not technically at war with Japan. The crew consisted of Major Edward J. York, Lieutenant Nolan A. Herndon, Lieutenant Robert G. Emmens, Sergeant Theodore H. Leban and Staff Sergeant David W. Pohl. To spend a day or two with them would make a fine story. I applied to the press section of the Foreign Office and received the usual suave, "The matter will be taken up." I asked our Military Attaché if there was any objection from his standpoint, and General Michela said frankly that it was entirely up to the Soviet officials.

I asked Ambassador Standley if he could help me to get to the men. He shook his head smilingly. Nor would he discuss the matter at all beyond saying very earnestly, "Believe me when I say that the members of the crew have, since the day they landed, received all the courtesies and the best possible treatment from Soviet officials."

I never did get to see them, but I did find out quite a bit about them and how they were being treated. I got none of this information officially; in fact, General Michela closed up whenever I broached the subject. Neither Ambassador Standley nor his staff would discuss it. But a bit of information from an RAF man who knew them, a hint from here, a scrap of news from there, and it wasn't long before I had in my possession one of the best stories of the war. It will keep until after the war. This business of censoring oneself is very trying.

But this much can be told. From Khabarovsk the five men were moved in a special railroad car to Penza. They were given fine food and plenty of vodka which they didn't like much. They were in good spirits. None of them had been wounded, and they told Red Army officers accompanying them that they hadn't even been shot at. The red circle in our air force insignia was evidently mistaken by Japanese ack-ack men for their own red markings. The boys thought that a great joke.

The boys were given a *dacha* outside of Penza. It was a

comfortable house, and the food was excellent. They had all the caviar they wanted and they had plenty of meat, vegetables and wine. They were under the direct care of General Koblents, Commander of the Penza garrison. Every week a Red Army doctor came to see them, but their health was so good that his services were never needed. The *dacha* had a pool table, and a volley-ball court was fixed up for the men. Everything possible was done to make them comfortable. They had nothing but praise for the Red Army men under whose "guard" they were placed. They learned chess and spent a lot of time playing with the officers. A month after they arrived at Penza, Ambassador Standley and Second Secretary Edward Page went to visit them. Lieutenant Emmens was a bit worried because his wife had borne him a son in his absence and he was anxious for details. The Ambassador was able to reassure him.

In the summer of 1942 the military situation in the vicinity of Penza became critical. The Germans were getting too close for comfort. The crew was moved to Okhansk, a relatively small village some seventy miles southwest of Molotov, on the Kama River. In September, Ambassador Standley, General Bradley, then in Moscow on a mission, Eddie Page and General Michela again visited the boys. They brought plenty of cigarettes and American canned food with them. The Soviet government flew the American officials in a special plane from Kuibyshev to Molotov. There they were met by the Chairman of the Executive Committee of the Molotov Oblast and he acted as host on the boat trip down the river to Okhansk, a delightful journey. On their arrival they were immediately taken to the crew.

The boys were living in a well-built, comfortable, one-story house. They had a good staff of servants to care for them. They were all in good health but all impatient at the enforced idleness. They begged the Ambassador to use his influence and see that they be put to work. They wanted to do something. They know the B-25s backwards and they knew that the Russians were using some of these medium bombers of ours. Couldn't the Soviets use their specialized knowledge? They'd act as mechanics, advisors, pilots—anything, to have something to do. This lush, easy living was getting on their nerves.

The Ambassador said he would try to do something about it. He did, and the Soviet government said they'd allow the men to work with the Civil Air Fleet. Under international law, of course, they could not allow the men to engage in combat or in work even directly connected with combat. Two months ago our embassy received a notice that the men were being transferred to Ashkhabad which is in southern Russia.

If you'll wait around until after the war I'll tell you the rest. It's really a lovely story.

April 24 (Easter Sunday):

At eleven o'clock last night the Easter cry of "Kristos Voskres" was heard from the altars of the twenty-six churches in Moscow which have not been turned into museums or warehouses. Then from the throngs which filled every church and every square outside the churches came the answer from the devout, "Voistina Voskres." Twice more the priests cried "Christ Is Arisen," and twice the swelling chorus answered, "Indeed he has arisen."

From the Kremlin tower the bells played the "Internationale" as they do here in Moscow every night at eleven.* Usually, in the still night air, the sound of the Soviet national anthem carried through loudspeakers to every large square dominates the city. That was not true last night. They formed a weak, faintly heard chorus to the Easter greeting by the

* In December, 1943, a new national anthem replaced "The Internationale."

largest crowd to attend church services in Russia since pre-revolution days. Once there were 220 churches in the capital and old residents say that they were usually crowded at Easter Saturday night services. But never, they say, have there been such crowds as tried to enter the churches last night. Most of the correspondents had made arrangements to get into one church or another. Anticipating the crowded conditions, everyone started for the churches a good hour before the ceremonies were to start. But not one got within fifty yards of the entrance doors. Even at that distance the crowds were so tightly packed that devout worshipers were unable to bless themselves. Many women fainted in the packed masses of humanity, but so tightly packed were they that they were held up by those around them; there was no chance of falling.

During the past few days we have all noticed the Easter preparations. Our maids, secretaries and couriers were out looking for paint to decorate the Easter eggs, as much a part of Russian Easter tradition as of American. Women tried, for the most part in vain, to find woolen or muslin replicas of the Easter bunny for their children. Smiles were seen on the streets and in the hotel corridors. We all suspected that the churches would be crowded, and yet, surrounding the whole season, there has been a conspiracy of silence. The newspapers have not mentioned that there would be services. The radio has been silent. The midnight curfew in Moscow is a strict one, and to be found on the streets after that hour is a grievous offense. We all knew that the services began at eleven at night and usually lasted from three to five hours. Would these devout Moscovites defy the curfew? It looked very much as though even these completely regimented people would do just that.

Special Easter cakes were baked everywhere and the food shops, without explanation, offered raisins as an integral part of the special seasonal cake. Yesterday afternoon, according to ancient custom, the cakes and the eggs were brought to church to be blessed.

Then at six o'clock the Commandant of Moscow announced on the radio that the curfew would be suspended. It was the first intimation that the government was even unofficially cognizant of the holy season.

It was a soft spring night—the first we'd had—and the moon was high. As the thousands walked through the streets to their churches early in the evening the loudspeakers placed on every square were proclaiming the good news of Anglo-American advances in Tunisia. This was another raisin in the Easter cake. It was the most joyous night the Russians have had in many months. For the moment the front is static. The winter has gone and its scars are beginning to heal in the warm sun of the past week. Food rations have been slightly increased. There has been a definite feeling among the Russians recently that the British and Americans are actually contributing something really vital to the war effort. They did not have that feeling until recently.

It was strange walking home at 2 A.M. after the services. The streets were still crowded, although thousands remained in the churches waiting for the seven o'clock services in the morning. Nobody can ever call this place Godless Russia. The government by merely ignoring religion (although not forbidding worship) has most certainly hoped to see it eventually die out. No Red Army man was actually forbidden to attend services, but it was generally known that an officer lost "caste" if he appeared in church. Correspondents who have been here for a long time were amazed to see among the crowds last night a liberal sprinkling of Red Army men and officers, the first time, they say, that this has occurred. God has been a strict absentee in the educational program of the youth here in Moscow but, despite that, parents have never stopped implanting the faith of the Russian Orthodox Church into the hearts and minds of the young. There are no longer monasteries in Russia where young priests can be trained, but the priests themselves train young men in their own churches. By now the government probably realizes that attempting to kill faith is like trying to punch a hole in a pillow.

Walking home with David Nichol of the *Chicago Daily News* and Bill Downs of Columbia Broadcasting we turned into Red Square. The moon was fiery red above St. Basil's ten-domed church at the far end of the Square. We walked past the Lenin Museum to get a good look at Red Square by moonlight. It was an impressive sight. The Square was completely deserted. To the left stood the sturdy office building of the General Staff. To the right the Kremlin and Lenin's tomb. The small but impressive tomb with its alternate layers of red and black highly polished marble gleamed brightly in the light of the moon. Just behind it in the wall are buried the honored dead of the revolution, the American, John Reed, among them. Huge St. Basil's, now a museum, was silhouetted sharply against the moon, and in front of it the ugly white circular stone platform, famous because it was from here edicts of the Czar were read and it was here that enemies of the Czar were beheaded, was softened into ivory by the magic of this Easter moon. The night air was still and filled with weird fancies. Was Lenin really there in the tomb? Was he writhing because thousands of his fellow Muscovites were worshiping God tonight? Was he satisfied that the church as he knew it —a self-serving organization devoted more to the enrichment of the priests and to their political advancement than to the spiritual welfare of the people—was now dead and that a simple honest faith had taken its place? Whether Lenin's body still remained in the tomb we did not know, but we recalled the answer of Vice-Commissar Lozovsky when we asked him that question. He had merely said, "Lenin is always with us." There is no doubt of that.

[61]

This morning was almost like an Easter Sunday at home. People put on their best clothes and again attended church services. The morning papers did not mention the amazing crowds of last night. I went to Father Braun's Catholic Church to ten o'clock Mass. Like all other services his, too, were crowded. Incidentally his is the only Roman Catholic Church in Russia and he is the only Roman Catholic priest in the country. Today as every Sunday he held two masses and both were crowded. I have heard Russians say that his congregation consists mostly of Poles. It isn't true. He says that about seven-eighths of his regular church-goers are Russian. They certainly were this morning. Unlike the Russian churches, this one has pews. In every way it is like a church one would find in America. The devoutness of the congregation was too obvious to be ignored. More than five hundred of them received communion. The aisles and the back of the church were crowded with people standing in this lone Russian frontier of Catholicism.

Ambassador Standley and virtually his whole staff attended. They sat in the first few pews. Of course four NKVD men accompany the Ambassador wherever he goes. Their car follows his. The Foreign Office insists that this constant surveillance which all ambassadors and heads of missions are subjected to is for their protection. It is, in any case, an established custom here and the Admiral is so used to it that it doesn't bother him. His four guardians sat just behind the Ambassador and his group. They seemed very unhappy and uncomfortable in the strange surroundings. They watched surreptitiously and tried hard to follow others when they stood or knelt.

The popular Ambassador and his uniformed staff made a fine showing, and it was hard not to feel proud of them. His Naval Aide, Commander John Young, immaculate in what I think to be the best-looking uniform in the world, walked out at the side of the Ambassador. Young, I was surprised to see, wore on his left shoulder golden aiguillettes.

You seldom see beggars in Moscow except outside churches. I followed the Ambassador and his staff out. Six very old women, all looking alike, stood lined up on the steps holding out supplicating hands. Admiral Standley stopped and gave each of them a few rubles.

I asked John Young the significance of the gold aiguillettes. He explained that this was an official visit Admiral Standley was making to Father Braun's church; therefore he went as the President's representative and Young, by Naval custom on such official visits, wore his gold braid. It was a fine gesture toward the little priest and toward all religion when Standley, a non-Catholic, took the trouble to attend services —officially.

Father Leopold Braun was born in New Bedford, Mass., in 1903. At Sacred Heart School, at Holy Family High School in New Bedford, and at the Assumption College in Worcester his main interest was music. He was ordained a priest and then sent to Louvain to study music at the Augustinian Monastery. Incidentally he picked up a few languages. At this time Bishop Eugene Neven, a French cleric, was the Administrative Apostolic to Russia. The Bishop needed an assistant, for his domain was huge. The Bishop applied to the head of his Order and Father Braun was elected. He came to Russia with Ambassador Bullitt just after the Litvinov-Roosevelt pact guaranteeing religious freedom in Russia to American nationals was signed in 1933.

Not long after his arrival in Moscow the Bishop returned to France for a holiday. He was never given a visa to return, so the young priest from New Bedford found himself in the position of Administrative Apostolic to Russia. It was a great challenge for any young priest, and today Father Braun is high in his praise for Ambassador Bullitt but for whom his

position would have been impossible. Father Braun was tolerated but not helped by the Soviet government, and time after
time Bill Bullitt interceded and helped the priest with advice,
money and encouragement. Father Braun inherited the old
French church, St. Louis de Français, on Malaya Lubianka not
far from the center of Moscow. It is an old church which was
designed by the same architect who designed the magnificent
Bolshoi Theatre. It was rotting away from neglect, and the
first job of the absolutely penniless priest (according to the
rules of his Order he does not draw a salary but lives entirely
on charity) was to rehabilitate the old building. He found
that he had 25,000 parishioners in Moscow. Thousands,
through fear, refrained from attending services but gradually
he built up a substantial though poverty-stricken congregation.

A less vigorous man might have given up the fight in dis-
couragement as obstacle after obstacle was put in his way.
His church was robbed five times, the vandals even commit-
ting the sacrilege of stealing sacred church vessels from the
altar. He complained each time, but the only satisfaction he
received was a bill from the authorities. According to Soviet
law all church property (since 1917) belongs to the state and
Father Braun was held personally responsible for the loss.
He settled it by asserting truthfully his quite obvious poverty
and by waving the Litvinov-Roosevelt pact at the authorities.

Then he pulled the master stroke of quoting Stalin's own
constitution which insists that the state and the church are
quite separate. Obviously, if the church and state are separate,
the state has no claim to church property and no legal basis
for demanding that the church be responsible for property
that has been stolen. Father Braun won his case. Although
technically he is the American chaplain in Moscow and, as
such, a representative of our government, he is not accorded
the privileges of a diplomat. He had no fuel to heat his church

last winter. He has a car but no gasoline cards are issued to him as is the case with diplomats and correspondents.

Father Braun lives in what was once the French Embassy, a startling-looking ornate structure on Bolshaya Yakimanka. At present it is the Turkish legation. According to Russian standards, his four-room apartment is quite comfortable; his magnificent library, in part a heritage from his predecessor, is distinguished, but his food rations are the same as those of any Russian citizen. You take your life in your hands when you visit Father Braun. He owns the largest and loudest-barking dog in Moscow, a huge shepherd who answers to the incongruous name of Pax. Pax greeted me on my first visit with a very antagonistic demonstration which left me limp. But Pax worships his master and once she sees Father Braun acting friendly toward you her antagonism vanishes. The other day I was at Father Braun's and stayed late in the afternoon.

"If there is food enough I'd like you to stay for dinner," he said.

We went into the kitchen and found his cook fixing his meal. The dinner consisted of a small saucepan of bean soup. That and some black bread was all. I thought that we might do better at the Metropole. We set out. First there was a five-minute walk to the street car. Buses and street cars are invariably packed in Moscow, and it is seldom that you can get on the first one that comes along. After a long wait we managed to squeeze into a crowded street car. A ten-minute ride brought us to the subway. The subway was crowded too, but eventually we found room. Another fifteen minutes brought us to the Square of the Revolution station near the Metropole.

"Don't mind this trip," Father Braun laughed. "I do it at six o'clock every morning in order to get to church to say seven-o'clock Mass."

[65]

Visions of the little priest waiting for street cars, shivering in wintry blasts in the freezing Moscow mornings, came to me, and I shuddered. At the Metropole we have our principal meal at noon and that, most of the time, is good enough. The evening meal is usually but not always a cold meal. We were unlucky. It was a cold-meal night, but we did have caviar, salami, cheese and excellent Russian bread and, with a bottle of Caucasian wine, fared much better than we would have on his saucepan of bean soup.

May 3:

Alexander Werth and I went out to inspect an anti-aircraft battery yesterday and today both of us are much the worse off for our experience. When the Red Army has visitors, it entertains, the entertainment usually consisting of 10 percent music, 10 percent speeches, and 80 percent vodka.

Vodka is slightly more palatable than the drinking water, which is heavily chlorinated. It is well that it is chlorinated. When the snow melted some seven weeks ago hundreds of bodies were found rotting under it not far from Moscow, close to the source of the water supply. When the ice in the river broke, bodies began to come to the surface. We are grateful for the pure water we get from our taps, but it is very hard to drink. It goes down all right because it is very cold, but you taste the chlorine afterwards. It has a sickening taste. Actually, we drink a glass of water and then have a vodka chaser. The first makes us feel slightly ill; the second makes our eyes water and chokes us. There is virtually no mineral water left in Moscow. The wonderful Narzan water, quite equal and perhaps superior to any American brand, came from a district now occupied by the Germans.

The anti-aircraft battery was about thirty miles from Moscow and we rode out with Vasev, who is known to us all as the Vice-Goon. Nikolai Palgunov is his boss. We have to see Palgunov to arrange facilities for trips and we fight with him over cuts made in our stories; he is, in short, our only contact with official Russia. We have a test here which decides when a man has stayed too long in Russia or, to use the expression popularized by the British, has "missed too many boats." If a correspondent comes to the luncheon table after a visit to the Foreign Office and says, "Palgunov is not such a bad fellow, after all," we all know that he has missed too many boats and should be sent home. That is our infallible test. We accept it when someone says that he is being followed constantly or that his room was searched. We seldom believe it, but we accept it as a normal example of Moscow nerves. But no one can say to us "Palgunov is not such a bad fellow, after all." He represents everything that makes life difficult for a correspondent here. His name is pronounced Pal-goon-of, with emphasis on the middle syllable. It logically followed, of course, that he be called the Goon and now so widespread has that habit become that even ambassadors and heads of military missions talk about him quite seriously as the Goon. It naturally followed that his assistant Vasev be known as the Vice-Goon. He is a short, stocky man, and, if we knew him under different circumstances, we might even like him. But it is treason for us to like anyone from the press section of the Foreign Office. In any case, the Vice-Goon took Alex, Sofiano and me to the battery and an interesting trip it was. The location of these batteries is, of course, a strict military secret. You could pass within a quarter of a mile of this one and not realize there was anything there. Four slim barrels pointed to the sky—that was all. Everything else was underground and yet, when we arrived, a crew of about fifty men and girls appeared from nowhere. Twenty girls are members of this crew; twenty fresh, healthy-looking youngsters all under twenty-one. They were all students when war came and they were selected for their quick intelligence. Their job is a delicate one. They handle both the visual range finder and the precise radio detection finder. All four guns were 85 mm. guns which throw up a pretty heavy shell. All four of course are synchronized in the manner common to both British and American anti-aircraft batteries. These guns throw a shell up to about 27,000 feet and are effective at that height.

The battery has three German aircraft to its credit. If there is a mass raid at night they throw up a screen barrage protecting a specified zone. Other batteries in the same "ring" toss up similar barrages, and the various zones overlap so that there is little chance (theoretically) of German planes getting through. As a matter of fact no raiders have gotten through to Moscow for a long while now. Whether it is because they tried and failed or merely because they thought Moscow not worth the bombing no one knows. We all expect a big raid any time now, and no one is looking forward to it. But for home consumption Germany must bomb Moscow and hurt it. That would take some of the curse off the fact that (at the moment) the German Army has reached a sort of stalemate here in Russia. Goebbels must be urging a bombing of Moscow. I would, were I in his place. None of us here believes in the invincibility of any anti-aircraft defense. We remember London too vividly. We know what happened to Cologne and Essen. If the Germans are willing to accept a 15 percent loss they could undoubtedly hurt Moscow badly.

Back in 1941 the Germans did send 200 bombers against Moscow one night, according to official Soviet reports. That night twenty-two of them were downed. The damage done by the rest was not great. In fact, you have to look very carefully in Moscow to find any bomb damage at all. This is in part due to the rapidity with which repairs are made. Moscow is protected by two rings of anti-aircraft guns and, in addition, guns are mounted on the roofs of most large buildings. I noticed that during the bombing here in the fall of 1941. It would be startling to stand in front of the National Hotel across from the Kremlin, look up and see jets of flame burst over the Moscow Hotel to the left of the Square. These were from big guns atop the hotel. We knew they were big not only from the sound of the blast but from the crack of spent shrapnel pieces which fell on the pavements.

The colonel who was in charge of anti-aircraft in the area we visited explained the working and co-ordination of guns and finders to us. It was quite the same as in Britain. He showed us the quarters under the ground where the crews lived. The twenty girls lived in two large dugouts lined with logs and planks and immaculately clean. The walls were decorated with pictures of Soviet leaders and a Holland stove stood in a corner. It was hard to believe that we were below ground. A series of passageways all wooden lined and floored led to each of the guns, to the visual and radio finders and to the men's quarters equally clean and comfortable. They all slept on cots which were covered with excellent blankets. The favorite recreation of the crew was volley ball. They had fixed up a court just a few feet from the guns and the men played the girls. The girls won easily. It was pleasant in the spring warmth watching the laughing girls in uniform and the soldiers getting grimmer and grimmer as the game progressed. The sun glinted on the barrels of the guns and only the fact that two men remained at each gun served as a reminder that the war wasn't too far away. Fresh green patches were beginning to show in the tawny brown of the earth and a clump of birch trees not far off gleamed whitely. The laughter of the girls rang out in the still air. It was spring and difficult to think of war.

The colonel asked if we would stay for "a cup of tea." Alex Werth groaned and said, "Now we're in for it."

[69]

When a Red Army group asks you casually to remain for "a cup of tea" it means a great deal more than a cup of tea. We climbed down into the dugout and, after traversing one of the passageways, entered a large, comfortable room. I winced when I saw the table. It was set for about twenty-five people and in front of each place was a bottle of vodka. We sat down and drank our first toast. The colonel gave that. It was the one you hear most often, "To Victory with Stalin." You have to drink Russian toasts bottoms up. As you bring your glass to your lips there is always a shout of "*Pei do dna*," which means, literally, "drink to the bottom." Alex nudged me and told me to answer the toast. He speaks Russian well so I protested, but Alex explained that he'd give one later. So I got up and cried out, "To Victory with Stalin, Roosevelt and Churchill." That met with a roar of approval and then we went to work on the food. There was caviar and herring, both of which go well with vodka. There was a magnificent salad, the chief feature of which was fresh cucumbers. Fresh cucumbers came to Moscow a week ago and we have them whenever we can.

Now more toasts followed. Every man there gave a toast and always the cry of "*Pei do dna*" or merely "*do dna*." Sofiano, the only woman present, doesn't drink more than one or two glasses of vodka so she was all right, but Werth and I were in a tough spot. Let us turn away from a half-finished glass but for a moment and someone would fill it. Conversation was loud now and everyone was smiling.

It was yesterday that the Anglo-American victory at Bizerte was announced and we had to toast General Eisenhower and General Montgomery. We toasted everyone but Rommel. Then came the music. One of the men brought in an accordion and he could play it as only a Russian can play that instrument. The men sang and now everyone was friendly and everyone was laughing and a remembered song would bring forth a dozen lusty voices. We had a sort of veal cutlet with French-fried potatoes and more vodka. The accordion player had a few drinks and the tempo heightened. He began to sing. He sang *Vecher na Reide* ("Enemy in the Harbor") and the soldiers shouted for Ivan Borisovich to dance. A smiling blond lieutenant got up a bit unsteadily, but there was nothing unsteady about the way he danced. We clapped our hands in time to the music and shouted and his feet twinkled as he threw them out from under him in the classic movement which even we in America know as an integral part of any Cossack or Ukrainian dance. He whirled and leaped and the soldiers roared with laughter and brought him more vodka. He downed the vodka without stopping the cadence of his semi-acrobatic gyrations. Everything seemed a bit unreal now. We were underground, but you wouldn't know it. The long room was snug, and by now it seemed as if we had all been friends for years. The accordion player swung into "Merry Men," a popular song with troops, and the soldiers danced a sort of wild waltz with each other as partners.

"How are you doing?" Alex Werth asked.

"I'd hate to have to thread a needle," I told him. My colonel friend never let my glass lower its vodka content—and it would be losing considerable face if I refused his smiling "*do dna.*" A delightful atmosphere of happy confusion filled the air. The highest extravagances in toasts seemed quite normal. Poor Vasev* sat by himself, a bit bewildered. As a Foreign Office official he felt out of place; he couldn't join in this hilarious gaiety. It was impossible not to love these good-looking, gay Red Army soldiers. All were young, well built, and very frankly happy, because the daily monotony of their Army existence was being broken. This was the Rus-

---

* Two months later Vasev was killed when his car hit a mine near the front.

sia that lay beneath the unsmiling faces one saw by the thousand in Moscow. Give them food, music, vodka, and the real spirit of *joie de vivre* came out. They were, in short, having a hell of a time. So was I.

Then the girls came in. Everyone cheered. We pushed the table back and danced some more. None of the girls would drink the vodka. None of them smoked. Soldiers get a ration of both vodka and cigarettes, but these youngsters said they had arranged to get chocolate instead. But they were gay and laughing, and they sang the sad words of the songs the accordion player was thumping out. The soldiers danced with them and with each other and all of a sudden I found myself dancing with the colonel and he was singing at the top of his voice. Red Army soldiers often dance together.

The colonel took me home in his car, and he insisted upon coming up to my room for a nightcap. I had perhaps two inches of vodka left in a bottle and the nightcap fitted him. We were blood brothers now, and when he left he ceremoniously kissed me on both cheeks. It's just an old Russian custom, especially among army men. It was a good day. It's always good here when you can get away from Moscow and the horrible bureaucracy of the Foreign Office and actually get to know real Russians. They're wonderful people, and they deserve so much more than they have or will have for years and years.

June 1:

At home the kids would be getting out baseball bats and gloves and hurrying to the nearest vacant lot. Here in Moscow, the youngsters just out of school were hurrying to the embankment across the narrow river. They laughed and yelled, and then a soldier gave an order and the laughter stopped.

The kids lined up. There were about sixty of them, one-third of them girls. Not one was more than fourteen. The soldier gave crisp orders. The kids marched smartly up and down the embankment. They marched by twos and fours, with their drillmaster barking out military commands. They drilled for one hour—these children of Mars—and then they were dismissed. When their time came, these youngsters would already have considerable basic military training.

As the kids hurried away from the drill ground, again laughing gaily, it was not to a baseball diamond or playground. Their real work of the day was just commencing. Children in Moscow have no time for play. Time after time they have heard their parents and teachers say, "This is your war, too. What are you doing about it?"

The children of Russia are organized into a society called the Pioneers. The duties of Pioneers are not nearly so pleasant as those of our Boy or Girl Scouts. During wartime there's no play, no long hikes in the country, no lessons in knot-tying or woodcraft. These Pioneers do not even have uniforms. Their job is not one which would appeal to an ordinary American boy, but it's a mighty essential one.

When school is done and drilling is finished, each group of Pioneers is assigned to a city block. They find out where families need help. They go into homes and do what is needed. If the woman of the house is too ill or elderly, or is nursing a child, they do the marketing, sweep the floors, help with the dishes and sometimes (to allow the wife a night off to visit friends) they remain and mind the babies.

Within the Pioneers there is a secret group, the envy of all the others. These are called the Timurs. Some years ago, a motion picture depicted a boy named Timur who had very great powers. He often visited the dirty homes of mortals and merely by waving a wand would make the house immaculate. If there was wood to be chopped, why, that was a cinch. He'd wave his wand again and there would be a neat pile of logs all ready for the stove.

When the family came home to find the house clean and wood piled in the bin, they would know that Timur had been visiting. Timur was a great favorite with Russian youngsters, and the Pioneers adopted his name for their secret society.

A flying group of Timur lads will descend on a house, give it a thorough cleaning, chop enough wood to last a week—and then vanish. The housewife comes home and looks at her now clean and tidy house and thinks that the age of miracles has come again.

Although discouraged by military authority, the children have actually done a job in combat at the front. I met fifteen-year-old Vassya, who was just back from the front. He was a baby-faced kid with wide-open eyes. He was very unhappy. He was being sent to school. However, he said stoutly, a good soldier must always obey orders.

Vassya lived the life of an ordinary country lad in the region around Kharkov. The Germans came and killed his father, and Vassya ran away to join the guerrillas. At first, he acted as a scout for them—a spy who could go into occupied villages without fear of detection. But many of his comrades in the guerrillas were killed, and young Vassya picked up the gun of one who had fallen. In time he became an expert Tommy-gunner, incidentally using a Thompson machine gun made in Bridgeport, Connecticut. Vassya liked the gun very much, he told me, and wished to thank the workers in Bridgeport who made such a wonderful weapon.

Oh, yes, he had killed many Germans—so many, in fact, that the Germans heard of him and learned his name and took their typical revenge. They hanged his mother and sister, who were still in Kharkov. Fearing the boy would do something really rash now, the guerrilla chief made him go to Moscow. He'd never been to Moscow before and was having the time of his life.

A group of Pioneers became heroes not long ago in an occupied region near Kursk. The kids there had a swimming hole, and when spring came, they spent most of their time in it. Unfortunately, the Germans also discovered the hole, ordered the kids to run along and swam there every day themselves. There was only one road leading from the town to the swimming paradise. The kids thought of a bright idea.

They found some very old and dirty phonograph records. They planted these on the road traversed by the Germans. Both the Germans and the Russians have an anti-personnel mine which looks like a phonograph record. When the Germans saw some of these half-buried records, they suspected that the guerrillas had been active. The Germans have a healthy respect for Russian mines. They brought up a machine-gun detachment and sprayed the road with bullets, hoping to explode the "mines." But no explosion resulted. They brought up heavier guns and sent barrage after barrage into the road. This took some days, during which the kids swam happily in the pool.

Pioneer ingenuity triumphed again in the Kursk neighborhood, and all Russia is laughing about another stunt perpetrated by the youngsters. The kids heard some nature-loving Germans discussing a report that there was a nightingale in a small woods just outside the town. They would bring a recording machine to the woods and record the song of the nightingale. Clever young Ivan Pechnikov had a bright idea. He was an expert at imitating bird songs. He would go into the woods and warble his tunes. The Germans would come along, and the guerrillas would capture them. He ran to a guerrilla detachment near by and they agreed to his plan.

It worked beautifully. Ivan and his whistling led the Germans to where the guerrillas were waiting. The unsuspecting Nazis were blissfully recording the song of the youngster, thinking it a Russian nightingale, when the guerrillas came. They captured the small detachment of Germans and the truck which contained the recording machine. They played the record back. It began with the lovely notes of young Ivan and then came shouts and curses and the sound of gunfire and the wail of captured Germans. They hadn't had a chance to turn off their recording machine.

A youngster whose story is told wherever Pioneers gather is fourteen-year-old Misha Nikolaev. His family, too, was wiped out and he joined a band of guerrillas. A Russian war correspondent from *Pravda* was wandering around looking for material when he met young Misha on the road. They walked along, and soon the kid was telling the correspondent a fantastic story, none of which the correspondent believed. He told of going behind the German lines and stealing six horses. Oh, yes, he got the horses back to his detachment. He told how he had surprised three Germans chopping wood in a forest. They had laid their guns on the ground. He had crawled up close, grabbed one of the guns, captured the three Germans and then brought them back to his guerrilla group.

"Go on, young Munchausen!" the correspondent laughed. "Tell me more."

"In all, I have killed fourteen Germans," the boy said earnestly, "and once I captured a machine-gun nest alone by sneaking in close and throwing a hand grenade."

They parted, the correspondent laughing at the youngster's boastfulness. He reached a near-by guerrilla outfit and asked the commander for some of his experiences.

"We have only one person here who is worth a story," the commander said. "That's young Misha. We took him in because all his family had been killed. He had orders just to help with the cooking, but we found him sneaking off on his own. Once he brought back six horses. Again he came in with three captured Germans. Only the other day he actually put out of commission a machine-gun nest that had been giving us a lot of trouble. He's a very shy youngster, and I'm afraid you will have trouble getting his story from him."

"Shy!" the correspondent exploded. "He's the most boastful little brat I ever saw. I met him down the road, and he told me the whole story, none of which I believed."

"The general is visiting us tomorrow," the commander explained, "and he is going to give young Misha a decoration. I told him that the general would wish to hear the whole story of his exploits. For a week, the kid has been in terror. He has been rehearsing his story and today he told me he was going for a long walk and that he would try the story out on the first man he met. He thought that would give him some practice in telling it."

The correspondent mentally apologized to the kid and then brought the story to Moscow. Needless to say, the Pioneers adopted Misha as their No. 1 hero.

Another youngster much respected by Russian kids is ten-year-old Vadim. He quite unwittingly played a practical joke on the Germans, one which appealed greatly to the robust sense of humor of his countrymen. Vadim lived in a small village called Uspenskoe. The Germans were approaching and Vadim was greatly worried. He had a small pig which had become a pet to him. There aren't many dogs left in Russia—dogs have to eat meat and meat is scarce. But pigs can get along nicely without meat. The thought that his beloved pig might fall into the hands of the Nazis filled Vadim with terror. He would hide it somewhere. But where? He knew how thoroughly the Germans searched all farmhouses when they entered a village. Vadim finally solved the difficulty. He hid the pig in the kitchen behind the huge Holland stove. (Incidentally, in Holland the same stove is called a Russian stove.)

The Germans came and they searched the house. Vadim held his breath as they went through the kitchen, afraid that the pig might squeal and reveal his presence. But the little pig never uttered a sound. When the Germans left, Vadim found out the reason for the porker's silence. The heat from the stove had smothered the poor pig, and he was quite dead.

Vadim, his heart heavy, decided to bury his pet. Another difficulty arose. Germans always dug up any spot which showed fresh earth because they knew that the farmers often buried food and weapons. Then, too, parachutists often buried their telltale silk parachutes. Vadim didn't want his pig to be found by the hated Germans. But a bright thought struck him. He went out of the village and into the fields beyond. The fighting had been heavy here and Vadim soon found what he wanted. He wanted a German helmet and an iron cross. At night he buried his dead pet. He pushed a stick into the ground at the head of the grave and placed the steel helmet on it. He hung the iron cross over the helmet. This grave he was sure would not be defiled by the Germans. But the general in command of this sector of the front decided to move his headquarters to the village of Uspenskoe. He wasn't there long before he held an inspection of the graves of the Nazi dead. He came to the grave which Vadim had dug. Curious, he turned over the iron cross and then cried out with grief when he saw the name engraved upon it.

"This is the grave of my son," he said. "It is unfitting that he lie in hated Russian earth."

He gave orders. His staff brought a nice pine coffin on which was emblazoned the swastika. Soldiers came hurrying with shovels. They dug into the fresh earth. As they came to the remains the General bowed his head in sorrow and a guard of honor set off a volley of twenty rifle shots in honor of the son of their general. The General leaned over the grave only to be confronted with the contented face of Vadim's pig.

The story was heard by a guerrilla band, which spread it over the countryside. It even came to Moscow. It spread through this sector of the German Army, and the poor general was never able to command the respect from his men he had hitherto enjoyed.

When Pioneer youngsters take their oath of allegiance, the ceremonies are mighty solemn. In the presence of comrades and always with some ranking Red Army officer in attendance, the boy or girl takes this oath: "I, a young Pioneer of Soviet Russia, before my comrades, solemnly promise the Great Stalin and the Party of Lenin to live, study and work so as to justify the high name of Young Leninist. I promise to be decent, hard working and brave. With all my heart I hate the Fascist invaders. I will always be ready to defend the Fatherland. I serve in the names of fighters who gave their lives for our happiness. I will remember eternally that their blood burns on my Pioneer scarf and on the red banner." (God, of course, is an absentee when any official oath is taken in Russia.)

Then the commander of the group cries out the slogan of the Pioneers: "*Bud Gotov.*" Like our Boy Scout motto, this means literally: "Be Prepared."

The candidate answers: "*Vsegda Gotov,*" or "Always Prepared."

There are ten rules which form the Pioneer credo and they are similar to our Boy Scout articles of behavior, except for the first two, which are quite startling.

The ten commandments are: One: A Pioneer is true to the cause of Lenin and Stalin. Two: A Pioneer passionately loves his Fatherland and hates its enemies. Three: A Pioneer considers it an honor to become a member of Lenin's Komsomol. Four: A Pioneer is honest and truthful; his word is as firm as steel. Five: A Pioneer is as brave as an eagle; he despises cowards. Six: A Pioneer has a sharp eye, iron muscles and steel nerves. Seven: A Pioneer needs knowledge as soldiers need arms in battle. Eight: A Pioneer is unafraid of hard work.

Nine: A Pioneer is the pride of the family and his school. Ten: A Pioneer is an example to all children.

June 8:

Joseph E. Davies left today after a two-week visit which has left us bewildered. Mr. Davies said that he had come merely to deliver a letter to Stalin. Although he didn't say what the letter contained, we are all convinced that it was a suggestion from President Roosevelt that he, Stalin and Churchill meet. What bewilders us (and we are sure bewilders Stalin) is the fact that the President had sent Mr. Davies to deliver the letter. Our embassy is just across the street from the Kremlin and Ambassador Standley is never too busy to walk over to the Kremlin with a letter.

There was a distinct Hollywood tinge to the whole Davies visit. The huge DC-4 which brought Davies to Moscow must weigh about 56,000 pounds. It had a crack crew of nine men. Mr. Davies brought his nephew with him to act as his secretary (his nephew is Lieutenant Stamm, a naval officer). Mr. Davies brought his former valet with him to supervise the preparation of his food. (His former valet is now a corporal in the U. S. Army.) Mr. Davies brought his personal physician with him, a necessary precaution because Mr. Davies is not in good health. We all admired the courage of Mr. Davies in undertaking a very difficult 16,000-mile trip by air. No one here questions his need of a secretary, a valet and a physician. But everyone in journalistic and diplomatic circles here questions the necessity of such a formidable entourage to deliver two ounces of mail.

Maxim Litvinov arrived a day or so after Mr. Davies, and Litvinov brought a print of the Warner Brothers picture, *Mission to Moscow*, with him. Stalin tendered a dinner to Mr. Davies at the Kremlin a few days after his arrival. It was a typical Kremlin show reserved for visiting big shots with the usual twenty or so courses and thirty or so toasts. The press, of course, is never permitted to breathe the rarefied air of Kremlin dinners, but our friends in the various embassies always give us accurate reports of such dinners. To us the real big news of the dinner was the fact that Nikolai Palgunov attended. That meant that he was still in high favor. We had been hoping that his inefficiency and poor judgment would by now have percolated up to the sacrosanct presence of Vyshinsky or Molotov and that he might be on his way out. The fact that he was at the dinner meant that he was still the white-haired boy in the press department of the Foreign Office, which is depressing news for us. The other news was that the film, *Mission to Moscow*, was shown in Stalin's private projection room after the dinner. Some of the British and Americans who have been here for many, many years and who really know Russia told us that Stalin gave a magnificent performance during the showing of the picture.

"Walter Huston was fine," a British member of the diplomatic corps told us, "but he couldn't compare with Stalin. Do you know that Stalin kept a straight face throughout the showing? He didn't laugh once."

A few days later the film was shown at our embassy at one of the usual Saturday-afternoon shows. It was a beautiful technical job and the performances of the character actors who figured in the trial scenes were especially magnificent. But the film portrayed a Russia that none of us had ever seen. This would have been all right, except that the picture purported to be factual and the Russia shown in the film had as much relation to the Russia we all knew as Shang-ri-la would have to the real Tibet.

Correspondents like Henry Shapiro, Jean Champenois and Alfred Cholerton who had been in Moscow for many years were bewildered. The film had telescoped two purge trials into one and had not presented them with any degree of accuracy; no fault of course in a picture which did not claim to be factual. But this picture did. We all had copies (in English) of the testimony given at the trials and it varied considerably from what was shown on the screen. In the actual trials Radek's defense had been impassioned and brilliant and Bukharin's vituperative comebacks at Prosecutor Vyshinsky's expense masterpieces of invective. The Warner Brothers' or Davies' version differed considerably. In the film Radek is condemned to death. Actually he was sentenced to ten years' imprisonment.

The veteran diplomats were also astounded at the treatment given Lord Chislen in the picture. Chislen was British Ambassador to Russia during Mr. Davies' tenure of the American ambassadorship. In the film Chislen was made out to be a halfwit. Veteran embassy officials and correspondents couldn't understand that at all.

"Litvinov once told me during those days," a correspondent said, "that there were only two foreign diplomats in Moscow he had any respect for. They were Chislen and the German Ambassador, Von Schulenberg."

We were all frankly embarrassed by the picture. I was especially amazed because I know the Warner brothers and their brilliant staff that so faithfully mirrored the careers of men like Dr. Erlich, Pasteur, Zola and others whom they made subjects of pictures. It was hard to believe that they had made this factually incorrect film. It would have been so easy for Warner Brothers to have called in any correspondent who had spent some time in Russia to check up on factual details. If the purpose of the picture was to improve relations between America and Russia it was completely defeated by the obvious inaccuracies shown on the screen. It was such a pity that no one with any knowledge of Russia was called in to advise on the story. It could have been a great picture and an honest one.

I met one of the officials of Voks the day after the picture was shown to us. Voks passes on all foreign pictures before they are shown in Russia. I asked him if *Mission to Moscow* would be released to the public.

"Well," he hesitated, "we'd like to release it, but of course," he added in perfect seriousness, "we'd have to cut a great deal of the Russian part out of it."

Mr. Davies was right on Russia. He played a long shot, the long shot came through, and one must respect his judgment for that. He has done everything possible to "sell" Russia to America in books, magazine articles, radio talks and speeches. But Russia is so magnificent in her courage, her endurance, and her stubborn refusal to ever admit that she is beaten that she doesn't need conventional propaganda to make America respect her. Her six million dead speak more eloquently for her cause than could any mere propaganda film, no matter how beautifully acted or directed. But then *Mission to Moscow* was not really a picture about Russia; it was a picture about Mr. Davies.

We had two press conferences with Mr. Davies at the lovely guest house where distinguished visitors are quartered in Moscow. Recently we have all been greatly disturbed at the lack of co-operation our military authorities were getting from the Kremlin. Time after time our War Department has cabled our representatives in Moscow asking them to get information concerning captured German material. To date, virtually all of these requests have been politely parried by Kremlin officials. Standley has been greatly perturbed about it. Several of us at the press conference with Mr. Davies suggested that he ask Stalin for a little more co-operation. Mr. Davies didn't seem to believe that we were informing him accurately as to the lack of co-operation our officials were getting—a situation which is common knowledge in Moscow. We all left the press conference pretty discouraged. Mr.

Davies had been charming and a fine host, but his lack of knowledge regarding Russia shocked us all. We correspondents without exception admire and like the Russians enormously—so much so that we have taken unto ourselves one of their greatest characteristics, that of realistic thinking. Like Standley, we too think of Lend-Lease as a two-way street. We didn't want much material from Russia and when we did and Russia had it, she gave without stint. The ships which brought Lend-Lease material to Murmansk all went home carrying lumber and some raw materials which Russia could spare. But what we really wanted was information; information from the Red Army about German weapons that would help our men defend themselves when the time came for that so-called second front. We wanted our military representatives to live at the front as our observers lived at the British front even before we were in the war. It might be too much to expect that Russia give us the design of her magnificent new gun, the "Katusha," but we thought it not unreasonable that our representatives be shown every weapon captured by the Russians from the Germans. Mr. Davies didn't seem to understand our point of view. Unfortunately, his press conference was "off the record." So was a subsequent conference he held with Eddy Gilmore of the AP, David Nichol of the *Chicago Daily News* and myself.

It would be very easy at this point to accuse us (the correspondents) of being too officious, of taking too much upon ourselves, of trying to act as amateur diplomats when we were, after all, nothing but reporters. What right had we to attempt to influence Mr. Davies or any other emissary coming from Washington? Well, frankly, we had every right in the world. We were Americans first—and correspondents second. We knew Moscow by now the way we knew our own home towns. Because our position was unofficial, we were given information and we picked up gossip that even our own embassy and G-2 people could not by virtue of their official position have access to. If we couldn't be doing something useful we should, we all felt, be in uniform. That's why we all tried to give Mr. Davies the real picture of the difficulties under which our official representatives were laboring. We hoped that he'd go right to Stalin with a strong complaint. We thought that Stalin, if informed by Mr. Davies, might with one slash cut the absurd red tape that was preventing us from being 100 percent partners in this enterprise of war. As it was, we were members of the same corporation but we all felt our relationship should be that of partners; the relationship Britain and America enjoy, with mutual trust and respect. We hoped that Mr. Davies would report what we had said to the President. We weren't talking opinions. A reporter can't indulge in the luxury of opinion. We were talking facts and, if we were a little rough on Mr. Davies, he realized we meant no discourtesy; we were merely trying to emphasize the importance of what we wanted to convey.

Anyhow, Mr. Davies and his entourage have gone now, flying off in the beautiful DC-4 which now has the phrase "Mission to Moscow" painted on its nose. The crew had intended naming their ship "The Kremlin Gremlin." Last night Lieutenant Stamm, on behalf of Mr. Davies, came to my room to distribute largesse. He left us a lovely bottle of brandy and some twenty cartons of American cigarettes. It was a gracious gesture, appreciated by all of us because the embassy has virtually run out of cigarettes and ours went long ago. From our selfish point of view it justified the whole Davies visit.

June 10:

The more I get to know Ambassador Standley the more impressed I am with him. Every British and American correspondent here feels the same way. Standley has the rugged, uncompromising honesty that the pioneers must have had. I knew him when I came to Russia two years ago as a member of the Averell Harriman-Lord Beaverbrook commission in 1941. I doubt if there is a man in Moscow who doesn't admire our Ambassador. It is thrilling to have dinner with Sir Archibald Clarke-Kerr and listen to the British Ambassador extol this great American.

"He has done more to promote real American-Russian relations than any one man," Clarke-Kerr said the other night. "And I for one never hesitate to go to him for advice when I need it."

The world became conscious of Standley in March, 1943, when he gave his now famous statement to the correspondents in which he charged that the Russian government was not telling the people of Russia how much aid we were giving the country in the form of Lend-Lease.

It wasn't a formal press conference. Ambassador Standley had just returned to Moscow from Kuibyshev and the correspondents thought they'd drop in to see him. Sure he'd be glad to see them, but he had no news. They sat in the comfortable library of Spasso House and the Ambassador told them of his long train ride back from Kuibyshev; how the snow was melting in the old city; how living conditions had improved. It was so informal that none of the correspondents were taking notes. Eddie Page, Second Secretary of the embassy, who usually takes a transcript of press conferences, didn't have a notebook out.

It was Eddy Gilmore who asked casually, "We're sending quite a lot of stuff over here, aren't we, Mr. Ambassador?"

The Ambassador said that was true. He quoted from the Lend-Lease report which had recently been made by Ed Stettinius. And then the Ambassador dropped a bomb that exploded in that comfortable library and was heard all over the world.

"Ever since I've been here," he said slowly, obviously

[86]

choosing his words, "I've been carefully looking for recognition in the Russian press of the fact that they are getting material help not only through Lend-Lease but through Red Cross and Russian-American relief, but I've yet to find any acknowledgment of that."

Eddie Page, reared in the careful standard of the State Department, swallowed twice and looked stricken. The correspondents stopped smiling and then Henry Shapiro of the United Press asked, "Is that off the record, Mr. Ambassador, or may we use it?"

"Use it," the Admiral's eyes twinkled as the boys grabbed for pencils and paper. "It's not fair to mislead the American people into giving millions from their pockets to help the Russian people, and the Russian people not even know about it. The American people are doing it because of their friendly feeling toward the Russians, but the Russian people don't know a thing about it. The Soviet authorities seem to be trying to create the impression at home as well as abroad that they are fighting the war alone with their own resources only."

Correspondents no longer have automobiles in Moscow. They had to rush from the Ambassador's residence two blocks to the subway. They rushed, all right. They knew they had one of the biggest stories of the year. They hurried to the Foreign Office where stories are censored and threw the Ambassador's quotes into typewriters. The censors looked and went white. The correspondents were smart enough not to comment, not to embellish the story. That could be censored. They merely sent the exact wording of the Ambassador's remarks, and even the censors, who so cheerfully use their red pencils on our stories, could not censor a statement made by an Ambassador. They passed the story in full.

The next day the storm broke. Standley knew that he'd be criticized for his outspokenness. He knew that the protocol-minded, soft-tongued State Department would be horrified. The communist newspapers in New York and London hit the Ambassador with pens of vitriol. But no one said that he had told anything but the truth. The Moscow papers did not comment at first and then suddenly there was daily mention in the papers of American material being used on the front and on the home front. The Stettinius report was published in full. Millions of Russians who hadn't known of this material help warmed toward America which was giving so freely. The effect of Ambassador Standley's statement was far reaching. The account of America's participation in the Tunis campaign was played up to a greater extent than before and all of this culminated in Stalin's friendly May Day proclamation to the Red Army. Stalin knew something which the misguided communists of New York and London didn't know: he knew that William Standley was a damn good friend of Russia but that Standley, like himself, was a realist and not a fairy godfather who liked to distribute gifts anonymously. Stalin perhaps knew the whole story of Standley's statement and what was behind it and was probably chuckling, "Good for you, Admiral."

It all began last October when smart Henry Cassidy of the Associated Press sent a series of questions to Stalin which Stalin answered. In answer to a question regarding American aid, Stalin wrote bluntly, "In comparison with the assistance which the Soviet Union, drawing off the main forces of the Fascist troops, is rendering to its allies, the assistance from the allies to the Soviet Union is meanwhile of little effect."

This statement, given wide publication, bothered Standley, who knew exactly what aid America had sent. Shortly afterwards, official Washington asked Standley to get expressions of opinion from Soviet authorities as to the effectiveness of American material being sent to the Soviet Union. Standley sent his Naval Aide, Admiral John Duncan, his Military Aide,

General J. A. Michela, and the chief of the supply mission, General Phillip Faymonville, to ask the Soviet military, naval and trade authorities for such expressions of opinion. The Soviet authorities refused to comment. By now Standley's blood was up.

He told the Soviet authorities that the Lend-Lease appropriation bill was to come up shortly before Congress and that Congress, though generous, was apt to be sensitive if it believed that the money it appropriated for Russian Lend-Lease material was going down the well—that it was doing no good at all. The Soviet officials did not reply to Standley's request. Molotov was noncommittal. Standley, knowing how desperately the Russians needed more and more war material from us, was worried about how Congress would react to this conspiracy of silence on the part of Soviet officials. Standley consulted nobody. Standley is a straight thinker not interested in the devious involved intellectual processes of State Departments or diplomats. He would smoke them out. And smoke them out he did that afternoon early in March in the comfortable library in Spasso House. Congress, reading how Russian papers had printed all of the Stettinius report; Congress, reading of the acknowledgment by Soviet authorities of the helpfulness of our material, unanimously voted the full appropriation to Russia. Standley, the "enemy of Russia," had done a great deal more for Russia than the American communists, who so glibly give the Soviet Union ineffectual lip service. The reason is, of course, that Standley knows and loves Russia.

Standley today is a very young seventy-one. He has the affection and admiration of every correspondent in Moscow and he has the respect of every Soviet official. Standley and Stalin have a lot in common. Both are men of action who hate red tape. Each has only one interest—the welfare of his own country.

"During war time," Standley says, "diplomacy must go by the board. We are whole-hearted allies of Russia. Of what use is diplomacy between allies and friends? The truth is the only kind of diplomacy worth a damn in war time."

✳✳✳✳✳✳✳✳✳✳✳✳✳✳✳✳✳✳✳✳✳✳✳✳

Chapter IV

THE ROAD TO VYAZMA

THE MOSCOW papers were filled with atrocity stories. Skepticism is the natural viewpoint of any correspondent. To begin with, we hate to accept handouts. We want to see for ourselves. We didn't disbelieve the atrocity stories carried by *Pravda* and *Izvestia* nearly every day—we merely wanted to verify them. Before I arrived the correspondents were taken to several villages recently evacuated by the Germans. They were allowed to see for themselves. They believed. They had seen the bodies of civilians; many had starved to death—others had been shot or hung. The bodies did not lie. The survivors told horrible stories of what had happened to them and to others during the German occupation, and the correspondents were unanimous in saying that these survivors did not lie. I still wanted to see for myself or, to be more honest, I wanted to get the same story they had gotten—a better one if possible. I applied to the Narkomindel for permission to do a half dozen articles. I wanted to see our Lend-

Lease material in action. I wanted to interview three or four Russian women heroes. I wanted to go to Leningrad. Then finally I wanted, if possible, to enter some Russian city with the Red Army and get the story of the German occupation from the civilians who had remained in the city. I didn't name any particular city. I was surprised when the Nark phoned and said arrangements had been made for me to go to Vyazma which had been recaptured only a few days before. I made a strong plea that I be allowed to bring Tania Sofiano with me to act as interpreter. The Nark agreed to let her make the trip.

It would be especially interesting, Sofiano said, because we would travel the Smolensk road, through Mozhaisk and Borodino—we would travel the road traveled by Napoleon's army in its retreat of 1812-13. I had just finished *War and Peace*. I hadn't merely read it—I had studied it.

We were to leave at 7 A.M. The Nark was furnishing a car and a driver. One of the censors, Nikolai Borisovich Andreyev, would accompany us. When you go on a trip in Russia these days you bring with you everything that you will need. You cannot live off the land, unless the Red Army invites you to meals. Sofiano had to arrange food for five or six days—not a simple matter. She finally got some bread, sausage and *balik*. She got some chocolate and two bottles of vodka, and we thought ourselves lucky to have that. It takes quite a while to get under way in Russia. The car never showed up at seven. It came around at nine, but the driver didn't have any gasoline coupons. He could get his coupons the following day he said. But today—no. That would have downed anyone less resourceful than Sofiano. She phoned General Michela and asked to borrow his gasoline coupons for a few days. She would guarantee to return them. Mike was agreeable. The coupons were duly obtained, the car filled with gas and oil and off we went. The car was a **very** tired old car which made strange abdominal noises. We passed through the city and over the bridge leading out of the city. Napoleon's army had once retreated across this bridge. I had my copy of *War and Peace* with me and it was thrilling to follow the route through Tolstoy's eyes. *War and Peace* is, in truth, the Russian Bible and Sofiano, whose copy I had borrowed, knew the book backwards, both in Russian and in English. About six miles out of the city, she told our driver to stop.

"Here is Poklonnaya," she said. "You remember toward the end of the book just before the French Army moved into Moscow, Napoleon stood here waiting? Remember?"

I remembered and I climbed out of the car to look at the hill. It was hard to believe that the destiny of a huge nation was once settled here on this gentle hill. Snow fringed it at the base but, as it sloped gently upward, the snow gave place to brown earth and, at the top, green grass was already showing. Three women were plowing on the flat top of the hill. It was only perhaps fifty feet high, this hill by the road. On September 2, 1812, Napoleon stood here looking toward Moscow. The whole city lay spread out before him. He had sent emissaries ahead to tell the city fathers that he was here. He ordered them to come and surrender to him. He waited there, confident, arrogant, but impatient on that September morning.

By those indefinable tokens by which one can infallibly tell from a distance a live body from a dead one, Napoleon could detect from Poklonnaya Hill the throb of life in the town and could feel as it were the breathing of the beautiful great being.

Napoleon waited and the sun climbed in the heavens and a chill came into the air and Napoleon called for his great-coat and angrily demanded the reason for the delay. None knew, and then his adjutants came galloping from the city with the news that Moscow was deserted. Only a few families remained and these too were preparing to flee. The city was deserted and Napoleon would be cheated of the type of triumphant entry he liked so well. He didn't know it then, but he lost an empire standing there on Poklonnaya Hill. Had the city fathers come and surrendered, Napoleon would have entered the city as Emperor. Instead, he entered the city merely as an invader. Had he entered as an Emperor he could have imposed terms on the Russian commander, General Kutuzov, and the Czar. It would have meant that the war was over. But he entered merely as an intruder.

Now the hill was, in a sense, roaring defiance to another would-be conqueror. Across its base in white-washed stones was traced out the most popular of all Soviet slogans: "*Pod Voditelstvom Stalina K Pobyede*" which means "To Victory with Stalin." I climbed back in our car and we rolled along the six-lane highway on the road to Vyazma. If one could get this road to unlock its secrets as Tolstoy had done, one might yet learn something about Russia. The calendar said that spring had come, but the country we drove through was still tawny and brown. Russia is no respecter of calendars. Our car wheezed along, choking and spitting. Every time we came to a slope, it was a matter of conjecture whether we'd make it or not. The noises became more and more alarming. As a kid I always had a broken-down, ancient wreck like this and the noises coming from under the hood were strangely familiar. Twice we just stopped, and each time our driver got out slowly, separated the gas line from the carburetor and then sucked the dirt out of the gas line. Obviously the gasoline was of such poor quality that it kept clogging the strainer leading to the carburetor. Then we'd go off again.

"This car needs to have its valves ground," I told Sofiano. "Its gears are stripped and we are a cinch to blow a gasket."

"*Nitchevo*," Sofiano said indifferently. That is the Russian equivalent of "So what?"

We reached the village of Kubinka and there the car gave a throaty rattle and expired. Our driver smiled happily and told us, "It is finished. I will need new parts to fix it and we can get no new parts here." Our Foreign Office representative, Nikolai Borisovich Andreyev, was very embarrassed until I told him that these things happened in my country too—all the time. By some miracle, there was a railroad station in the village and a telephone. Nikolai Borisovich went off and came back beaming. He had gotten the Foreign Office on the phone (no mean triumph) and another car was en route. Sofiano and I went exploring. Back in 1941, the advance units of the German Army had reached this small village. Motorcycle squads and some tanks had lumbered into the age-old collection of thatched huts. This was only thirty miles from Moscow. A small stream flowed brightly through the village and women were washing clothes in it. Kubinka was a village of old men, women and children. You never see any young men in Russian villages. They have long since disappeared into the great silence of the vast front.

We sat by the stream and soon a very young child, dressed in voluminous folds of tattered clothing, came and joined us. He looked at us unabashed out of large solemn eyes and accepted a piece of chocolate graciously, almost condescendingly. His name was Vova he told Sofiano. Vova is the diminutive for Vladimir. Vova didn't know how old he was. Sofiano said he was about six.

"My father and my two brothers are in the army killing Fritzies," he said proudly. Just as British youngsters call Germans "Jerries" so do Russian youngsters call them "Fritzies." Vova added, "When they come back they'll tell me how old I am."

He shook his head vaguely when Sofiano asked where his

mother was. Perhaps his mother was working in a defense plant in Moscow; perhaps the Germans had looked upon her and decided that she would be useful.

A frog hopped out from the marshy grass that bordered the stream and leaped out onto a flat stone in the stream. The child squealed with delight. In villages like Kubinka, children do not have toys. They must fashion a world of their own and people it with whatever is at hand. Airplanes that constantly patrol above on watch for daylight raiders; tanks that roar by and then fade into clouds of dust; men in greenish-gray uniforms who march by singing "*Sviaschennaia Voina*" (Sacred War); rabbits darting nimbly out of the birch trees that fringe the village and a frog leaping out to a flat rock in a stream—these are the characters that make up a child's world in a village such as Kubinka.

"The Fritzies were there," Vova said unexpectedly, pointing to the birch trees that gleamed whitely in the spring sun. Luckily the memory of a child is short and Vova had forgotten the guns that had roared, the machine guns that had rattled when the Red Army drove the Germans from the woods. Vova never knew that had those Germans surged on to Moscow and taken the city, he would have grown up a slave.

Our car finally arrived from Moscow, and I shuddered when I saw it. But the driver looked competent enough. He had some spare parts which he gave to our first driver, and we went on toward Vyazma. Now and then we would pass a village that had been completely burned by the Germans in their retreat in 1942. Occasionally partially burned villages, with roofless farmhouses, gave evidence that the German bombers had been active here. In the fall of 1941 they had managed to penetrate the outer defenses of Moscow and bomb the city, but recently they had been stopped before reaching even the outskirts of Moscow by the terrific anti-aircraft barrage. When that happened they jettisoned their bombs and hurried home. Often their bombs found farmhouses on the road to Vyazma. Now that the snow had melted, farmers were repairing their barns and homes, building thatched roofs—small protection against bombs, perhaps, but excellent protection against the burning sun that would come soon in midsummer and the intense cold of the winters. We went on and then turned off the road and we were at Borodino. Borodino leaped right out of the pages of *War and Peace*. It couldn't have changed much since that fateful September 7, 1812, when the Russians chose to stand and fight Napoleon. For twelve hours the two armies fought.

A mist hung over the scene, melting, parting, shimmering with light in the bright sunshine and giving fairylike beauty to the shapes seen through it. The smoke of the guns mingled with the mist and everywhere gleams of sunlight sparkled in it from the water, from the dew, from the bayonets of the soldiers crowding on the river. Through this mist could be seen a white church and here and there roofs of cottages in Borodino . . . and the whole scene moved or seemed to move as the mist and smoke trailed over the wide plain.

It was here that Prince Bagration, perhaps the best of General Kutuzov's generals, received a wound that caused his death two years later. It was exciting to stand there on the banks of the river and visualize Napoleon giving crisp, arrogant orders to Murat and Ney and Davoust. Napoleon won a battle here on these plains—but he lost a war. He lost 32,000 of his crack troops and he never recovered from that loss. He swept on to Moscow, but the Russian Army retreated in orderly fashion to winter quarters east of the capital. Tolstoy realized that:

The maggot may gnaw at the cabbage, but the maggot dies before it has killed the cabbage.

The Russian Army had lost nearly half its men at Borodino, but it kept gaining strength as Napoleon lost it. Then Moscow was burned and Napoleon retreated down this road through this very plain. He retreated, fleeing not from Kutuzov but from the inevitable, for his army carried the germs of ruin. It was a dissatisfied-looking army. It had reached its goal—Moscow—but the fruits of victory turned sour under the sullen, passive resistance of the conquered who refused to acknowledge that they had been conquered.

The army could not have recovered itself in any way. From the battle of Borodino and the sacking of Moscow, it bore within itself the chemical element of dissolution . . . There was no general engagement nor even a skirmish of any importance, yet the French Army ceased to exist . . . Victories are not always an invariable sign of conquest.

We drove on down the road and I felt as excited as the day I found my first bicycle under the Christmas tree. I was so steeped in *War and Peace* that whole passages came to mind. It was as though Tolstoy was taking me along this road himself; as though he had written *War and Peace* especially as a guide book for me to use. One hundred and thirty years before, the French had hurried along this road, looking over their shoulders, seeing menace in the birch trees that lined the road, afraid to straggle lest they fall and be pinioned by the knife or club of a Russian partisan. And two years before the Germans had retreated along the same road, accompanied by the same fear—and yet they too had suffered no real military defeat. Both armies had found Russia too big for them. Both armies dwindled as they marched away from Moscow. Why? How? The answer was in Tolstoy:

Just as water flowing over dry land is absorbed by the dry land, so did Russia absorb the French Army.

Our car rumbled along the wide road. We saw steeples in the distance and the roofs of houses and soon we were in Mozhaisk. The Germans had captured this city, only sixty miles from Moscow, in October, 1941, and those of us who were in the capital then were pretty sure that they'd come right on through and take Moscow. There was little to stop them and they had that fine wide road to roll their tanks along. We were all evacuated to Kuibyshev then. Everyone left Moscow—except Stalin. He remained in the Kremlin. Voroshilov's hastily trained army of reserves was thrown into the breach and by some military miracle they stopped the main body of the Germans here at this rather shabby city with its muddy, unpaved streets and its shabby-looking buildings. The main street was bordered by two-storied houses. It was getting dark now. Perhaps in protest at the unaccustomed work it had done this day, our car shivered a bit and then wheezed to a stop.

"It is the carburetor," Sofiano translated, as our driver let go a calm stream of Russian. "He also says the axle is bent. But the army is here and they can take care of it."

"Do you mind staying the night here?" Nikolai Borisovich asked unhappily.

"Not at all," I told him. "Anyhow, we have no alternative."

He wandered off to contact the head man. We stood around, watching the driver take off the front wheel. He was calm, unhurried and not a bit worried. Oh, the military people would have a repair shop here; he would get what he needed. It was getting quite dark now and Mozhaisk was blacking out. A group of children, attracted by the unusual sign of strangers, gradually circled us and then came closer. There were ten of them ranging (Mother Sofiano, an expert on such things, said) from three to eleven. These children had lived under German rule for eighteen months and yet they all looked plump and healthy. Sofiano gave them each a piece of chocolate and their eyes widened incredulously. She chatted with them and soon had them laughing, their shyness gone. I fell completely for Natasha, who was four. She sucked unbelievingly on her square of chocolate, making it last as long as possible. She huddled close to her brother, Nikolai, aged seven, and with her free hand clutched that of her other brother, Peter, who was nine.

"Were the Germans good to you?" I asked, and Sofiano translated.

"We didn't see them very much," Peter said. "We stayed in our cellar during the day. If we came out they would find excuses to kick us."

The other children were quiet now, staring at Peter solemnly.

"What did they give you to eat?"

"Nothing," Peter said, "but every day we had *lepeshki.*"

That surprised me. *Lepeshki* means Russian pancakes and there is nothing better or more nourishing. I was almost on the point of having the first charitable thought toward the Germans I'd felt in some years.

"Where did you get the flour to make the *lepeshki?*" Sofiano asked.

"There was no flour," Peter said stolidly. "Mother made *lepeshki* out of grass and potato mash. She chopped the grass up fine. That is all we ever had to eat because the soldiers ate all the bread."

For eighteen months these youngsters had lived on grass and potatoes, not a diet recommended by our better dietitians, yet all seemed healthy enough. It takes a lot to kill a child.

"There was our church," Peter said, pointing to a heap of rubble across the square, hardly discernible in the waning light. "When they left here they blew it up. It was a brick church and the bricks flew all around and one of them hit mother and killed her."

I might emphasize again that this was no conducted tour I

was on in which one could talk only to those hand-picked by the Soviet authorities. These youngsters had merely wandered over to us. You had to believe them. Peter's father? The inevitable reply. He was in the army "killing Fritzies." We asked the other children the same question. The father of each one was in the army. Perhaps that is why they were wandering around the town at eight o'clock at night.

Nikolai Borisovich finally came back, very pleased with himself. The Commandant would be glad to find us lodgings for the night. We stumbled across the square to a sturdy-looking, one-storied house. There were three rooms in the house, two bedrooms and a kitchen. There was also a primitive bathroom, holding neither bathtub nor sink. The living room was immaculately clean and tidy. It was lit by a single oil lamp. One might have found this room in any small New England farmhouse. Lace curtains framed the two windows. A comfortable-looking, single bed stood along one wall and there was also a sofa, heavily upholstered with damask material. There was a heavy dresser and on it were two empty perfume bottles, a small glass frame on which had been painted a red and white rose, an imitation ivory elephant and a framed picture of three smiling lads, all in the uniform of the Red Army. There was a small table and around it were four chairs. Three of the chairs each lacked one leg.

"When the Germans left they broke almost everything," Maria Petrichenko, our temporary landlady, said without emotion, but with a rather puzzled look on her face. "I don't know why they broke the legs off the chairs. And of course they took all of our oil lamps except this one which I hid. They always take oil lamps to use in their dugouts. When they left they blew up our power plant, so we have no electric light."

Maria was a pleasant and intelligent-looking woman of perhaps fifty. She was small, but there was a quiet strength about her and occasionally she smiled confidently. She had been through a lot, but she had survived and she knew that nothing could ever be worse. Her three sons and her husband were in the army; she hadn't heard from any of them for nearly a year. But her letters to them had not been returned. When a man has been killed, mail sent to him is always returned, and thousands of women in Russia know by that token that a son or husband is dead. In the beginning the major or colonel commanding always wrote to widows or mothers of men under him who had been killed, but when the losses amounted to a hundred thousand or more a month this could not be done. Maria Petrichenko had been lucky. A German general had commandeered her house and she had been spared certain indignities that might have come her way otherwise. She made tea for us, and it was pleasant sitting there around the table (I was given the chair with all four legs intact). The radio played music from the Moscow station and, listening to the news broadcast, you could shut your eyes and almost visualize yourself in an American farmhouse. Of course there was one great difference. You couldn't turn the dial on this radio and get another station. This wasn't a radio, it was merely a loudspeaker. The Moscow station was connected with a central town radio that piped it through. There are no private radios in Russia any more. We correspondents and the embassies alone had them.

A friend of Maria's came in and stopped with surprise when she saw us. Mozhaisk is only ninety miles from Moscow, but even so strangers from the capital were a rare sight. Maria introduced her as Nadezhda Smirnova. Maria poured tea from the huge samovar that seemed to have no bottom.

Nadezhda was tall and dark, and her hair kept tumbling down over her forehead. With unconscious grace she brushed it back as she talked. She looked very young to have four children, and her calm face showed nothing of what she must have gone through, except that she never smiled. She didn't mind talking about her experiences.

"I couldn't leave when they came," she said thoughtfully. "It's hard to move four children. But we kept out of their way as much as possible. We lived in the cellar. I had to go out every day, of course, to get food, and that was bad. Some of the men in the town wouldn't work for the Germans. They were hanged. I saw six bodies hanging from a gallows they had put up. Those of us with children had to do what they said. Me? Oh, they left me alone—most of the time."

They had left her alone—most of the time. Looking at her graceful, supple figure and her dark comeliness you hesitated to ask any further. You couldn't read the past, not even the agonizing past of the last eighteen months, in her inscrutable, heavily lashed eyes. She talked of the future, of the time when the beasts would be driven from the land, when peaceful country folk could return to their soil.

We drank tea and had vodka, which they hadn't seen for a long time. Outside of Moscow there is very little vodka in Russia. We ate our dreary *balik* and our sausage and Nikolai Borisovich brought out some butter and white bread. Meanwhile Maria had produced an army cot and had set it up. She put blankets on the sofa. I was to have the bed. No, she wouldn't let us draw lots. The cot was too short for me; Nikolai Borisovich would be comfortable there. The sofa was too short—it would fit Tania Sofiano admirably. I should have the bed. I couldn't argue.

"It's a good bed," Maria said a little bitterly. "Even the German general found it comfortable."

The sheets were clean and cool. Maria turned the lamp down and left us. Sofiano said we would leave about eight in the morning. She took off her shoes and, for all I know, slipped off her dress, and then crawled under the covers. Nikolai Borisovich followed suit. So did I. Somehow it didn't seem strange to sleep three in a room; it seemed quite matter of fact. And before I could give it a second thought there were others in the room: Sonya and Natasha and Pierre and the men who had fought at Borodino in 1812; the duel between Dolohov and Bezuhov was refought again and once more Natasha sat dry-eyed beside the sick bed of Prince Andrey, but in my dream I was more charitable than Tolstoy had been. In my dream Prince Andrey lived, and he and Natasha laughed and loved as they were destined to do. These characters were so real to me that, when I awoke in the morning, I lay for a time wondering where I was and wondering why Tolstoy hadn't been kinder to Natasha. But Tolstoy was so terribly moral, so Godlike, that he gave real happiness only to Princess Marya, the long-suffering, but even she had moments of doubt when she remembered that there "was another happiness unobtainable in this life."

Then Nikolai Borisovich called cheerfully, "*Gospadine* Reynolds, the tea is ready," and ruefully I stopped trying to rewrite Tolstoy, decided to let *War and Peace* stand as it was, and went to wash. Tania had long since been up and she reported that the car was fixed, that the commandant had phoned Vyazma and that we would be expected for lunch.

"Will it be one of those lunches, Tania?" I said in dismay.

"It will be," she said cheerfully. "When you give a toast, remember to say, *Lei do dna.*"

The morning was still and clear and smoke rose lazily from the chimneys of the farmhouses about us. There was much rebuilding to be done in Mozhaisk, but for the moment there was no extra wood, no concrete, no hands that could be spared. Meanwhile people did their best and life went on and if you hadn't known that this town had lived for eighteen months in slavery, you wouldn't have guessed it. We said good-bye to kind Maria Petrichenko. I tried to give her three hundred rubles for our night's lodging. She looked puzzled, and I called on Sofiano for help, but she shook her head sharply.

"Of course not," she said. "We were guests of Maria Petrichenko, not paid boarders. You would insult her by offering her money. I have given her some butter and some chocolate. She is very happy about that and well satisfied."

Of course I had been wrong. Would you offer money to the wife of a New Mexico rancher who had taken you in for the night? Would you have offered money to the wife of a New England farmer because she had given you a glass of milk or a bed? It was the same with Maria Petrichenko. It is not that Russians are more dreamy-eyed about money than we are. No doubt Maria could drive as shrewd a bargain as the next one. However, she was not in the business of renting rooms—that was only a friendly gesture extended toward three travelers who were in need of shelter.

We drove down the road to Vyazma. It was no longer smooth and wide. From here on this would be a military road. In retreating, the German Army had smashed the smooth concrete, had blown up each of the twenty bridges that the road crossed from Mozhaisk to Vyazma. We bumped along the rough surface, sometimes sinking hub-deep in tracks worn by giant tanks. On either side of the road were signs of the speed of the retreating German Army. There were thousands of shallow slit trenches and well-fortified dugouts which had been the homes of German soldiers. There were abandoned tanks, field kitchens, smashed gun carriages, and now and then, the long barrel of a German gun would point futilely toward Moscow. Red Army engineers had thrown up temporary plank bridges across the streams. Huge craters on both banks showed that the Germans had been lavish in their use of dynamite when they came to their demolition work. They are thorough at that job. But beside every temporary wooden bridge, Red Army engineers were working fast and establishing bridges more substantial and permanent.

Every few miles we were stopped by sentries—invariably women sentries. One would ask sharply for our credentials; another would stand with gun leveled. These women wore the usual Red Army uniform, with the exception of skirts instead of trousers.

"They're the best-looking dames I've seen in Russia," I said to Tania, and she agreed. They were young and slim, and their outdoor life had given their cheeks a color lacking in the faces of factory workers one saw in Moscow.

As we got closer to Vyazma, the road became more congested. Truck convoys shot by us, traveling fast. Often we overtook convoys of tanks which lumbered along slowly but steadily. Huge guns crawled on toward Vyazma and the front. Red Army men were still looking for mines on either side of the road and in the birch and pine forests beyond. "When the Germans retreated down this road, our guerrilla fighters killed a great many of them," Tania reminded me. "Just as in 1813, the guerrilla partisans killed stragglers of Napoleon's army."

I was back in the world of Tolstoy again. Through his eyes I saw eighty-year-old General Kutuzov, discredited by his czar, despised by his generals, considered a coward by his own troops, following the army of Napoleon cautiously, content to allow Russia to absorb the French army just as "earth absorbs water that flows over it." Kutuzov refused to follow the rules of organized warfare. Napoleon was so enraged by his unorthodox conduct that he actually complained to the Emperor Alexander. Kutuzov never attacked directly (neither did the guerrillas who harried Von Bock's retreating army in the spring of 1942). Kutuzov was master of the oblique retreat (this brought victory to the Red Army at Stalingrad when their "retreat" developed into an encirclement). And, of course, Kutuzov was master of partisan or guerrilla warfare. On paper, partisan warfare should never succeed. From the time of Genghis Khan and Hannibal, through Alexander the Great and Napoleon and even to the time of the German Clausewitz, there was one fundamental military theory never ignored: "The attacking party must concentrate his forces in order to be stronger than his opponent at the moment of conflict." Partisan warfare acts in direct contradiction to this rule. Military science has always assumed that the strength of an army was in direct proportion to its numbers. That is, the more soldiers, the greater the strength. Military science sometimes forgets that often the mass of an army does not correspond to its force. In warfare, the attacking force of an army is the product of the mass multiplied by something else—an unknown X. This unknown X is the combination of several factors which might be called the spirit of the army. The factors include the hatred they bear for their enemy, the absence of that feeling so universal to soldiers that they will weaken at the decisive moment, the excellence or poorness of their training and equipment. Add these all together and you get that unknown X or spirit of an army. Multiply that by the number of soldiers you have at your disposal and you can approximate what the attacking force will be.

A small army with a very powerful spirit can be much more effective than a large army which lacks this spirit or has it in only a small degree. This success of the partisan bands in 1813 and again in 1942 is due to the fact that their spirit multiplied by their numbers created a terrific striking force. The same is true of our Rangers and Commandos. Such groups almost literally explode against an enemy.*

---

* Anon. critic: You realize, Reynolds, that you have lifted this theory almost verbatim from Tolstoy.
Reynolds: Well, anyhow, if I steal from Tolstoy, nobody can accuse me of petty larceny.

Partisan groups are difficult to capture. They hurl themselves at an enemy, do their damage, and then, like a ball thrown with great force at a concrete wall, they bounce back. Casualties among the Russian partisans have been relatively light. The German Army is repeating Napoleon's pathetic complaint that the Russians do not fight according to the rules. Their complaint takes a more lethal form than did Napoleon's. They do not treat captured partisans as prisoners of war. They execute them immediately.

We continued on down the road that was so full of military history. In the distance we saw thin spirals of smoke rising. We crossed our twentieth bridge and then went up a short hill. A railroad crossed the road just before the top of the hill was reached and Red Army engineers and labor battalions were tearing up twisted rails and laying new tracks. They worked with incredible speed and quiet; there was no shouting of orders. Everyone seemed to know just what to do. Here, where the railroad crossed the road, there were some eighty women, old men and children sitting among the disorder of their household possessions. They had all left Vyazma before the Germans had entered the city, and they had brought such household goods as they were able to cart away. Yes, they were going back to the city where they had been born and wed and had children. What if the city was ruined? Step on an anthill and crush it, scatter it and within a few hours you'll see the ants hurrying back. If that homing instinct is so strong in an ant, it is even stronger in a human being. Vyazma meant home to these people sitting there on the roadside. Somehow or other they had gotten this far. Vyazma was only two miles away. They waited patiently until there would be room on the military trucks that constantly rumbled past. Occasionally a truck that was only half loaded stopped and the driver and soldiers would load the sewing machines, the chairs, the bundles of bedding, the pots and pans—and another family would be almost home. Virtually every family there had a sewing machine. They all looked happy, too. There was no trace even on the faces of the smallest children of the life all must have led during the past eighteen months. Where had they lived? We questioned them. Some had found shelter in small villages, but most had hidden in the woods. They had fashioned dugouts for themselves and had lived on grass, herbs and berries and occasional bread made with flour, brought to them by the partisans.

Then we reached the top of the hill. The sun was high and it shone down whitely on what had once been Vyazma. Nothing I had ever seen in Coventry, Plymouth or London had prepared me for this. When Vyazma first broke upon your consciousness you could only draw an involuntary breath of horror. The sight below us was so horrible as to be unreal. Had this shapeless, jagged mass of rubble, out of which rose only a few chimneys, ever been a thriving, living city? It was hard to believe that it had once lived. None of us said anything. In silence we drove into the dead city.

The smell of destruction hung heavily in the still, clear air. There is no smell to compare with the sickening smell of a city that has been destroyed. The unwholesome smell of the killer lingers after he is gone. We drove through the heavily rutted streets with difficulty. An effort had been made to clear them, but rubble of all kind covered what had once been paved streets, and the dust and debris thrown over the road when the Germans dynamited the houses were in some places three to four feet deep.

It was seldom that we passed a house which had more than one wall standing. Chimneys resist the pressure of dynamite better than do walls or roofs, but very few chimneys stood above the ruins. An unearthly silence hung over the city, as though the Red Army men whom we passed felt that to speak loudly here would be as undecorous as to sing ribald songs in the presence of the dead. We drove through the city and reached a small wooden shack on the other side of it—on the outskirts. Major Peter Smolin was in charge of Vyazma now. He had marched into the city just two weeks before at the head of the Red Army. He and several companies had remained behind to bring some sort of order out of the chaos. The rest of the army went on and was now holding a position some fifteen miles beyond. Major Smolin was young, handsome and likable. On his breast there gleamed the Order of the Red Star. Only twenty-six, he was a veteran of two years of fighting.

"I don't have to tell you what happened to Vyazma," he said. "Walk around and see for yourself. There were 716 civilians left when we entered. Talk to any or all of them. Hear their stories and doubt them if you can. Go where you wish—alone, if you wish. There are no secrets in Vyazma. There were three buildings standing when we entered the city," he explained. "The Germans had left them. But they destroyed the rest of the city."

Vyazma was not killed because it was a military center. It's true that a railroad from Moscow had its terminus here, and one expected that the Germans would blow up some fifteen miles of railroad tracks. That is accepted military procedure. One expected that they would slaughter livestock, strip the city of scrap metal and grain, and use all the household furniture for fuel. These, too, are stringent, but accepted military practices.

But the Germans went far beyond that. When they finally knew they would have to leave, German sappers began with the railroad station on the outskirts, blew that up, and systematically worked toward the center of the city, destroying every building. From the center, they worked through side streets of the old city. Some of the buildings died hard. The Germans worked on the power plant for two days before it was reduced to debris. They worked thoroughly. All but the cathedral and two other large buildings were absolutely destroyed; they had a purpose in leaving those nearly intact.

"There was a fine brick building," Major Smolin went on, "which we thought we would fix up as a hospital. There were seven hundred and sixteen men, women and children here then, most of whom either had typhus or were starved almost to death. Many were weak from beatings and others from wounds. Twenty-six doctors and nurses went into this brick building to convert it to a hospital, and then too late we realized why the Germans had left the building intact.

"A large delayed-action mine exploded. It killed them all. Two days later a second intact building blew up. Sixteen men were killed. Those who had remained in the city were anxious to hold church services. Before I allowed them to enter the cathedral, I had my sappers inspect it. They found a thousand-pound time bomb there. Like all the mines and bombs left, it was a chemical-action bomb. We got it out into the fields and exploded it. Then the people held their services. Only the cathedral is intact, you see.

"The Germans buried mines everywhere. They still explode. They buried them under debris in ruined houses. They buried them under the street mud. We have dug up hundreds of them. We still search for them."

The city was deathly silent as I walked around. Old women sat apathetically in the ruins that had been their homes. Their children, unconscious of disaster, played happily in the debris, occasionally crying out when they unearthed some remembered household article—a dish, a broken chair, the remains of a stove. Already seven thousand people had returned from their hiding places in neighboring forests and villages.

A few days after the Red Army recaptured the place, the government appointed a committee to investigate stories told by the 716 who had remained. Their stories were checked, one against another, and printed in Moscow papers. Ever since our own government admitted that fantastic stories of German atrocities given out in the last war were manufactured in Washington, we as a nation have been rightfully skeptical of such hand-outs.

It was so with the Soviet report. I read stories of almost incredible torture, rape and murder with some skepticism. After two days in Vyazma, talking to dozens of survivors picked at random, I now believe every word of that report and could support it with twenty additional stories of horror—a few of which could be printed.

Come along with me into the ruins of Vyazma and talk to men, women and children. We are under no supervision. We will talk to those we find huddled around fires, to those searching amid the ruins for something to salvage, to anyone we wish. Here is a very old man trying to repair a chair with only two of its legs left. He sits beside what was once his house and talks in a matter-of-fact tone.

"When they came in," he says, "I escaped to a village not far away. But they came there so quickly that no one could leave. They gathered people from other villages near by and said they were going to send them to Germany to work. One hundred and forty refused to go. The Germans put them into a house and then set fire to it. I saw this happen. They all burned to death."

"Is this true? Will you swear that it's true?"

The old man looked at me, a bit puzzled. Why should he be inventing such a tale? He didn't answer, just shrugged his shoulders and looked past me. It was nothing to him whether or not I believed his story. He got on with his job of repairing the chair.

I went on and there was a sad-faced woman with heavy lines of suffering etched on her face. Her name was Alexandra Ivanovna Khokhlova. She, her husband and her son had remained behind. She talked of those eighteen months as though they were something out of another world.

"When they first came," she said tonelessly, "they went from house to house, taking everything they could use and killing all our hens and dogs. They broke all our glasses—I don't know why. It got worse later. There is a bridge just outside the city; you can see it from the cathedral. There were two sentries there. Often men from neighboring villages or from the woods would come in starving and ask the two sentries for food. The sentries told them they could have food if they would chop wood. They would chop wood, and the sentries would actually give them food.

"Then the sentries would tell them to leave the city and go back across the bridge. When they would get halfway across the bridge, the sentries would shoot them and laugh as the bodies fell into the snow. When the snow began to melt, they made us go there to clear the stream and its banks under the bridge. We found more than fifty bodies."

The woman told her story unemotionally, as though recounting a tale seen in a motion picture. Doctor Goebbels always labels such stories as lies and says they are inspired by Soviet propaganda bureaus. This woman wasn't hand-picked by Soviet officials. No Soviet officials were with me. The old woman raised her hand and brushed it across the scar on her cheek. I asked what had caused the scar.

"I was home one night when a very young and drunken officer came into the house," she said. "He told me that he was going to sleep with me. I said that I was an old woman and had sons older than he was. It didn't matter. He grabbed me. When I resisted, he picked up a glass from the table and smashed it into my face. He pulled the tablecloth from the table and smashed my plates and glasses. I ran away and he followed me, but he was so drunk that he fell down. I hid in the barn for three days and he never came back.

"They made all the young girls sleep with them, and if they wouldn't, they would beat them. As soon as a girl would get pregnant, the soldiers would tell her to go away. A lot of them had babies," she added thoughtfully.

I walked another hundred yards and stopped Anna Yakovievna Sorokina, a middle-aged, placid-looking woman. She, her husband and her twenty-nine-year-old daughter were caught when the Germans came in. They hid for a time in their cellar, but eventually the Germans found them and put them to work. One day the enemy soldiers came into the house and, while she watched, killed her daughter.

"They said she was a guerrilla," Anna told us in a flat voice. "My daughter was not a guerrilla."

Do you want more stories? Could you stomach the story of Natalia Osipovna Kiriushina, who carried a three-months-old child in her arms, or the story of Nina Petrovna Ospova, who lay for weeks on filthy straw in a room with sixty others who also had typhus? Most of the others died.

Story followed story, all of the same pattern. A dozen repeated the story of the two sentries who laughed when the bodies fell from the bridge into the icy stream below. You can hear a thousand stories—no, several thousand—of how the Germans treated the citizens of Vyazma and of the surrounding villages. They vary only in detail.

Late that afternoon, I ate with some Russian officers. They were incredulous when I told them that a good part of America thought that Japan was our principal enemy. I told them that sometimes I worried because my countrymen did not seem to have a healthy capacity for hating Nazi Germany, which is needed for waging total war.

"Perhaps," one of the officers said gently, "if your countrymen could see this city and talk to its survivors, they might realize what manner of men the Germans are. The other day one of our generals visited us. We passed a sentry, and the sentry neglected to salute the general. 'What are you dreaming about that you forgot your discipline?' the general said to him. 'I was daydreaming,' the sentry admitted. 'I was thinking what a great idea it would be to leave this ruined city exactly as it is. Then we could build a high wall around it, so nothing would be disturbed. Future generations would come to see the city, and then they would realize the kind of beasts that invaded their country during this war. That's what I was dreaming of, Tovarisch General.' "

With one of the officers, I walked to the outskirts of the city near the destroyed railroad station. There was a large cross there.

"We were looking for unexploded mines and bombs," the officer explained, when I asked him about it. "Here there was a patch of soft earth, and we though perhaps it covered a time bomb. We dug into the earth, and before we were finished, we had found the bodies of six hundred men, women and children. Many had been shot or hanged. Many had obviously died either of typhus or starvation."

He paused, then said quietly, "You do not blame us, I trust, for hating the Germans?"

Napoleon's army had spent two months here before hurrying on in panic to Smolensk. General Kutuzov, very old and feeble, had ridden into Vyazma at the head of his army. Kutuzov had cried out, "There can be no peace, for such is the people's will." That was so much truer today than it was even in 1812-13. And yet I knew that even as I talked to survivors in Vyazma, thousands of my own countrymen were asking themselves, "Will the Russians make a separate peace? Can we trust the Russians? Will they keep on fighting?"

We walked back in silence. It was six o'clock. A hundred fires burned amid the ruins, and families huddled around them. There is no blackout in Vyazma—there is no way of

[115]

blacking out a dead city. From the distance came the sound of heavy guns. The front was not too far away. Each day the people wake up to the sound of the dawn barrage, and late each afternoon, they again hear the rumble of drums. From right outside the town came the angry barking of anti-aircraft guns. Perhaps they were only being tested, perhaps some stray raider was trying to get through to the city.

Bombing Vyazma would be silly. Like putting a knife into the heart of a corpse, I thought. Then over the echo of the guns came the sound of singing. It came from the center of town. The officer saw my puzzled glance.

"Today is Sunday," he explained. "They're holding services. Would you like to join them?"

We went toward the sound of the singing. It led us to a cathedral which was up a slight hill, so that it completely dominated the city. It alone was untouched, and there was something majestic about its calm solidness. Germans find it easy to kill men and women and cities and they have been known to kill countries, but not even Germans can kill faith.

Services were just ending. Church was crowded, mostly with children and women, among whom was a sprinkling of old men. There are no young men left in Vyazma. We stood on the steps, watching them. These people had been through suffering quite comparable to that endured by any martyred saints. Yet no sign of suffering showed on the faces of any of them. They looked calm and serene. Faith which burned within showed so plainly on their faces. They looked like people who, for a brief time, had walked with their God and who had been granted the inner peace that only comes to those who have faith. They streamed downhill toward the cellars and debris where they would sleep tonight. We watched them from the church steps.

We stood silently. The sun was gone and now the valley lay dim in shadow. Distant hills, on which the sun had been streaming all day, now seemed insubstantial, ghostly shapes. Strange and peaceful silence had settled over the city. The city no longer seemed to be dead and lifeless. Perhaps I had been wrong about Vyazma. Perhaps it was not really dead. Perhaps a miracle might come to pass and Vyazma too might live again.

Major Smolin drove us to the outskirts of the city when we left. We left about six and it was already getting dark. We came to the edge of the city and he said good-bye to us.

"You know, if I were you," he said quite seriously, "I'd keep my brightest headlights on. The road for many miles is very rough and pitted with mine craters and shell holes. If you drive without lights you are apt to fall into one of them, or worse, are apt to bump into some tank or truck that is parked for the night."

"Don't German planes ever strafe this road?" I asked, amazed at his lack of concern regarding any blackout. Back in Moscow, you might well be shouted at by a warden if you as much as lit a cigarette on the streets at night.

"Oh, yes, sometimes," he said carelessly, "but the danger is slight. You risk being hit by them if you turn on your headlights, but if you drive without lights you are certain to hit something. Of the two, I think the danger of German planes is much less."

We drove on through the dusk toward Moscow. Red Army men were encamped on both sides of the roads and now and then a group of them were singing beside their open fires. Sentries occasionally challenged; silently we showed our passes, received their crisp salutes and then went on.

"They should raise a monument outside Vyazma," I said to Tania Sofiano, though in reality I was talking to myself. "On it should be engraven:

"Vyazma was a city of 60,000 inhabitants. It was 500 years old. Vyazma was killed by the Germans in March, 1943. At the time of its death, only 716 citizens of Vyazma were left."

Future generations will no doubt hear stories of ruthless and unnecessary cruelty practiced by the Germans in this war. But they may be more civilized than we are now, and incredulous of such stories. The epitaph will bear witness that the stories are true.

Moscow, June, 1943

****

Chapter V

THREE RUSSIAN WOMEN

In FICTION, all heroines are slim and beautiful; their eyes are provocative and their hair is as soft as moonlight. It happens that way occasionally in real life, too, but now I speak of a heroine who is neither slim nor beautiful; her eyes are not provocative but, instead, are weary with the pain she has seen and suffered, and her hair is concealed under a shawl. She has no glamorous past and, as for her future, there is little chance of her surviving another year. This, then, is Uliana Alexandrovna Golubkovar, soldier of Russia.

At first glance, Uliana looks like almost any middle-aged peasant woman. She sits hunched over a little, the way women do who have spent too many years bending over the soil, coaxing it to yield wheat and corn and potatoes. Until she tells you, you don't know that she bends forward slightly because that eases the pain of a half-healed wound. Until she tells you that she is only thirty-three, you would indeed think of her as just another middle-aged peasant woman. And you might mistakenly think of her as stupid, until she tells of the time she was left for dead by the Germans, or of an agonizing escape she made, with death often within a few feet of her, or of Germans she and her group of guerrilla fighters had killed.

She was born in the village of Putivl, which is in the soft, lush region of the Ukraine. She had two young sisters, Alexandra and Maria. They were trained as nurses. Uliana herself was a brilliant student and fervent patriot. Her father was postmaster of the village, and he took great pride in the intellectual achievements of young Uliana. So did the rest of the village, for when the old mayor (who had held office for twenty years) died, they elected young Uliana in his place.

In Russia they do not call the head of a community mayor; they call him president of the local soviet; but it means the same thing. She was enrolled as a party member when she was twenty-four, a great honor in the Soviet Union, for there are only two million party members in the whole country. That is one percent of the population. There is a waiting list of more than a million.

As mayor, Uliana settled local disputes over land boundaries, she administered justice, and the village of Putivl was indeed a happy and contented community. And then the German juggernaut rolled through the smooth plains of the Ukraine. Many in the village quite sensibly left, but not Uliana. When the Germans roared into Putivl, Uliana was there, calm and serene, prepared to do her best to make life easier for her fellow villagers.

But the Germans gave her no chance. They took Uliana and some of the other leading citizens, led them to a near-by monastery, lined them up against a wall and shot them.

"There were eight of us," Uliana told me in a peculiarly detached voice, as though she were telling of something which had happened to someone else. "Three of us, two teachers and

I, were women. They marched us to an old monastery. They told us to face the wall and to take off our clothes. By now, of course, I knew that we were going to be shot. The Germans usually make people they are going to shoot or hang take off all their clothes first. It saves them a lot of trouble afterward.

"I undressed slowly, and then the shots came. I still had my stockings and underwear on. Nobody cried out when the shots came. Then I felt something hit me in the side and I fell forward. Things became confused. I half remember being carried into the monastery and down a staircase, then I lost consciousness.

"When I came to, it was dark and there was a weight on me. When my mind began to work, I realized that there were bodies on top of me. Upstairs, soldiers were arguing about the clothes. I could hear them and then I heard someone groaning near me. It was one of the men, a doctor, and he was not dead, though the others were. He cried out to the Germans to come and finish him off, but they didn't hear him. I crawled over to him and said that we should try to get out. We were in the cellar of the monastery."

"How did you get out of there?" I asked.

"When the soldiers left," she continued, "I crawled up the stairs very slowly because my side hurt and I was losing a lot of blood. The doctor followed me. It was night now. We crawled to a farmhouse near by. I couldn't stand up to knock at the door. I lay there, trying to cry out and fearing that the Germans would hear me, but they didn't. The people in the farmhouse took us in. The doctor had a bad wound. He died that night.

"The following night they put me in a wagon, piled hay on top of me and sent me to a farmhouse a few miles away. Each night I would be transferred farther away from my village, farther away from the Germans. Then I reached an unoccupied town which had a hospital. The bullet had gone through my side and had injured my lung, and they didn't think I would live. I did, though, and then when I was better I decided to join the partisans. People in our villages always knew where they could be found."

"Were you expert with a gun?" I asked.

She smiled faintly. "I had never held a gun in my hands before, but I soon learned. We were usually behind the German lines. We kept in touch with the people of the occupied villages. Sometimes we raided these villages. There was a great shortage of salt in the Ukraine. I imagine the Germans sent it back to their country. Once we heard that they had a stock of salt in a certain village. We raided the village, took the salt and distributed it among the people of the neighboring villages. We were well armed, but food, of course, was a problem."

"How would you get food?" I asked her.

"They put me in charge of that," she said. "My wound was giving me trouble and I couldn't go on quick marches. I'd take a few men and lie in wait beside a road. When a convoy of German food trucks came along, we would ambush them and run the loaded trucks back to our headquarters. We shifted headquarters every few nights. We slept by day usually, and fought by night."

"What was the partisans' main job?"

She shrugged her shoulders. "Our main job was to blow up railroads and bridges. We blew up a lot of them, hindering the German advance. They decided to send a good force after us. We heard about it. They sent twenty tanks into the valley where we were, but we outflanked them and blew up five of them with hand grenades. Then we moved somewhere else. We were always on the move."

Uliana lived and fought with the partisans for nearly two years. She doesn't know yet what happened to her mother or to her two younger sisters. She would rather not think about that, she said. Why was she in Moscow? Uliana was a little ashamed of it. Her old wound had given her a lot of trouble, so she had been sent to specialists in the capital. But she would be back with the partisans soon, she said grimly, and then, rather surprisingly, she lost her placidity and became vibrant, alive, dynamic.

"Do your American women know the kinds of beasts we are fighting?" Her eyes flashed now and she no longer bent forward. She no longer looked like a middle-aged peasant woman. She was filled with a righteous hatred of the men who had invaded her country.

"Do they know that every time Germans occupy a village they hang or shoot a group of women just as a lesson to the others?" she said. "As a lesson to make others fall into line and obey them. Their motto is, 'Women and children first.' Yes, first hang the women and starve the children. Have American women ever seen the bodies of children who have starved to death? I have—in many villages of the Ukraine." Uliana breathed heavily and put her hand to her side. She got up and bowed, and there was a certain majesty about this stocky Russian who couldn't quite stand up straight. She walked out of the room.

Katia has chestnut hair that tumbles gaily over her forehead, and it is difficult to resist the impulse to run your hand through it. Katia has gray eyes that twinkle when she laughs, and she has even, white teeth and a dimple in her right cheek. She has a slim figure and soft hands, beautifully cared for. She is twenty-four but looks younger.

Katia wears the shining Order of the Red Star and the gold and crimson of it gleam against the dark blue of her uniform. She is a lieutenant and one of the best combat pilots in Russia. She has just returned from the Stalingrad front to receive another decoration. She has been in Moscow ten days and is very bored. Moscow must seem dull to a pilot who has made 160 operational flights and downed six "certain" German aircraft and received credit for many "probables."

"It will be good to get back," Katia says, her gray eyes gleaming. "Moscow is nice, but it is no place for a fighter pilot to be. Once you've seen the ballet and heard the opera, what else is there to do in Moscow?"

"You might do this," I suggested. "You might tell me the story of how you became a pilot."

Katia was born on a farm near Vyazma in the village of Konoplianka. Her father died when she was very young, and her mother, with five daughters to bring up, had a difficult time. Katia began to work when she was eight. She did housework for a more prosperous family in the village. She had no time to play, no real girlhood, and it is doubtful whether she ever had any dreams. Her dismal future was too obvious. Fortune had destined her to be a household drudge.

Then came Stalin's first great innovation—the collective farm. That meant a great deal to small farmers. It meant a certain amount of security, for one thing.

Katia immediately went to work on a collective farm. Now life was better. She had friends of her own age with whom to talk and play, and she was allowed to attend school for the first time in her life.

Then one day Katia met her destiny. She was walking home from school and, looking up, she saw an airplane. It was the first plane she had ever seen. It circled lazily above her as though it were there for her special benefit. She stared, fascinated.

The pilot glided low, so that she could see the graceful outlines of the plane easily, and then he opened the throttle and roared away, leaving a singing heart below. Katia told herself that one day she, too, would fly an airplane. It was a fantastic ambition for a young girl in an obscure Russian village, but she nursed it, and henceforth everything she did was directed toward that one aim. By now, Katia's older sister, Olga, was working in a Moscow factory—an aircraft factory. Katia headed for the capital.

Her sister laughed when Katia told her of her ambition. Katia had it all planned. She would work in an aircraft factory and her work would be so outstanding that they would immediately send her to a flying school.

"Everyone here is a specialist," Olga told the dismayed Katia. "Everyone has been to a technical school to learn the use of precision instruments. You'll have to go to school before you can get work in an aircraft factory."

Katia went around to technical schools, but found that they had closed for the summer. Then she made the round of factories looking for any kind of job. When you apply for factory work as a pupil in Russia, you must fill out a formal application. Among other questions, you are asked, "What do you want to be?" Invariably Katia wrote down, "Pilot."

One personnel manager grew impatient. "This is a shoe factory," he said. "If you want to be a pilot, it's no place for you."

She went back again to her sister's factory. She pleaded for any kind of job at all. Her persistence was finally rewarded, and Katia was given a job as messenger between departments. Nothing mattered as long as she could hear the roar of engines of planes landing and taking off on the airport which was also part of the factory.

Katia was a good citizen. She became a Pioneer leader— Pioneers are much like our Boy and Girl Scout organizations. She loved children and she worked hard, all of it voluntary unpaid work. In addition, she became a member of the Komsomol (Young Communist League), and she attended night school. But always she kept sight of her main ambition.

At the factory airport, they taught young pilots to fly. Katia never stopped badgering the officials in charge to give her a chance and finally, again perhaps impressed by her persistence or maybe just tired out by it, they reluctantly allowed her to enroll in the school. She didn't mind the tedious months of ground instruction. Soon she would actually fly in a plane.

Then the day when she began her dual instruction finally arrived. She proved an apt pupil, and one spring afternoon when her instructor climbed out of the plane, he waved her back and said casually, "Take it up yourself. See what you can do."

"That was the greatest moment of my life," Katia says, her gray eyes shining. "I took it, and it obeyed me. It was wonderful to be high above Moscow in a plane that did everything you told it to do. I landed, and it was all right, but the instructor said, 'That landing was probably an accident. Take it up again.' And, thank goodness, my second landing was all right, too."

From then on, Katia did nothing but fly. She resented the hours of darkness when she couldn't fly and she became a good pilot, so good that within six months she was acting as an instructor. About this time, aviation clubs were springing up all over Russia. She was given a post as head instructor at one of these clubs. She turned out more than one hundred pilots, some of whom became her colleagues in her squadron at Stalingrad.

"Then one morning," Katia says, "I heard Molotov tell us on the radio that the Germans had invaded us and that we were in a state of war. I said to myself, 'Be calm. Be calm.' But it was hard to be calm. I knew now that I wanted to be a fighter pilot. How? I didn't know. But I would become one."

And, despite every difficulty, she did become a fighter pilot. She found the speedy Yak, the best of all Russian fighters, not much more difficult to fly than the sport planes

she had been accustomed to. Gunnery was a little more difficult, but she soon mastered the ground targets, and finally
the targets towed in the air by other planes. She was given
her wings. Stalingrad was taking a bad beating in those days,
and fighter pilots were urgently needed there to stop the
German bombers. Katia, wearing her new dark-blue uniform
and her new wings, was sent to the Stalingrad squadron.

"Men laughed at first," she said. "They thought it a joke,
but not a very good joke. We usually fly in pairs, with each
pilot looking after his partner. None of the men wanted to
fly with me."

But discipline is discipline, and one of them had to accept
her as a flying mate. They took off on a reconnaissance flight,
and when they returned an hour later, her partner smiled
and cried out, "*Khorosho*," which meant, "Okay." She had
been accepted and henceforth she was one of them.

She got her taste of battle very soon. Alone, she came out
of a cloud and was startled to see a full squadron of German
bombers just below her. They were heading for Stalingrad.
She really had no right to risk herself and her plane against
twelve bombers, but if she didn't, these Germans might get
to Stalingrad and drop those eggs. She dived, got a German
in her sights and pressed the little red button. Smoke poured
from the German plane in a lazy trail, and she zoomed above
the squadron and into a friendly cloud. She thought she'd
try it again. Apparently their fighter escort was very high.
She banked and returned to attack.

This time she hit the leader, probably hit his gas tank, for
the plane blew up in an orange ball of fire. She saw that the
remaining German planes were dropping their bombs. They
always did this when they anticipated an attack by a force
of fighters. She saw bombs burst harmlessly in white flowers
of smoke on the countryside below and then she thought it
high time to be getting home.

[127]

She had her miraculous escapes as all pilots do. There was the time when she was attacked by two Messerschmitt 109Fs, an awfully good German fighter. She got one of them nicely, and then she and the remaining Messerschmitt, with the sky to themselves, fought for twenty-five minutes—a long time for a dogfight. Each tried to maneuver into good positions. Each cleverly averted and countered every offensive trick.

Finally Katia got him in her sights. She pressed the button—and nothing happened. She was out of ammunition. Well, she would try to make him think she still had ammunition. She circled and climbed and dived, and then he managed to get behind her, and she had a horrible moment when she realized that he was in a beautiful position. She dived. He followed, but the expected fusillade didn't come. Then she realized that he, too, had run out of ammunition.

"It was very silly," Katia says gravely. "There we were flying close to each other and neither of us could do anything about it."

Katia laughed. She had to go, really she did. She had an appointment—at the Kremlin. Rather shyly she confessed that. Yes, she was going to the Kremlin to be decorated again. She was to receive the second Order of the Red Star, and then she would be off to the front again.

Our third Russian woman isn't really a woman at all. She says she is nineteen. She looks fifteen. She seems far too small to carry the long name of Ekaterina Stepanovna Novikova about with her, so it seems quite natural to call her by her diminutive of Katiusha, which really means Kathie. Katiusha always wanted to be a parachutist. She did make one jump. It was from the roof of her parents' farmhouse in the Yaroslavl region, and her parachute was her mother's pet possession—a silk umbrella. The jump was not exactly a success. The umbrella caught on a shutter, and young Katiusha (she was eleven then) landed in very soft mud which injured nothing but her clothes and her feelings.

As a youngster, she never liked dolls, but she did like dogs. Katiusha was the freshest tomboy in the neighborhood and at a very early age she flatly declared her intention of becoming a member of the Red Army. "You're too short," they mocked, and that was true enough. At twelve, she was only a tiny thing with very short legs. She heard of some pills which would make her grow and somehow she managed to get a boxful of them. The instructions said to take one every day. Katiusha took ten at once, which sent her straight to the hospital.

Her parents moved to Moscow to find work in the factories, and Katiusha went to school. There were shooting clubs then in Russia, and Katiusha joined one. At least she would learn to shoot a rifle. She did learn to shoot a rifle, and when she was sixteen she learned to shoot a machine gun. Like any enthusiast, she wanted to spread her gospel, and one day the school authorities were horrified to hear shots in the schoolyard. They hurried out to find Katiusha teaching her young schoolmates how to handle a machine gun.

When war came, sixteen-year-old Katiusha tried hard to enlist. "We have enough men to shoot guns," they told her, "but we need people on the labor front."

She heard the magic word "front," and that was enough. She immediately enlisted in a labor battalion.

"I thought we were going right to the front," Katiusha wails now, "but it was quite different."

She was sent just outside of Moscow with thousands of others who were building trenches and gun sites. It was hard work even for sturdy little Katiusha who had been brought up on a farm. There was an anti-aircraft battery in the vicinity and she and others were given strict orders not to go near the battery. Anyone who broke the rule would be

[129]

brought up before the commandant. As soon as she heard that, Katiusha's short legs carried her as quickly as possible to the forbidden zone. She was immediately hauled before the angry commandant.

"Why did you go into that section?" he asked.

"It was the only way I could think of to meet you, Tovarisch Commandant," Katiusha said humbly. "I am a machine gunner. I want to go to the front."

"How old are you?" he asked, finding it hard to be stern.

"Nineteen," she lied gravely, and when he asked for her passport (all citizens carry passports for identification purposes) she handed him instead her certificates which told of her proficiency with a rifle and machine gun.

"We have plenty of machine gunners," the commandant told her, "but we do need nurses. Will you join us as a nurse?"

To get to the front, Katiusha would have joined anything. Luckily, she had studied nursing at school. A group of infantrymen were just leaving for the front. Katiusha went with them. Her baptism of fire came quickly. They had advanced only a few miles when they were dive-bombed and then strafed by low-flying German planes.

"I just stood there and shook my fist at the planes and yelled at them," Katiusha says. "How I wished I had a gun! All I had were bandages. I did what I could, but it was the first time I had ever seen blood, and it was pretty awful."

Closer to the front, disaster struck again. A group of German parachutists landed behind her detachment and cut them off. They had landed tanks, too, and for six days Katiusha's group held out. There was no question now of what she was to do. She crept out to where a machine gunner had been wounded. His hands still clenched the handles of the gun, but he was dead. Katiusha disengaged his fingers and took the gun in her own hands. Henceforth, she would never be anything but a machine gunner. This was at Belyi in the

Smolensk region where fighting was exceptionally heavy.

"I knew the region well," Katiusha says, smiling, and when Katiusha smiles, she shows small white teeth and wide blue eyes. Katiusha has three big freckles on her stubby nose and these make her look even younger than she is.

She was often sent on reconnaissance because she knew the section so well. On one of these long forays she found a cool swimming hole. She used to visit it often, to bathe. One day she found a soldier preparing for a swim. She cried out, "*Zdorovya, tovarisch*," or "Hello, pal," but his answer was in guttural German, and he went for his gun.

"I had dropped my gun," Katiusha says, frowning as though reproaching herself for her carelessness, "so I reached into my boot and pulled out my knife. I threw myself at him, and just before he got his gun, I stabbed him. He died immediately," Katiusha added grimly.

"Was he the first German you ever killed?" I asked the child.

"Oh, no," Katiusha said. "I had kept track. He was the sixty-seventh one I had killed."

At the front, it was kill or be killed, and killing became commonplace for this youngster. Twice she was wounded, and then a third time she was sent to a hospital with a shell splinter in her head. They found out that she was only seventeen. They told her sternly to go back to Moscow; they wanted no children here at the front.

She started for Moscow but made a detour to wind up with a guerrilla detachment near Sychevka. She spent five months with the guerrillas. During that time she killed, she says almost apologetically, only twelve Germans. Then she was sent to officers' school. The training was ridiculously easy after her practical experience and, within three months, she was made a lieutenant.

Since then, she has been at the front constantly. She received the Order of the Red Star and has another decoration coming up. She has seen the hardest fighting of the war and took part in the defense of Kharkov. The fighting was bitter on the western front when the Russians advanced.

Not long ago Katiusha and her group were given orders to capture a village. They entered it and had to capture house after house. Katiusha, with grenades in her belt, with a revolver at her side and with a Tommy gun in her hands, crashed into one house. She swept the room with her gun, killing two out of three Germans. The third, an officer, held up his hands.

"I walked close to him to get his gun," Katiusha says, "and then he noticed that I was a woman. He was enraged and he hit me on the side of my head. I went sprawling. Well, I was pretty mad, too, so I emptied a whole drum of bullets into him before he could raise his gun. That is seventy bullets. Have you seen *Lady Hamilton?*"

At the moment, the film *Lady Hamilton* was the most popular picture in Russia. Katiusha had just seen it. She would really rather talk of how beautiful Vivien Leigh looked and how handsome Laurence Olivier was, than she would of the Germans she had killed. That was the commonplace part of everyday existence.

"I have seen *Lady Hamilton* three times," she said, and she looked like any schoolgirl now (except for her wound stripes and her decorations and her uniform). "And now I'm going to see it again. Then tomorrow"—she smiled happily— "I'm going back to the front."

These are three women of Russia I thought you might like to meet.

Moscow, June, 1943

****

Chapter VI

POLAND BELIEVED GOEBBELS

LATE LAST April Dr. Goebbels announced on his radio that
the bodies of 10,000 Poles had been found buried near Smolensk. He charged that these bodies had been identified as
Polish officers listed as missing since the Russian occupation
of Eastern Poland in 1939. Dr. Goebbels charged that these
Poles had been executed by the Red Army and tossed into
the graves which the German Army had now discovered.
When we first heard this (we listened constantly to the
German radio because it came to us so clearly) we yawned
and switched over to the Rome station. It was, we thought,
just another one of the good doctor's bedtime stories. But
he hammered away at it again and again. He suggested that the
International Red Cross be sent to Smolensk to see for itself.
We laughed at that too. To begin with Russia was not a
member of the International Red Cross. Then, too, we knew
that any Red Cross commission sent to the occupied territory
around Smolensk would see exactly what Goebbels wanted

[133]

it to see—and nothing else. It was an absurd suggestion in line with the Goebbels tactics of the past four years.

Then we were shocked to see that the Polish government in London was actually taking the story seriously. We heard on the BBC that Vladimir Kot, former professor of law at the University of Cracow, later Polish Ambassador to Russia, and now Minister of Information in London, had published a statement by the Polish Minister of War, denouncing the atrocity. This was followed by an official request by the Polish government that the Red Cross be allowed to investigate.

There is an old Russian saying, "What's the use of being a Pole if you can't be stupid." The alacrity with which the Polish government in London so stupidly walked into the Goebbels trap made us wonder if perhaps the proverb didn't have some meaning. Whether the atrocity story were true (and Goebbels never produced proof that it was true), the Poles certainly did everything they could to handle it in the most undiplomatic way possible. The diplomacy of the Poles is as subtle as the path of a Mark VI tank through a flower garden.

For years the Russian-Polish pot has been simmering dangerously and this incident caused the lid to pop right off. On May 8th we were all called to the Foreign Office and handed a copy of a letter sent to Polish Ambassador Romer by Molotov that afternoon. This marked the end of Russian-Polish diplomatic relations, though there was some doubt at first whether this was a mere suspension of relations or a definite break.

The letter was given to us in Russian, and the confusion arose in regard to the wording used. All of the correspondents, translating freely, wrote that diplomatic relations had been broken off by the Soviets. The censors refused to allow this to go through. They insisted that the boys use the word "suspended." They pointed to the word in Molotov's letter. The word was "*prerivat*" which, by dictionary definition means, "to suspend." The word "*porviat*" (to break) was not used, the censors insisted. However, it all came to the same thing.

Alexander Werth, Marjorie Shaw, Ralph Parker and two or three others who knew the Polish Ambassador well hurried to his embassy. Ambassador Romer has been a charming, well-liked member of the diplomatic corps. Romer is the ideal diplomat—a great rarity in a Pole. He is smooth, tactful and he has the knack of seeing the other man's viewpoint. Even that night he never lost his temper. He was sad at having to leave. He regretted the whole incident exceedingly, but he emphasized the courteous treatment he had always received from the Soviet officials. He would leave in the morning, he said. He would not comment on the attitude his government in London had taken, but he told Alexander Werth that he did not for a moment believe the Dr. Goebbels story of the 10,000 dead Polish officers.

Werth and the others hurried to send the story, but the censors refused to allow them to quote Romer.

"We do not have diplomatic relations between Russia and Poland at the moment," Palgunov explained, "therefore Romer is not an ambassador. He is merely a private citizen and you cannot quote him."

That was, I regret to say, typical of the petty bureaucracy we were exposed to from Palgunov and his censors. The quote from Romer would have helped Russia enormously. But unfortunately, and despite what so many Americans think, the Russians are the worst propagandists in the world. They sometimes seem to go out of their way to show themselves in an unfavorable light.

Anyhow, Romer left the country. Clarke-Kerr and Standley went to the railroad station to see him off. Standley gave

Romer a carton of American cigarettes as a going-away present, while Clarke-Kerr gave him a bottle of Scotch.

The open rupture between the two countries is only the culmination of an underground diplomatic war that has been waging since the end of the first war. It is pretty difficult to bring their fundamental differences into the open because they have been so befogged by petty quarrels.

If you look at their struggle objectively and realistically the whole conflict boils down to power politics. It is a conflict between a first-rate power determined and able to wield overwhelming force, and a second-rate state trying to perform a first-rate role with the aid of coalitions.

Poland was afraid of Germany because the leaders of Germany were, for the most part, Prussians, and the Prussians have traditionally hated Poland. When Hitler came into power, Poland felt new hopes that she might get along with Germany. Hitler was an Austrian by origin; Goering a Bavarian; Goebbels a Rhinelander and Hess came from a German family which had settled in Egypt. Poland was sure that these men would not be imbued with the anti-Polish feeling of the Prussians who had hitherto ruled Germany. Josef Lipski was the Polish Ambassador to Germany then (1934), and the Germans wooed him with soft words. In the *Polish White Book*, a collection of all official documents and agreements concerning Polish-German and Polish-Russian relations, Ambassador Lipski writes to his boss, Foreign Minister Beck: "Hitler said to me . . . 'The theory of hereditary German-Polish enmity is very unsound. In the history of our two countries there have been periods of co-operation against the mutual danger threatening from the East . . . (Russia had recently made great progress with her military preparations.) . . . The moment may come when both our countries might be compelled to defend ourselves against aggression from the East.'" Hitler told Lipski that in his opinion the policy of former German governments (especially the Reichswehr) which had wished to unite with Russia against Poland was unsound. He knew Bolshevism well, the Chancellor added; he had fought it from the very beginning, and he recalled his struggle against communism in Bavaria. Lipski apparently fell hard for Hitler. Josef Beck, always a hater of communism, too, listened to Hitler and fell into a poppylike dream induced by the opium of his words.

Then came the Polish-German declaration of January 29, 1934. It was a beautiful document of less than 300 words— but what pretty words of neighborly love they were! Such phrases as, "The maintenance of a lasting peace between the two nations is an essential prerequisite for the general peace of Europe," abound in the declaration. It added: "Both governments announce their intention to settle directly all questions of whatever nature which concern their mutual relations." Four days later Hitler spoke in the Reichstag. He paid a glowing tribute to Marshal Pilsudski and he wound up his sweet speech by saying that the whole thing "fills us with *especial joy*."

And of course Poland had a pact with Russia too—a non-aggression pact signed in 1932 and ratified in 1934 with the added provision that it would remain in force until 1945. She was officially, at least, on very good terms with her two big neighbors, and she could hardly be blamed if she had some wistful secret thoughts to the effect that she held the balance of power.

Poland felt pretty comfortable now. Yeah man, she had a partner, big Germany. Hitler was her pal and that nasty Stalin man had better not start anything. Pal Adolf would slap him down if he did. Meanwhile Pal Adolf was bringing in German-born residents of Poland and showing them how to shoot little guns; how to undermine Polish authority; how to sabotage; how to organize a strong minority so that when

[137]

the time came it could handle a large unorganized majority. Poland, thinking of its nice declaration all sealed and tied with red ribbons, continued its complacent way. Complacency was the style in the 1930's anyhow.

Then at 4:45 A.M., the morning of Sept. 1, 1939, the complacency of Poland was disturbed by the roar of bombs dropped on the city of Westerplatte. Germany was waging an undeclared war on Poland, and the lovely 1934 declaration lay in the Foreign Office gathering dust on its pretty red ribbons.

In ten days Poland had folded up. Her resistance was heroic if futile. But Warsaw no longer existed as the capital of Poland. Her industrial areas melted before the mechanized strength of the man who had murmured such sweet nothings to Ambassador Lipski. For all practical purposes the Polish government had ceased to exist.

Poland melted before the Germans and then on September 17, 1939, Russia moved her troops across the border into Poland. Poland was between the devil and the deep blue sea. It was a pitiable position and the world sympathized. Russia undoubtedly moved in only in self-defense. She needed the security which possession of those 76,500 miles would give her, should Germany ever attempt to invade her. Of course Stalin used the sweet talk of diplomacy when he sent his troops into Poland. He said, "The Soviet Government further cannot view with indifference the fact that the kindred Ukrainian and White Russian people who live on Polish territory and who are at the mercy of fate, are left defenseless."

On October 29, 1939, a plebiscite was held in the Russian occupied territory, and the citizens voted a 90 percent majority to the Soviets. How accurate the count was no one knows. Elections held under the shadows of guns are hardly ever strictly the will of the people, and there were Russian guns about. The Russians say that the population of this territory was 12,800,000 of whom 7,000,000 were Ukrainians, 3,000,000 White Russians, 1,000,000 Poles and 1,000,000 Jews. Correspondents in Moscow think those figures are reasonably accurate. I have heard the same figures given in London. Assuming them to be reasonably accurate, perhaps the overwhelming vote was not out of line. In any case, the incorporation took place and my bet will be that it is there to stay.

Ethnographically, the Russians have an excellent case for keeping this territory. But we might as well be realistic about it: Russia wants that belt of land to act as a margin of safety against future aggression.

Now let's get to 1941. Soviet-Polish relations got off to a fresh and favorable start under the agreement of July 30th of that year. The Sikorsky government said, in effect, "Well, for the moment we're allies fighting the same enemy. Let's let bygones be bygones until we sit at the peace table." All embassies were stationed in Kuibyshev then. Moscow was too near the front. The Sikorsky government made the mistake of staffing its embassy and its military mission with diplomats and officers who had always been identified with the avowedly anti-Soviet policies of Josef Beck. These gentlemen entirely lacked the gift of reticence.

[*From here on my story is one which has not been told before. None of the following facts came to me from Soviet sources. I have checked on everything as much as possible and I am convinced that everything that follows is one hundred percent true.*]

I was in Kuibyshev during those days. In a sense Kuibyshev was a small town. Everyone ate at the Grand Hotel and drank at the Grand Hotel and for the most part lived at the Grand Hotel. Correspondents, military attachés, ambassadors, ministers—Grand Hotel was headquarters. Correspondents have what we call "sources of information." We learned an awful lot sitting around after dinner at the Grand Hotel when vodka had loosened tongues. We used to hear the Poles talk. The Poles hated Russia and made no effort to conceal their feelings. Well, perhaps if I had been a Pole I would have felt as they did.

The first problem the Poles had to tackle was that of the 750,000 Poles the Russians had transferred from the eastern provinces to the northern and central parts of Siberia and to southwestern Asia. Those among them who were military or political prisoners were placed in labor camps—the Russian term for concentration camps. The civilians had been removed to distant villages. The incorporation decree of October 29, 1939, said that any Poles living in Russian territory as of October 30, 1941, were Soviet citizens, which complicated matters no end. After prolonged negotiations the Russians permitted the Poles to establish relief organizations with the aid of Lend-Lease supplies. Eventually the Poles had 520 agents throughout the country. They were organized into committees, each committee headed by a selected agent who was called in the language of diplomats "*homme de confiance*." Many of these committee chairmen were given Polish diplomatic passports.

Meanwhile the Sikorsky government in London said that it wanted to raise a Polish Army from the Poles incarcerated in Russia. An agreement was concluded with the Kremlin on August 14, 1941, which provided for the raising of an army of 30,000 men. This agreement was subsequently amplified by accord and the figure was raised to 96,000 men. General Vladislas Anders, bald-headed, eagle-eyed and ribbon-bedecked, weak after nearly two years of confinement in Russian prisons and labor camps, began to organize this army.

Meanwhile the Polish relief organization groups were work-

ing. The *"hommes de confiance"* with their diplomatic passports were the only foreigners permitted to travel through
such hitherto forbidden regions as Siberia and southwestern
Asia. A scandal of major proportions broke out in connection
with the relief organization. Correspondents knew about it
and embassy officials gossiped about it, but it was hushed up
by Soviet officials and a strict censorship ban placed on any
mention of it.

One day in Kuibyshev the Russians arrested a Polish "relief
worker" named Piwowarczvk. On him was found a letter
from General Wolikowski, Chief of the Polish Military Mission. The letter contained instructions of an intelligence
nature. The Soviet government asked General Wolikowski
and his two aides, Major Jacyna and Captain Przewlecki, to
leave Russia immediately. They left.

A short time later a Polish relief delegate named Rola-
Janicki arrived in Kuibyshev from Tashkent. The Grand
Hotel seemed very lovely to him after Tashkent. He ate
well and listened to the dulcet music of the four-piece
orchestra and so rapt was his attention that he departed from
the hotel, leaving his wallet on the table. The Russians found
the wallet and it was sent to the police station to be called for
by the owner. But it was never called for. One reason, perhaps, was the fact that it contained locations of new railroads
of military importance which had never been shown on any
known map. Rola-Janicki was given three days to leave the
country. He left.

The Russians rather understandably became annoyed. They
inaugurated a systematic check-up of all relief delegates.
They found a large number of them in possession of diplomatic passports. Close surveillance was put upon them, and
the Russians are very good in that "close surveillance" department. One hundred and twenty Poles were eventually
arrested, charged with espionage, anti-Soviet propaganda

[141]

among the Poles, and attempting to spread panic among the Russians. All this happened at a critical time. The Germans had just launched their great offensive against Stalingrad and the Caucasus. The Germans were doing very well then, and the Russians were in no mood to humor those who were spreading anti-Soviet propaganda. One can see their point.

Those who were arrested included Wiencek, delegate to Alma Ata; Professor Heitzmann, delegate to Samarkand; Wisinski, delegate to Kirov; Glogowski, delegate to Ahkabad; Winiarczyk, delegate to Sistifkar; and Zachjasiewicz and Dr. Slowikowski, members of the Relief Committee in Kuibyshev. Arlet, first secretary of the Polish Embassy, was arrested and expelled from the country. So were Zelinski, Polish consul in Vladivostok, and the consul in Archangel, whose name I could not obtain. Of the one hundred and twenty who were arrested, seventy-five were expelled from Russia, twenty were acquitted, several were convicted of espionage. There are still at this writing (June, 1943) fifteen awaiting trial. Ambassador Kot's weak explanation to Vyshinsky that he personally disapproved of relief workers doing intelligence work, hardly endeared the former law professor to the second-in-command of the Russian Foreign Office. The Soviet government asked the Polish Embassy to send new delegates who would work under the supervision of local Soviet authorities.

Meanwhile what of that Polish Army Anders was training? General Anders had little faith in the ability of the Red Army to withstand the full impact of the German blows which were increasing in fury each week. He told friends repeatedly that the German Army would eventually smash Russia. That is why he liked his training quarters—the middle Volga region. The Russians say they continually pressed Anders for a date when he would be ready to fight. He gave no definite answer, and the Russians began to suspect that he was staying there in the middle Volga all set to fly to the Caspian and to Iran should the Germans break through.

Russia was supposed to feed and clothe the Polish Army; to give it the essentials. The other allies were to provide heavy equipment. Finally Anders and his army moved to Iran. He said it was because the Russians failed to properly feed and equip his troops. Vyshinsky countered by asserting that when the Russians finally realized that Anders had no intention of fighting on Russian soil, instead of furnishing his troops with the rations given to combat units they gave them the rations ordinarily given troops which were resting. You pays your money and you makes your choice. As to which side is right, your guess is as good as mine—if not better.

Russian-Polish relations continued to go downhill. The Polish papers in London started tossing right-hand punches at Russia. It can be assumed that these papers, published under the aegis of the Polish Ministry of Information, represented the opinion of the Sikorsky government. The Russian press took it for awhile and then swung into action. They criticized Poles in Britain and America for making statements which were designed to undermine the public's confidence in Russia's ability to resist. They accused the Poles of sitting on the sidelines, hoping that Germany and Russia would knock each other out (that same old cry still raised occasionally by contemptible Britons and Americans) so that Poland could wind up the dominant factor in any Russian-German situation after the war. They attacked the Poles in the Middle East and in London as fascists and said that they sought to establish a fascist Polish government in London completely anti-Soviet.

The whole acrimonious discussion was disheartening to one like myself who had seen the magnificent Polish fighter squadrons in action during the battle of Britain and who had seen their hatred for the Germans expressed in practical terms. They were great fliers and courageous men who died bravely. But then too I had talked with Poles in Iran who were all the Russians said they were. I knew, as everyone in Teheran knew, what the Poles did with some of our Lend-Lease and Red Cross equipment. I know they cared for the Poles one way in Teheran and for Jewish Poles in quite a different way. Oh, a very different way indeed. That brings us up to the open rupture and the departure of Ambassador Romer.

Now a new figure emerged in Russia—the commanding figure of the Polish writer and spellbinder, Wanda Wasilievska. Madame Wasilievska is the wife of Alexander Korniechuk, a successful Ukrainian playwright and at present one of the Vice Commissars of Foreign Affairs. Although Wanda was born Polish, she became a Soviet citizen, a state of affairs which might tend to make her observations on Polish-Russian relations slightly prejudicial. She became president of the Union of Polish Patriots and announced that a new army of Poles would be formed under Soviet auspices. Colonel Zigmunt Berling, former Chief of Staff of Anders' Fifth Division, was revealed as the new Commander in Chief. A congress of the Union of Polish Patriots was held, with Wanda presiding, and resolutions were passed that the congress would henceforth march under the spiritual guidance of the late Tadeuscz Andrzej Bonawentura Kosciuszko, under the Polish National flag, and that it would fight to the death on Russian soil. It was also decided that copies of these resolutions be forwarded to Prime Minister Churchill and President Roosevelt.

Well, that's where the situation stands at the moment. I have only presented the facts of the case and those briefly, because I have only gone back as far as 1934. Poland was always unfortunate in having powerful, predatory neighbors. She was unfortunate, too, because the word "partition" seems to have been coined just to be applied to her. Boleslaus the Third, who ruled Poland from 1102 until 1139, divided his country into no fewer than eight parts when he died. This began the so-called "partitional period." Slices of her land and her population have been cut off periodically ever since. In 1309 the whole Polish population of Danzig was massacred by the Teutonic Knights. In 1790 Frederick William of Prussia extended a helping hand and made an alliance with Poland only to repudiate it three years later when he joined with Russia in yet another partition of the unhappy country. So it went through the centuries. The Treaty of Versailles (March 20, 1931) fixed the status of Poland anew, making it an independent republic and giving it territories which had belonged since 1815 to Prussia, Austria and Russia. With the backing of the League of Nations, Poland began to feel pretty frisky. Looking at her big neighbors, she came to the conclusion that in case they ever went to war with each other, she, little Poland, would cast the deciding vote. She could give victory to whichever side she favored, whichever side she gave free entry. She would protect herself by coalition. If she signed up with Germany, Russia would respect her rights. If she signed with Russia, Germany would respect her rights. That was her theory, anyway. So she signed with both, and a layman, looking at it dispassionately, might be pardoned for thinking that she was playing both ends against the middle.

Now she is in an unhappy condition. The world bleeds for the cruelties practiced upon her people. But the fact remains that diplomatically Poland is and has been out of step with her allies and especially with her biggest ally—Russia. Leaving the equities of the case severely alone, the conclusion is unescapable that Poland isn't big enough or strong enough to get out of step. When you get out of step you march alone. No one is big enough to march alone in this year of our Lord, 1943.

Moscow, June, 1943

****

Chapter VII

RUSSIAN FAMILY

IF YOU DON'T mind walking up five flights of stairs come along with me and meet the Starostina family. They are not an extraordinary family at all. They are much like the Smiths or the Joneses on your block if you happen to live in a community of factory workers. They are an average Russian family and, if you put about twenty million families like the Starostinas together, you have the Russia of today—just as if you put twenty million typical American families together you'd have the America of today. The real fundamental strength of a country does not lie in its leaders or in its armies. It lies in the cumulative faith and patriotism of the Smiths and the Joneses and here in Russia it lies in the ability of the Starostina family to hold out, to produce, to fight on the home front.

Suppose we go into their home, meet them and find out how they live and what they do, how much food they get and what they pay for it. Let's find out how they dress and what their amusements are and what they think of the war and its outcome.

I was quite out of breath when I climbed the five flights in the large apartment house in the factory district of Moscow. This is not a particularly beautiful section of the city, but today we aren't looking for the superficial beauty of park or boulevard or the man-made beauty of buildings like the Bolshoi Theatre or of the magnificent clean stateliness of the Lenin Library. We are in the neighborhood dominated by factories and workers' flats, for only in such a neighborhood can we find an average family of Russian workers.

Grandma Ekaterina Filipovna Starostina opened the door and smiled when she heard my panting after the long climb. Grandma Starostina looks much like any other grandmother whether she lives in Russia or Dublin, Ireland or Middletown, Ohio. At sixty-four there are lines in her face that record a lifetime of work, but she stands straight and her smile of welcome lights up her face as she murmurs the typical Russian word of welcome, "*Mozhno*," which means much more than the literal "You may come in."

Grandma Starostina worked in the textile factory which is just across the street. She worked there for thirty-five years and she married a fellow workman and bore him five children. Since his death she receives an old-age pension and keeps house for two of her married daughters and her two grandchildren. She presides over her immaculately clean three-room apartment and very definitely she is head of the family. She had a huge samovar on the table and the tea was ready. I sat down with the two married daughters and the two shy grandchildren while Grandma Starostina busied herself with the cutting of bread and sausage. Occasionally, as we talked, she would put in a word or half consciously pat one of the children on the head.

We sat in a room that was half dining room, half bedroom.

[147]

It was about twenty feet long and ten feet wide—the whole apartment had an area of twenty-five square yards, for it is by square yards that apartments are rented. There was another bedroom in addition to this room and a kitchen. The kitchen was shared by a family of three who lived in a room across the hall. This would be a typical arrangement for a worker's family in Moscow. The war interrupted a huge building campaign, and until the war is over the half-completed apartment houses designed to give workers larger quarters, which one sees everywhere, must remain incompleted.

One daughter, thirty-one-year-old Alexandra Fedorovna, with black eyes and dark hair, urged her eight-year-old son, Vladimir, to talk to me. Her husband died four years ago and now she and Vladimir lived with Grandma Starostina. Vladimir is at kindergarten. He has all of his meals there and this costs his mother sixty rubles a month. The rate of exchange, a rather artificial one, out of line with buying power, is five rubles to the dollar, which means that Vladimir gets three meals a day for twelve dollars a month. He was a tall, dark-eyed youngster, very solemn and a little shy because he was wearing his best suit and a white Buster Brown collar. I asked him what they'd given him to eat at school that day.

"Today for breakfast we had two slices of bread with butter, an omelet and tea with sugar," the youngster said very seriously. "At noon we had noodle soup, potatoes and apple jam. At three o'clock we had tea but no sugar and a piece of bread with more apple jam. When we left at five o'clock we had kasha (porridge) with milk on it and bread. I like apple jam," he said, unbending for the first time.

"The little rascal," Grandma Starostina laughed and ruffled his hair. "He eats all that and then comes home and always wants something with us at our evening meal."

Vladimir's mother. Alexandra, explained that she worked

in the same textile factory across the street in which her mother had once worked. She began in 1928 as a weaver but has recently been promoted to the job of testing the finished product to determine if it is up to standard. Her salary is 600 rubles a month ($125) but invariably she makes more than that. All Soviet factories have bonus systems and, if the plant exceeds the scheduled production, each worker receives additional compensation, according to his position. Alexandra, for instance, earned 800 rubles ($160) this past month. Originally, she and all of her fellow workers were on eight-hour shifts, but now the hours are determined entirely by the need for production. She usually works ten or eleven hours a day.

"But we don't work by the clock," she says scornfully. "Our men at the front don't fight by the clock."

Alexandra is also a blood donor. Virtually every widow or wife of a Red Army man is a blood donor. Every six weeks she travels to the Central Blood Clinic to give a pint of blood. She would do it more often, but the doctors allow no one to act as donor more than once in six weeks. Each time she gives blood she gets 270 rubles ($54) in cash and an extra ration card entitling her to an extra pound and a half of butter, pound and a half of sugar, pound of meat and pound of cereals each month.

Recreation? Strangely enough, Alexandra is no ballet or opera enthusiast. Nor does she especially care for the movies. Alexandra is strictly a theatre fan and she attends whenever she can. Chekov's *The Cherry Tree* and Moscow's current hit play, *The Front*, are her two favorites. She doesn't go out much at night. Usually she is too tired and she'd rather romp with young Vladimir and gossip with girl friends who live in the apartment house.

"I go to bed early," she says, smiling a little sadly. "The sooner you get to sleep the sooner you forget your troubles.

Time goes quicker and the end of the war will seem to come more quickly."

While we were talking, her twenty-seven-year-old sister, Klavdia, was romping with her son, a rolypoly, laughing-eyed five-year-old, Vitali. Vitali is the kind of youngster whom you want to wrap up and take home with you. He climbs on your lap, gurgling with happiness and then, suddenly remembering something, he'll dash out into the hall and ride triumphantly into the room on his three-wheeled bicycle. His mother is slim, fine-featured, with soft blonde hair and very light blue eyes. She too works in the textile factory across the street. It is called the Trekgornaya Manufactura and in peacetime her foreman was a tall, very dark Moscovite who was very popular with the workers—especially the women workers. But his eyes fell on the blonde beauty of Klavdia, and seven years ago they were married. They had an apartment next door to Grandma Starostina. Then the war came. He enlisted, and lonely Klavdia and her son moved in with Grandma.

"I couldn't stand being alone," she says, smiling ruefully, as though ashamed of her weakness. "I moved in here and now at least Grandma and I can talk about him. In bad times like these you want to be with your own people. It makes life easier."

Klavdia began in the factory as a clerk and now has become an inspector of textiles. Her salary is 500 rubles ($100) a month, but this month she made 600 ($120). She, too, is a blood donor, and has given blood twelve times. Despite her almost frail blonde beauty, Klavdia is a very serious-minded girl. She was a member of the Komsomol (League of Young Communists) when younger and is now studying to become a member of the Communist Party. Klavdia goes to school three nights a week when she is finished at the factory. She studies history, political economy, the principles of Marx and

[150]

Lenin, the history of the party, and then she has to take a stiff examination which not all manage to pass. But she is confident that she will pass and be admitted to membership. It must be remembered that the Communist Party in Russia is not a political party in the sense that we at home understand political parties. Here one must earn membership either by study or by giving special meritorious service to the country. If Klavdia makes it, she will be the envy of her fellow factory workers.

Klavdia is a movie fan who especially liked the present film, *Actress*, the story of a musical-comedy star who gave up her career to act as a nurse. She heard hundreds of wounded soldiers criticize her for not staying at her real job. As an actress she could give so much joy to workers and soldiers who desperately needed the mental relaxation furnished by the films and the theatre. Finally she goes back to her real job. The film is an interesting commentary on a condition which we haven't recognized at home as yet. The Soviet authorities class the opera, the ballet, the theatre and the films as essential industries necessary to the war effort and leading lights are not only exempt from service but are almost considered slackers if they do enlist. *Actress* points out the government policy on this. Klavdia wholeheartedly agreed that the girl in the film was of more use on the stage than she would be in a hospital. Klavdia showed me a letter from her husband. He had been sent from the front to an officers' training camp, and Klavdia was very proud (just as your neighbor Mrs. Smith or Mrs. Jones would be proud). The letter also told of the good food the men enjoy at the front.

"We have a lot of canned food from America," he wrote, "and it is excellent." Because of that one line in the letter Klavdia had become an ardent friend of America as an ally.

"We all celebrated when we heard the wonderful news from Tunis," she said. "In our newspapers we first read our own war news, then eagerly look for stories of American and British victories and bombing raids over Germany. Ah, that is good news to read about our allies."

Grandma Starostina, who had been listening, interrupted to say that lately she had been getting a lot of canned milk, lard, sugar and chocolate, all of which came from America. This food, obtained on ordinary ration cards, had made millions of Russian friends of America. Strangely enough it is the American lard which is most highly prized. Strangely enough to me, that is, because I don't even know what lard is used for, but here there is a scarcity of it, and American lard has been a great boon. Klavdia and Alexandra have two older married sisters, Natasha and Sonya. They live together not far from the Starostina apartment. No home in Russia has managed to escape tragedy and the Starostinas are no exception. The husbands of both Natasha and Sonya are listed as missing.

"But it may be," Grandma Starostina says hopefully, "that they were cut off and are now back of the German lines with the guerrilla groups."

Let us consider the economic situation of the family. With the eighty-two-ruble pension Grandma receives, their total average earnings are 1,600 rubles ($350) a month. Their rent is fifty-three rubles ($10.50) a month, which is the average rent of any worker's family in Russia. That includes heating, water and radio. Lighting is another eight rubles ($1.60). Their ration cards allow them twelve and a half pounds of meat per month, which will cost an average of sixty rubles ($12) monthly. Mutton is quite cheap, averaging four rubles a pound, while pork, of which there is a scarcity, costs eight rubles a pound. Their ration cards permit them thirteen pounds of cereal a month at an average cost of four rubles per pound, a total of fifty-two rubles ($10). They are allowed five pounds of butter at eight rubles a pound; five pounds of bread daily at eighty kopeks (fifteen cents) a pound, and three pounds of sugar a month at two rubles (forty cents) a pound. No milk is allowed for adults, but five-year-old Vitali, in addition to his meals at kindergarten, is allowed two glasses of milk a day (twenty cents). Grandma Starostina went over last month's housekeeping accounts with me. Last month the family living expenses, including rent, food and the children's fees, came to 535 rubles ($107), which left quite a comfortable margin for clothing and extras.

Outside of the government shops, where ration cards are honored, there is an open market in Moscow. Here farmers who have produced a surplus, or people who have commodity goods to sell second-hand gather and they may charge anything they wish. Their prices would make a New York or Detroit millionaire blink, but actually, of course, few Moscow families either need or can afford to patronize the market. Typical prices at the open market are: milk—seven dollars a quart; potatoes—six dollars a pound; sugar—eighty dollars a pound; butter and lard about the same, while a pound of meat would cost about one hundred and eighty rubles ($16). A pair of second-hand shoes costs anywhere from one thousand to four thousand rubles. Divide by five and you have it in dollars. The open market with the fantastic prices charged seemed to me to be a negation of the whole communistic philosophy. Sometimes farmers made great fortunes selling their surplus produce in the Moscow market where ration cards were not needed. The papers were filled with the story of how a collective farmer had bought one million rubles worth of Soviet war bonds ($200,000) and had then presented the bonds to the Red Army. I asked a Soviet official how he had accumulated that much money.

"The open market, of course," he shrugged. "We don't like the open market much, but it is a necessary evil and, of

[153]

course," he added seriously, "it does have the effect of encouraging individual enterprise."

What price communism? I am afraid that American and British communists would be very bewildered by things that happen in Moscow. But then citizens of Moscow might be pardoned if the American party line at times bewildered them.

The Starostina family, however, never patronizes the open market. Because both daughters are factory workers and blood donors their ration cards amply supply the family with food. They get necessary clothing through their factory department store at reasonable prices. Girls aren't buying new frocks or silk stockings in Russia these days. All fabrics are needed for uniforms and other war purposes, while silk and its substitutes are used for making parachutes or radio equipment. Russian women through long practice have the knack of making clothes last longer and now that it is spring millions of them go barelegged to save their cotton stockings. Only last week Grandma Starostina received eighteen yards of material from the factory to make suits for the two boys. She also received a pair of shoes for each child. This cost 250 rubles—twenty-five dollars.

There are few consumers' goods on the shelves of the Moscow stores, and the prices of the few goods they have are far beyond anyone's purse. Workers look to the factory for everything, and the factory does take care of them. The recreational, educational and economic life of a family revolves around the factory, and the workers do get whatever is available in the form of commodity goods. If these goods are scanty and not up to pre-war standards that is not the fault of the government or of the factory. It is the fault of the war and no one complains, least of all the Starostina family, which considers itself fairly well off.

We talked of many things, but we didn't talk about the war—except once. I asked, "Do you think we have a fair chance of beating Hitler?" There was an astonished silence, and then a peal of laughter from Grandma, from Alexandra, from Klavdia. Even Vitali, not knowing what the laughter was about, but knowing that everyone was happy and that life was good, joined in and then climbed up on my lap, still laughing happily.

"We cannot lose," Klavdia said simply. "We just cannot lose."

I imagined the Smiths and the Joneses saying the same thing at home. Any military strategist could show such families a dozen ways in which the war can be lost, but wars, in the long run, are won by families like the Smiths, Joneses, and the Starostinas and millions like them while the armchair strategists are drawing military diagrams on luncheon tablecloths. Anyhow, we didn't talk about the war beyond that. People in Moscow are much too busy working to help the war effort to waste time talking about war. We didn't even talk about nineteen-year-old Boris Starostina, the fifth child. He enlisted at seventeen and has been missing for nearly a year now. Sometimes men listed as missing do come back. Not often, but often enough to keep a spark of hope from dying. No, we didn't talk about him any more than you would talk to the Smiths or Joneses about a son listed as "missing." There's nothing you can say.

I left them finally because it was time for the kids to go to bed. I left them well fed, contented, the two children playing happily on the floor. The walk down those five flights wasn't nearly as hard as the climb up. I regretted only one thing. I wasn't able to kidnap young Vitali and bring him down the stairs under my arm. You've probably felt the same way about the Smith kid next door or that Jones youngster down the street.

Moscow, June, 1943

[155]

Chapter VIII

IT HAPPENS IN MOSCOW

JEAN CHAMPENOIS, who writes for the Free French Agency, is one of the most popular correspondents in Moscow. He has a comfortable apartment, and one day he held a cocktail party. Actually, of course, there are no cocktails in Moscow. But the party was a success. Two ambassadors and three generals were present as well as several correspondents. We sipped sweet wine, and conversation in French, Russian and English filled the room. A Soviet general was discoursing with considerable knowledge on the strategy of the Stalingrad victory when he was interrupted by the shrill crowing of a rooster.

A moment later, there came the unmistakable triumphant cackle of a hen. Both sounds seemed a bit out of place in an apartment in the center of Moscow. I asked Champenois where the noise came from.

"I keep a rooster and a hen," he said casually. "Didn't you know? They're in the kitchen. Come along."

I went into the next room and, sure enough, there was a belligerent-looking rooster that made ominous, throaty noises when we walked in, and a plump motherly-looking hen that had just deposited an egg on the floor.

"I get three eggs a week from the hen," Jean said proudly, quite unconscious of the incongruity of turning a kitchen into a farmyard. "I may get rid of the rooster. He doesn't like me. I think I'll have him for dinner some night."

"If you could only get a cow now, Jean, you could have milk and butter and an occasional steak," I suggested.

"I wish I had a cow," Jean said wistfully. "I could keep her here in the living room. But how would I get her up the stairs?"

Things like that happen in Moscow. The ambassadors and the British, American and Soviet generals saw nothing out of the ordinary in Jean's sharing his apartment with the hen and the rooster. In Moscow, the unusual seems normal, and daily life is a series of paradoxes. Technically, Moscow is still a city under siege, and martial law is still observed.

The midnight curfew rule is strictly enforced, even on correspondents, and, during the day, avenues are thronged with men and women in uniforms, armored cars, American jeeps and guns.

Yet, within the limits of military supervision, four and a half million people live fairly normal lives—as normal as life can be in a city dedicated one hundred percent to the war effort. Correspondents who share this existence have also come to regard life in Moscow as fairly normal, although they admit that outsiders would probably disagree with them.

One night the ballet *Swan Lake* was shown with the incomparable Ulanova as the prima ballerina. This is by far the most popular ballet in Russia, and the *Swan Lake* performance has all the glamor and éclat of an opening night at New York's Metropolitan Opera House. No member of the diplomatic corps would miss it. Neither would the British and American military missions stationed here. It was a gala occasion, for which tickets had to be purchased weeks in advance. Between acts, according to Russian custom, the audience paraded around the large lobby.

Two American correspondents, Bill Downs and David Nichol, were among the lucky ones to obtain tickets. They joined in the parade, jostling elbows with gold-epauletted Red Army generals, with American and British generals, with ambassadors and with the beauty and culture of Moscow. But they wanted to smoke, and neither one had a cigarette.

Everyone is strictly rationed on Russian cigarettes in Moscow. American cigarettes are available only when a visiting fireman arrives from America with a surplus supply. Downs had a package of smoking tobacco, but there's no cigarette paper in Moscow. Two great journalistic minds pondered the problem, and then canny Nichol, with a triumphant cry, drew from his pocket a book of subway tickets. These are printed on very thin paper.

The two master minds hurriedly rolled cigarettes and joined the moving circle, the cynosure of envious eyes. It is hardly a sight one would see at a fashionable New York opening, but it seemed quite normal in the lobby of the Filial Theatre.

The ballet theatre and motion-picture houses are packed every night in wartime Moscow. At present we have a large military mission in Moscow, and the boys are great ballet fans. Hard-boiled sergeants who a year ago were arguing as to the relative merits of Jack Dempsey and Joe Louis now argue just as heatedly about Ulanova, Lepeshinskaya and Semenova.

Moscow loves its theatre. In addition to the Moscow Art Theatre, the Maly, Filial, Stanislavski and other old-established theatres, there are many others situated in various Moscow parks. There are five in a park called the Hermitage, only a few minutes from the center of the city, and three in the Park of Culture and Rest. The huge Bolshoi Theatre, bombed more than a year ago, is still closed, but Moscow rejoices over rumors that it is going to reopen soon. In all, there are thirty theatres in Moscow and there's seldom an empty seat in any of them.

The most popular dramas are the old favorites: *Anna Karenina*, *The Marriage of Figaro*, and *The Cherry Orchard* (in which Chekhov's wife, for whom it was written, still appears), while in opera *The Queen of Spades* (Tchaikovsky), *Carmen* (Bizet), *A Life for the Czar* (Glinka), and *Traviata* (Verdi) bring in the crowds.

Dmitri Shostakovich, who lived across the square from me at the Moscow Hotel and whose Seventh Symphony won such rapturous praises when performed in New York last year, is not considered quite the greatest in Moscow, where the critical faculties are very well developed. Factory workers, street-car conductors, and Red Army men and women will argue that Dmitri, while a nice young guy, really doesn't belong in the same league with such big-timers as Tchaikovsky, Moussorgsky, Rachmaninoff or the brilliant Khachaturian. Toscanini, incidentally, sent Shostakovich the records of the New York Philharmonic playing his Seventh, but at a party given by Ilya Ehrenburg, the composer told one of the guests (a Russian war correspondent) that he hadn't heard the records yet. He didn't have a phonograph.

The Soviet Union has lost nearly one third of all European Russia, and six million of her people have been killed, captured or temporarily enslaved in occupied territory. Yet Moscow, much as she grieves in private, sees no reason for giving up her theatre and opera.

All our military people here speak the language. With typical army efficiency, they were all trained in Russian before being appointed to this post. It's strange to hear unmistakable Brooklyn or Middle Western accents arguing amiably in Russian. All correspondents, too (with the exception of this one), know Russian fairly well, and when we played hearts or gin rummy (our only dissipation), we usually played in Russian. Families of correspondents might blink in surprise if they heard fond sons or husband look at a hand and cry out with disgust, *"Ochen plokho!"* which means a very lousy hand.

The brightest minds in the American Embassy invented a drink composed of one-third vodka and two-thirds canned grapefruit juice, which was excellent. But the supply of grapefruit juice was soon exhausted. We did all we could to disguise the taste of vodka, but only one intrepid correspondent actually solved the problem.

I had a personal interest in his experiment because it was made on the occasion of my birthday. The scientist responsible is Walter Kerr, of the *New York Herald Tribune*. On such occasions we all contributed whatever we had. Most of us contributed vodka, but Eddy Gilmore of the Associated Press and Harold King of Reuter's each managed to snare a bottle of champagne. It was Kerr who invaded the kitchen of the Metropole Hotel to produce three lemons, an unheard-of luxury here. And then this genius went to work.

The idea, he said, came to him in a dream. He squeezed three lemons into a large glass pitcher, cut the rinds up and threw them in, poured in a bottle of vodka after that, and then filled the pitcher with champagne. The drink was *ochen khorosho*—as the boys say when they want to bestow particular praise on something. Kerr had one thing to add that made us regard him in awe. It proved the value of the scholarly influence of the *Herald Tribune*.

"I have named this drink Katusha!" he said solemnly. Katusha (a Russian gun) is a great anti-personnel weapon.

So was this drink, but it made a birthday for a very homesick correspondent.

Moscow never forgets that there's a war on and that this war is in her back yard. No bomb has dropped on Moscow for a year, but we all know that German bombers have attempted to get through the outer defenses of the city many times only to be repulsed by anti-aircraft guns and night fighters. Perhaps the enemy bombers will break through some night. Moscow is ready. Air wardens are on duty at every office building, factory and block of apartment houses. We would see them when we came home at night, standing alert in the still, pale light.

In the spring Moscow thinks of next winter. Every factory, every civil, social and political organization sends selected groups into the country for short periods. There they fell trees, cut trunks into logs and cart wood back to Moscow. There was a shortage of fuel last winter in Moscow, and thousands of apartments had to go without heat. There will be no shortage of wood next winter.

Moscow has inaugurated a tremendous back-to-the-land movement. Every Moscow citizen has been allotted a plot of land outside the city. Each Saturday afternoon, one would see strange processions trooping to various railroad stations. Hundreds of men, women and children walked along with hoes, spades and rakes over their shoulders, bound for their own little plots.

Special trains, with transportation costing virtually nothing, took them to the country. Urbane Moscovites developed into amateur farmers. Many spent the night sleeping in the open by their plots of ground and then worked all day Sunday on their potatoes, carrots and cabbages.

One day a paper carried a page-one story warning people that they only had five more days in which to plant potatoes, by far the most precious and sought-after vegetable in Moscow.

In the city itself, every back yard, every vacant lot has been cultivated. The American Embassy, on one of Moscow's main streets—Mokhovaia—had a ten-foot strip of grass in front of it. Even this was transformed into a truck farm which produced radishes, cabbage and carrots.

A portion of the grounds of Spasso House, residence of the American Ambassador, has been transformed into a farm. Under the skilled hand of Boston-bred Eddie Page, Second Secretary, thirty-three chickens, three rabbits and eight ducks were being fattened in the garage and in the yard back of the house.

Page thought he had made a ten-strike when he decided to breed rabbits. He had visions of hundreds of them scampering about and later gracing the embassy table. When weeks passed and the rabbits still remained three in number, a more rural-minded member of the embassy staff whispered into the ear of Page that, unfortunately, all his rabbits were of the same sex.

With the approach of summer, Moscow threw aside her somber raiment, and the streets became alive with color.

Flower stalls in the markets were gay with masses of peonies, lilies-of-the-valley, forget-me-nots, and buttercups brought in from the country by farmers. The flowers were eagerly snatched by people who wouldn't mind the lack of meat on their tables if they could decorate them with a few touches of summer.

Girls in bright print frocks mingled with crowds of uniformed men. The most common Red Army uniform is a green blouse, dark blue trousers, black boots, and khaki cap trimmed with red. Officers wear golden epaulettes on their shoulders. The immaculate whiteness of our own naval officers and trim U. S. Army uniforms were common sights on Gorky

Street. Occasionally, a tall Cossack swaggered by, complete with round fur hat and dagger hanging at his waist.

No one could ever accuse Moscovites of being hoarders. Secure in the knowledge that pensions will take care of them in their old age and that medical care is free should illness come, they spend every ruble they earn to make life more easy. If you mention the hard times inevitably ahead of them, they shrug their shoulders, smile, and murmur their favorite word, "*Nichevo!*" Money is merely something to be quickly transformed into commodity goods.

It is typical of Moscow that, although prices were fantastically high on unrationed goods, you could obtain a precious, almost priceless icon in exchange for two bars of soap. And a dressmaker, instead of charging you rubles for embroidering a blouse, would ask half a pound of sugar or a quart of vodka.

The Moscow maiden takes good care of her clothes. This is especially true of shoes, which are now virtually unobtainable except on the black market at a cost of $500. Obviously, all the leather is needed for the army.

Coming out of the opera one night, the crowd was greeted by a terrific downpour. In Moscow, everyone walks (no cabs or private cars, and the subway range is very limited).

Shoes do not last long if subjected to many downpours, and this night I saw a half dozen women remove their shoes nonchalantly, put them under their coats, and brave the rain barefooted. And one army officer, obviously wearing new boots, followed suit.

Things happen in Moscow which happen nowhere else. Janet Weaver, Moscow correspondent of the *New York Daily Worker*, is popular with her colleagues not only because she is the only American girl who has been in Moscow throughout the war, not only because of the charm which seems to be part of any Georgia-born girl, but because she

[163]

is the only woman in Russia who can make lemon meringue pie as we knew it at home.

One night there was a knock at the door of the apartment where Janet and her husband live. A fifteen-year-old girl stood there. Her name was Nadia Tomova and she was going to graduate from high school soon, she said. She had been selected to sing "The Star-Spangled Banner." Nadia had a copy of the words, but did not know the tune. Knowing that Janet was an American, she had come to ask her to teach her our national anthem.

Janet had once taught school in her native Georgia. She took the child to the home of a friend who had a piano; there she taught Nadia the tune and the correct pronunciation of the words. At the graduation exercises, Nadia Tomova was a terrific success.

One day, Captain Herbert Callis, skipper of an American merchant ship temporarily anchored in a Russian port, came to Moscow for a week's vacation. I showed him around town. Captain Callis, whose home address is Blakes, Virginia, made a rather profound observation on Russia's capital.

"Friendliest damn' town I ever did see," he declared enthusiastically, in his Southern drawl. "And it's the truth that anyone in this town big enough to walk is wearing a uniform."

That's almost literally true; and those who aren't in uniform are doing other war work. Moscow is a strange town, but it's a town of friendly people. No foreigner, and very few Russians, understand this country of paradox where the unusual is typical.

Once when I was very puzzled about something that had happened in Russia, when I was trying to rationalize something that just wouldn't add up, I brought my perplexity to my colleague, Leland Stowe.

Lee said, "Don't try to rationalize this country or you'll go nuts." There was a Russian poet named Tutchev who has been dead about one hundred years. A few lines from one of his poems have become a proverb in Russia: "You cannot understand Russia with your reason; you cannot measure Russia with a yardstick; you can only believe in Russia."

I have followed the poet's advice ever since. I think Russia has earned our faith. You don't have to understand the strange, paradoxical country to know that although she is dedicated to war, she has not allowed the scanty food, the lack of fuel, and the horror of battle to dampen her spirit or shake her faith in her eventual destiny.

Rumors reached us even in far-off Moscow that a big operation was due soon in the Mediterranean. I thought it was time I did some traveling with the American Army. I said good-bye to Russia, leaving the country with high faith in her destiny and with the conviction that when the war is over Stalin will be very easy for us to do business with. I headed for Cairo.

Moscow, June, 1943

****

Chapter IX

MIDDLE EAST INTERLUDE

CAIRO IS THE kind of place where someone is apt to sell you a street car; where you're apt to step off a curb and bump into a camel and where skirted Arabs (male) walk along the streets hand in hand. These, among other things, happened while I was in Cairo. The first night I arrived, Colonel Robert Parham, in charge of Press Relations for General Brereton and the Ninth Air Force, took me to a party. It was a nice party in a brightly lighted apartment in a pleasant part of the city. We left early. The street was dark. There were no lights and no moon. Parham had parked his jeep across the street, and we stepped confidently off the curb into the darkness. I bumped into something soft and big and smelly. Puzzled, I stepped back and tried it again. Once more I bumped into the same thing.

"It's a camel caravan," Cairo-wise Parham said. "We better wait until they pass."

Gradually, our eyes became accustomed to the gloom, and

[166]

we could see the dark outlines of the huge camels lumbering along. A camel undoubtedly has his qualities, but you would hardly pick one for a household pet. I had learned in school that a camel has a hump and that it can live, travel great distances and go practically forever without a drink. I didn't learn that a camel has a very bad breath and apparently never brushes his teeth. The camel is neither quaint nor picturesque—merely dirty. The camels in Egypt have the same attitude toward the country as do the Arabs—the whole land is their bathroom and neither demands the privacy that even a cat insists upon. The camel has only one inhibition. He does not mate in public. I have seen thousands of camels in my various trips to the Middle East, but even in the desert, where I was practically the only spectator, I never saw a boy camel so far forget the proprieties as to make a pass at a girl camel.

British troops who have been stationed in Egypt for years have told me gloomily that they have never been able to surprise a camel in what one might call an unguarded moment. This may seem to be a trivial matter, but troops are confirmed candid-camera fiends. This helps kill the boredom, and a picture of a couple of camels in *flagrante delicto* would have made several divisions happy.

Colonel Parham dropped me at Shepheard's Hotel. If you sit on the terrace of Shepheard's Hotel long enough, you are bound to meet the dullest and most unimportant men in the world. In that, it resembles the outdoor café of the bistro once known as the Café de la Paix. Being an avid reader of detective stories, I was quite familiar with Shepheard's long before my first visit to Cairo. Any time you picked up a thriller and saw on the cover, "A story of international love and intrigue," you just knew that the action would take place in Shepheard's. Actually, Shepheard's Hotel is about as glamorous as a dish of Spam. To begin with, it has telephones in only fourteen of its many rooms. My room was one without a phone. It was hot in Cairo, and I opened my huge French doors that led to a balcony. I slept the sleep of the pure in heart, until I was awakened in a rather rude fashion. I returned to semi-consciousness to find that something or someone was hammering at my chest with trip-hammer blows.

"I'll phone the manager," I started to say weakly, when the light flashed on. I thought I was dreaming. Two beautiful girls in evening dress were bending over my bed, laughing gaily, and pounding away at me with unladylike fists. I shook my head, but they were still there. I looked closer and saw that my assailants were Bea Lillie and Dorothy Dickson. Behind them, grinning like a cat, was another old friend from London, Leslie Henson, one of the funniest men alive. They had arrived in Cairo that night and had immediately gone to give a show at a camp some hundred miles out in the desert. They were working with an Ensa unit (Ensa is the British equivalent of our USO).

I didn't even have a bottle of beer to offer them. It is difficult to buy a bottle of anything in Cairo. I suggested we go down the hall to Frank Gervasi's room. He might have a drink. I was shocked to notice that Bea was not wearing her shoes but carrying them.

"This is a filthy country, Beattie," I stormed. "Put your shoes on, or you'll get athlete's foot or something."

"I've walked miles and miles today and my feet hurt," she said. "But what about you? Where's your pajama coat?"

I grabbed a robe and we walked down the hall to the room where my colleague from *Collier's*, Frank Gervasi, and Harry Zinder of *Time* lorded in regal splendor. They had the best room in the hotel. We never locked our doors at Shepheard's, and property was considered to be communal. We woke them up. Gervasi, half-asleep, blinked in the strong light, looked at Bea and Dorothy and said, "I must have died and gone to Heaven." Then he saw Leslie Henson and shook his head. "No, they'd never let Leslie in Heaven."

Gervasi had neither beer nor cigarettes. We sat and talked about London and about pals of ours there. There is a wonderful camaraderie among London theatrical people. Back in London I had gone around with an Ensa troupe with Bea, Henson and Dorothy, and it was exciting to hear gossip of the theatrical and Fleet Street crowd with whom I spent most of my time in London. Vivian Leigh had come out with Bea and the troupe, but she, sensible girl, had gone to sleep. We talked for hours, and it didn't matter that Gervasi and Zinder had long since dropped off to sleep. It was Henson who reminded the girls that at seven the next morning a plane was to take them on a five-hundred-mile jaunt to a desert airfield where they were to entertain. So off these great troupers went to get two hours of sleep.

Gervasi and I remained on in Cairo. He went on several bombing raids with General Lewis Brereton's Ninth Air Force. We knew that a big offensive was coming up soon, but we didn't know whether it would be across the Mediterranean to Sicily or Italy or whether it would be through the Balkans. In either case, we were strategically located here in Cairo, in a position to hop either north or northwest.

I mentioned earlier the astute gentleman who sold a passing street car. He did just that. He met an Arab just in from the desert—an Arab whose pockets were filled with Egyptian pounds. He explained that he owned the street cars and that he would sell any one of them for 200 pounds. The buyer then had the privilege of collecting fare from everyone who rode on the street car. The credulous Arab looked at the passing street cars which were bulging with passengers and quickly concluded the deal. His surprise was probably considerable when he attempted to eject the regular conductor and collect fares himself. The clever entrepreneur who had made the sale had vanished.

The sucker was a sadder but wiser man. The publicity he received in Cairo papers made him a public figure. Now the original rascal really showed his genius. Somehow he came and made peace with the sucker and expounded a great scheme. He had a tent in the Arab section, he said, and he would exhibit the sucker and charge sixpence admission. They would split the profits. They put large signs outside the tent and business was excellent. In fact, the sucker who was being exhibited finally got a bit weary of standing for hours being gaped at by his fellow Arabs, so he hired a stand-in who would undertake the arduous job of allowing the natives to look at him. Arabs are quite definitely allergic to work. It was then that the police swooped down and closed the exhibition on the ground that fraud was being practiced.

Bob Parham, his assistant, Captain George Kirksey, a former United Press sports writer, and Leon Kay, in charge of the Middle East UP bureau, and I decided to drive to Alexandria. The drive was across some 300 miles of sheer desert. Hollywood couldn't have done better with a desert. Parham comforted us with the thought that there was a restaurant halfway to Alexandria and that it sold cold beer. The temperature was about 110 when we arrived at the Halfway House, a square wooden building perched right in the middle of the desert. We were shocked to learn that even here license hours were enforced. It was after two o'clock in the afternoon and no drinks could be sold. The Greek bartender was apologetic but firm. Then Kirksey went to work on him with some New York double talk.

"Oh, no," he said, smiling. "It is all right to sell us beer because Horace Stoneham told us prosit and Mell Ott too. You know what Ottie hit last year and it was a bad year and he told us it was all right and frenken too you can't prevoot us that way . . ." He went on talking two hundred words to the minute, always emphasizing the name of Horace Stoneham. Why he picked on the owner of the New York Giants I don't know, but the Greek, evidently impressed by Kirksey's air of complete authority, his glibness with words that meant nothing at all and his intense manner, finally said, "Okay." He gave us a case of ice-cold beer (for two pounds) and the rest of the trip to Alex was pleasant enough.

We drove to the Red Cross headquarters immediately. You'll always receive a friendly welcome there and lemonade and sometimes ice cream—more highly prized in the Middle East than any drink. We were not disappointed. The Red Cross building was on the sea, and the cool breezes filled its immaculately clean rooms. A great many of our pilots, wearied after too many combat hours in North Africa, were sent here for a week's rest. They sat around the club room reading American magazines. The Red Cross had a private cabana on the beach, and the boys spent hours swimming and sunning themselves. They did a wonderful job with nerve-racked lads in Alexandria. They had sailing boats which went out three times a day filled with youngsters who needed this kind of relaxation to still quivering nerves. Pilots (especially bomber pilots) get "flak happy" after twenty or so missions. They need rest badly then, and our air-force generals are smart enough to follow the advice of the air corps medical men who watch the pilots carefully. If they see signs of nervousness or jitters, the medicos immediately recommend rest. Two pilots arrived while we were there. Both were very young and both looked worn. The woman in charge explained the routine. She found rooms for them and then suggested that they might like a cool sail in the Mediterranean that afternoon. To her amazement, one of the pilots fainted dead away.

"What's wrong?" she asked in alarm.

"Well, lady," the second pilot explained sheepishly, "my pal here was shot down last week, and he floated around in that damn Mediterranean for three days before he was picked up. I guess he's had enough of the Mediterranean."

"We'll get him a camel ride or a game of tennis instead," the harried Red Cross worker said.

Within limits, Alex was a gay place at night. The bars and restaurants were jammed with American and British fliers. There were quite a few New Zealanders in town too, a rather disturbing factor to the peace of the community. New Zealanders took special delight in beating up Americans. This was so true in Cairo that the M.P.'s were doubled in the section where the New Zealanders were located. New Zealanders are, for the most part, big, tough laddies who are very handy with their fists. It is with sorrow I record that they usually came off on top in their fights with our boys. I knew a great many New Zealanders who had fought in the desert with Friberg in the second Libyan campaign and a finer bunch of men I never met. Why, then, this antagonism toward Americans? Our boys were equally puzzled. I found out the reason. Clever Doctor Goebbels had been hammering away on the radio with his propaganda directed against American soldiers. He repeated again and again the story that Americans stationed in New Zealand had completely won not only the heart of the country but the women as well.

We dropped into a night club and stood at the bar for a while. Two New Zealanders came in. They sipped their beer moodily. One of them was especially downcast. He had just driven a truck from Cairo to Alex and on the way had hit an Arab. He felt very bad about it.

"Look, cobber," his pal said, "stop mooning about it. It wasn't your fault. He was hopped up with marihuana, probably. He stepped right into the middle of the road in front of us, didn't he?"

"Yeah," the other said, "but you hate to kill a guy like that, even if it's only an Arab." He pronounced it Ay-rab, as all troops do.

"Your lights were on. He should have seen them."

"And we didn't even stop," the driver said into his beer.

"You can't stop in a case like that. We'd have been killed. You know that," his pal said, and then he gave the clinching argument to dispel his friend's gloom. "And besides you hit him fair and square, didn't you?"

"Yeah, that's right," the driver said, cheering up. "I did hit him fair and square. There is that."

We drove back to Cairo the next day. The lull was continuing. Gervasi had been on a bombing raid over Sicily and he thought that Sicily might be next. We cabled *Collier's* for instructions but *Collier's* left it up to us. Gervasi was pretty much sold on his Balkan idea, and he wanted to be in on that show if it came off. The beauty of working for a magazine like *Collier's* is the fact that once you are in the field you can decide things for yourselves. This independence of action is one reason why men like Gervasi, Walter Davenport, Kyle Crichton, Bill Courtney, Jim Marshall, Frank Morris and I will continue to work for *Collier's* as long as they make typewriters.

There were no planes leaving immediately for Tunis or Algiers, so I decided to be a tourist and visit the Holy Land. An old friend, Frank Lynch, president of General Motors in the Middle East, had some business in Jerusalem, and I thought I'd go along with him. We talked Colonel Bob Parham into coming along. We thought it might be more interesting to drive instead of flying, so one bright morning we set off with our car bulging with lemonade-filled thermos bottles. We drove across the Arabian Desert, a dreary expanse of sun-baked sand, lacking only a few whitened horse skulls to remind you of Death Valley. The trip took ten

[173]

hours. Occasionally, we would pass long convoys of trucks or guns, but for the most part we had the desert to ourselves. After this seemingly endless trip we rolled into Tel-Aviv.

Tel-Aviv is the largest and only modern city in Palestine. It was founded in 1909 as a suburb of ancient Jaffa. Jaffa is a typical Arab city with crooked, filthy, winding streets. Tel-Aviv was immaculate with wide streets, modern houses and with the sidewalks filled with clean-looking Europeans.

"No beggars," I noticed.

"No kids yelling, 'backsheesh,' " Lynch said.

"No Arabs," Parham sighed happily.

Tel-Aviv is undoubtedly one of the cleanest-looking cities in the world. Cleanliness is rare in the Middle East. What these people (more than 90 percent Jewish) had done in the short space of thirty-four years was incredible. We drove all over the city and didn't even find any slums. Then we headed for the Red Cross headquarters. It was crowded, but the Red Cross people found us accommodations in a hotel called the Kaete Don right on the sea. I had stayed there one night a year before, and the handsome, white-haired proprietor, a German refugee, remembered me. To show that he did, he made us delicious Tom Collinses with real Gordon gin.

In the morning we put on bathing trunks and robes and stepped out of the little hotel onto the beach. The water was cool and we swam out and floated lazily and looked up toward the white houses with the flat roofs.

"Do you think we could get bacon and eggs for breakfast?" Lynch asked.

"I could eat horse meat," I said.

"What's wrong with horse meat?" Parham chimed in. "Every time we get a steak in the Middle East it's probably horse meat, but it's all right as long as we don't know it's horse meat."

We swam for an hour and went back to the little hotel. The smiling old man said, "I have a surprise for you for breakfast."

"What is it—Spam?" I asked.

"Sit down on the terrace and you'll see. Don't bother changing; there's no one here now but you three."

We sat down and first his waiter brought us large glasses of orange juice. It was good orange juice, too, not out of a can. Then he carried in three plates and when we saw what was on the plates, we couldn't believe it. Three steaks and on the top of each steak a fried egg.

"It's almost noon," the old gentleman said, "and I thought you'd be hungry. I have been saving those steaks. You'll find them good."

He was a wonderful old man. We stayed two days with him and had fine food, and the bill for the three of us (including meals) was fifteen dollars. Tel-Aviv was beginning to look like a dream city to us. There was a large American rest camp outside the city called Telawinski. We visited it. Our military men had built a garden spot in the desert and combat-weary men recovered their health here. Everything possible was done for them. The Red Cross, magnificent as always, took them on tours to the Holy Land. They had their own beaches and movies, and the food was far superior to ordinary rations. Ten weary Negro soldiers arrived while I was there. The lieutenant in charge (a Texas officer) treated those men as well as if they'd been his brothers. He showed them their quarters, a fine wooden-floored tent which held ten cots.

"Take it easy, boys," he said. "Just relax. You own this place while you're here. Sleep all day if you want. There's a library right over there with a few thousand books. We've got a car that goes to the beach twice a day. We got movies every night or, if you want to go to town, there's a bus that leaves at seven. If you want to see Jerusalem, let me know. I'll send you in. And the food is good. Eat your heads off, boys."

The C.O. was very proud of his hospital. We went through it and we saw his point. It would be a pleasure to be sick there. The doctor in charge was beaming. He had a girl patient—the first girl to be in the hospital.

"She has sand-fly fever, and she's been a pretty sick girl," he said. "She is a Red Cross worker and was on her way to Teheran when it hit her. She shouldn't go to any place that hot. They ought to transfer her to Alex or leave her here in Tel-Aviv where there is some breeze. But she won't let me recommend any change to her boss."

We went into a private room to see the girl. She looked pretty pale, but she smiled cheerfully enough. She was Kay Cerf of Long Island, and we told her that we were going to tell her boss in Cairo that she was in no shape to live in the murderous heat of Teheran. That made her real mad.

"I didn't come over here to be pampered," she said sharply. "I'll go where they send me. Besides," she smiled, "I come from Long Island. Iran can't be any hotter than our Long Island summers."

We left the hospital and headed for Jerusalem. The first thing that correspondents do when they enter Jerusalem is to contact Gershon Agronsky, publisher of the lively *Palestine Post* and one of the leading figures in the Zionist movement.

"I suppose you want to learn all about the Jewish-Arab question," stocky, smiling Gershon said. "I'm a bad one to ask, because I'm hopelessly prejudiced. I'm a confirmed Zionist. But meet me at the office tonight when I put the paper to bed and we'll go home. I've got a bottle or two of Scotch, about the only Scotch left in Palestine, and we can talk."

Rooms were scarce in Jerusalem but Frank Lynch knew a General Motors dealer in town, and he got us a room at the King David Hotel. Our room which held three beds opened on a terrace and the terrace overlooked the walled city and beyond to the Dead Sea. Lynch, Parham and I were enjoying the forgotten thrill of being wide-eyed tourists and it was a lot of fun. Our dinner at the King David was good, but my enjoyment was marred by the fact that the menu was printed in French, an affectation I have always found annoying.

"Have you any Frenchmen living in the hotel?" I asked the headwaiter.

He said there were no Frenchmen, the guests were mostly British officers.

"Then why do you print your menus in French?" I asked. "Why not in English or in German or in Hebrew? Why French?"

He looked bewildered. "I don't know," he confessed. "They've always been printed in French."

I've gotten that same answer in hotels in London, New York, Berlin, Cairo, Amsterdam and a dozen other cities. My one-man war against the absurd custom has gotten me nowhere. They still print menus in French all over the world, and no one has ever told me why. Frenchmen who travel abroad invariably know English, so it cannot be for their benefit. I hope some day to own a hotel and print menus in English. It would at least have the charm of novelty.

We picked up Agronsky at his office. His place was a beautiful model of what a small newspaper plant should be. Over his desk was a large autographed picture of Heywood Broun, which brought a nostalgic gasp from me. It also made me a complete Agronsky fan from then on. We went to his charming home and sat talking for hours, but never once did he mention the perplexing problem.

"I'm too prejudiced," Agronsky smiled in answer to a question I asked. "Stay around awhile. See for yourself. Get

[177]

both sides. I'll put you in touch with the leading Arabs. They're fine men. Get their side. Then visit our communal farms and talk to our men and women. But don't let me prejudice you."

Until the time we left, Agronsky, whose whole life is wrapped up in the Zionist cause, never tried to influence us, never volunteered information, never said one word of criticism of the Arabs. His fairness and his silence were two powerful advocates hard to resist. It would be presumptuous for anyone who has spent only a week in Palestine to discuss the question of Palestine as a national home for Jews. I did meet several intelligent Christian Arabs and they had just one argument. "This is our home and the home of our fathers, and their fathers. We object to turning our country over to foreigners. It is true that the Jews have done wonders with the land they farm here. They say that our methods are slow and backward. Our answer is that we are in no hurry. We have been here for thousands of years. They want us to turn our country over to them. No code of morals can justify the persecution of one people in an attempt to relieve the persecution of another. We are sorry for the Jews, but we insist that Palestine remain an Arab state."

The Moslem Arabs, on the whole, are completely pro-German, a result of the excellent brew distilled by Dr. Goebbels, a brew composed of one tenth logic, two tenths promises and seven tenths hatred. He shook it well, tossed it out over the ether waves and the poisonous concoction infected the Arabs by the thousands. If we win this war the Arabs believe their cause will be lost. If the Germans win they believe they will have freedom and complete control, a bit of wishful thinking seldom indulged in by any but the half-witted.

I heard many whispers in Palestine (from neutral correspondents) to the effect that the Arabs had large quantities of guns and ammunition cached away against the day when open warfare would come again. Mention this to an Arab and he will remind you that the communal Jewish farms had their own police forces, well-armed and organized. I visited several of the farms but saw no policemen carrying arms, a condition I am sure will be changed at the first sign of trouble.

The farms are "communistic" in the purest sense of that word. They are beautifully run, especially the large ones like Givaat Brenner located between Jerusalem and Tel-Aviv. Enzo Sirreni, one-time doctor of philosophy and professor in an Italian university, was the head man at Givaat Brenner. He has one rule for those who apply to become members of his farm. You must work on the land. Men who had formerly been lawyers, doctors, shopkeepers were working busily in the fields the day I visited the camp. Most of the fruit and vegetable produce of this farm was being sold to the British and American armies in Palestine. It was in every sense a model community—if you were willing to submerge your talents and your individuality and be merely one of the farm hands. These men and women were quite willing and anxious to do that because here they did find peace and self-respect. I stood on the roof of the administration building with Sirreni. From there we could see for miles in every direction. This had once been nothing but desert land. Most of it still was but occasionally a splotch of green would break the monotony of the dull expanse of sand and scrubby undergrowth.

"There is an Arab village." Sirreni pointed to a fertile-looking patch some four miles away. "We have taught them our methods of farming. We get along beautifully with them. As a matter of fact, I'm going over there this afternoon to help them repair a tractor that broke down. They have a fine farm because they work hard and because they know that the antiquated methods used for generations and generations by their forefathers are not good enough to coax things to grow in this soil. We taught them irrigation and even from here you can see how green and fine their fields are. But look there," he pointed to another village. "And there and there. They are other Arab villages and you see nothing but wasteland there. There are Arabs—and Arabs."

An interesting farm was the one called Maialeh Hahamisha (The Hill of Five). Here the custom was to use only first names. "Joseph" was the boss here. He had been born in Boston and he had been in Palestine for several years. He began this farm on the hill in 1936. One day he sent five men out beyond the community homes to start plowing. They were attacked by Arabs and all five were killed. The farm is now named in their memory. We sat in the community dining hall, drinking tea. I was slightly disconcerted as I raised my cup to see the head of a camel intruding through an open window.

"Don't look now," I said to Joseph, "but you have a guest."

He smiled when he saw the camel. A moment later an Arab walked in carrying a small boy on his shoulder. The youngster had a dirty rag wound round his hand. The red-sashed and sheeted Arab talked rapidly to Joseph and Joseph smiled reassuringly.

"Take them to the doctor," he called to one of the men at another table. "The kid has a cut that has become infected. Have the doctor fix it up."

A half hour later we left the hut. The Arab made his camel kneel and he and the boy now smiling proudly at a clean bandage mounted the evil-smelling beast. The Arab waved a smiling "good-bye" and a dozen friendly voices followed him as he went down the hill.

"Maybe that's the solution to the whole thing," I said to Joseph. "Look how grateful and friendly he is. If you could see more of them and have them get to know you and understand you there'd never be any trouble."

Joseph smiled a bit sadly. "Sure, sure. He is grateful. He's a fine man. I know him well. I know too, that he comes from the same village as did those Arabs who killed five of my people in 1936. We are good friends today. Tomorrow—who knows? If their leaders inflame them against us anything can happen."

By far the most impressive building in Jerusalem is the Y.M.C.A., just across the street from the King David Hotel. Some of our Arab friends had introduced us to the Christian Arab who ran the Y.M.C.A. He gave us the run of the place—no mean privilege with the temperature hovering around the hundred mark. To begin with there was a soda fountain there. None of us had had sodas for months. We had chocolate sodas, then strawberry sodas, then vanilla sodas—creamy wonderful sodas, the kind you dream about after you've been away from home for a few months. We went to the pool for a cool swim, and then we lay along the side of the pool, practically purring with pleasure. The white marble was cool on our bodies. Idly we watched some thirty or forty youngsters splashing happily in the water.

"Are these kids Arabs or Jews?" Lynch asked the attendant.

"About half and half," he said. "We don't make any distinction here. We have Jews and Christian Arabs and Moslems; as long as they behave themselves they can come."

"Do they ever have any fights?" I asked.

He looked puzzled. "No, why should they?"

"That's right," I repeated. "Why should they?"

Those kids, perhaps, had a wisdom denied their fathers. Jew, Christian, Moslem all played contentedly, racing each other up and down the pool, splashing each other noisily. We could feel the hopelessness of the situation. Clearly here was a conflict of two rights, an unhappy situation that might never be peacefully settled. That there will be armed conflict between the Jews and the Arabs when the war is over is a possibility too strong to be ignored. Both are proud, uncompromising people. Each thinks he is there by right and each denies the other's assumption. So few have studied the problem without prejudice. To complicate matters neither the Jews nor the Arabs are united among themselves in Palestine. The religious, orthodox Jews who mourn at the Wailing Wall feel nothing but horror at the farmers who, for the most part, have given up the practices of their fathers. The farmers look upon the orthodox Jews as relics of a past age.

There are many obstacles to any kind of union. One of them is the formidable figure of Ibn Saud, King of Saudi Arabia, head of the Wahabi or purely Moslem Arab sect. He likes to sit at the head of the table. He is on record as saying that the Jews should be ejected from Palestine immediately. There are more moderate Arab leaders like Nahas Pasha, who inclines toward the view that the Jews are in Palestine to stay and that the Arabs may as well make the best of it. The conflicting views held by Arab leaders have killed their dream of a Pan-Arab Federation, a union that might free them from the Western powers: the British in Palestine, Egypt, Iraq and the Arabian peninsula; the French in the Levant and North Africa. If the 60,000,000 Arabs can't agree among themselves, it is difficult to see how they can ever agree with any plan brought forth by the Jews. But as Gilbert Chesterton once said: "The nicest thing about miracles is—they sometimes happen."

The Christian Arabs look down upon the Moslems of the desert, and the latter think of the Christians as renegades. About a year ago, Judah L. Magnes wrote an article, "Toward Peace in Palestine," for *Foreign Affairs*. This made more sense than anything I ever read on the question. Magnes advocated a series of compromises based on a bi-national Palestine, with a union of Palestine, Transjordan, Syria and Lebanon all to be made part of an Anglo-American union.

If such compromises (and compromise is essential when two rights conflict) were effected, those kids we saw playing together in the Y.M.C.A. pool might not be killing each other five years from now.

The radio told us that Sicily had been invaded. I was in a hurry to reach there. We dropped our car and flew back to Cairo. Eddie Rickenbacker had just arrived. Rick had seen more in Russia in a few weeks than I had in as many months. They really let Rick go places and his account of the Red Air Force was especially fascinating. Rick came out of Russia completely sold on the ability of the Red Army to stand up against anything the Germans sent at it. This was the first time Rick and I had ever agreed. Rick and I are very old friends who disagree fundamentally on practically everything. I have always thought his attitude toward labor was childish and based on nothing but prejudice. He quite candidly thought I was completely lopsided in my attitude toward labor. But Rick and I have always enjoyed arguing and will, I hope, continue to enjoy arguing for many years to come. Rick is a great companion even if he is always (to me) on the wrong side of any argument. And even I will admit that Rick is a great American.

Rickenbacker was headed for home and it took a lot of will power to keep from going along with him. But he was going via Tunis and Algiers.

"You've got a passenger as far as Tunis, Rick," I told him.

"Of course," he agreed amiably. Edgar Snow of the *Saturday Evening Post* was hitch-hiking home with Rick. The night before we left Cairo I had a party for Rick at Shepheard's which I am sure jolted *Collier's* considerably when the expense account arrived. Frank Gervasi turned on his charm and made the hotel manager bring out wines that had been hidden; he even, by some miracle, persuaded the manager to get steaks for us. We really threw a party, and genial Rick signed a hundred autographs and answered a thousand questions. We ended the party with a toast to his (and my) old friend, Steve Hannagan.

"Just because I'm giving you this party doesn't mean I agree with you on anything," I warned Rick.

"That goes for me, double," Rick grinned.

Rick had been through a really tough couple of months. After Russia he had gone to China and India, and even for a veteran pilot that trip was a wearing one. But Rick had some indestructible store of energy hidden away in his lank body, and he was all set for the hot, ten-hour hop to Tunis.

"As your guest, I insist on having the cot for at least half the trip," I told Rick, when we climbed into the big Liberator. It had comfortable seats and one cot.

And so we took off in the glory of a cool dawn and headed for Tunis and Sicily. My Middle East vacation was over.

Cairo, July, 1943

Chapter X

WHILE ROME BURNED

No ONE AROUND American headquarters in North Africa fiddled while Rome burned for the second time. No one was excited, elated or triumphant. No one wanted to hurt Rome, yet it had to be done. General Carl Spaatz sat in his office in a white building on the shore of the Mediterranean. Now and then he looked at his watch. Members of his staff came and went, but no one said much more than "Five hundred planes over Rome now." Someone, consulting the schedule, would say: "B-17s hitting San Lorenzo now." A while later, another would speak: "B-26s over Ciampino now."

The raid was an anticlimax around headquarters. For weeks, the bombing of Rome had been considered, and then agreed upon. Then came two feverish weeks of planning and briefing. Only experienced crews were chosen. This would have to be the most accurate bombing ever accomplished, or Axis propaganda for once might have a legitimate weapon.

For two weeks the pilots and crews studied the air maps

of Rome made by Colonel Elliott Roosevelt and his photo-reconnaissance units. Even before they were told what their specific targets would be, they were made to memorize the positions of the Vatican, St. Peter's and other places of great religious or historical significance. These were to be avoided, regardless of the cost. They learned the positions of workers' districts and were warned not once but a dozen times not to damage civilian areas. They were told to bring their bombs back if they were unable to find the targets assigned. If visibility prevented pinprick bombing they were not to drop a single bomb haphazardly. This was not to be a raid on Rome but on the military objectives which unfortunately were located in Rome.

For two weeks General Spaatz and his staff studied pictures of the city. The aerial photography of Colonel Roosevelt's group is, I believe, the best in the world. When you looked at those photos through a sort of lighted stereopticon that enlarged them, Rome held no secrets from you. These pictures told General Spaatz and Air Chief Marshal Sir Arthur Tedder, with whom Spaatz worked, a significant story. The campaign in Sicily had begun. Those pictures told General Spaatz that our men in Sicily were in danger.

First, there were two "marshaling yards" in Rome. We civilians would call them freight yards, with sidings. Freight cars, loaded with military equipment, were constantly dispatched from these yards to bases where this equipment— guns, ammunition, bombs—could be used to kill the Americans, British and Canadians on Sicily. These yards were as much military objectives as would be Fort Knox or the War Department building in Washington, if the positions were reversed.

Other targets which had to be destroyed were the two airdromes at a point on the outskirts of Rome known as Ciampino. Fighter-bombers based there were harrying our men in Sicily and bombing ships headed for Sicily from North Africa. And so Rome had to be bombed.

Perfect flying weather on the day of the bombing meant that our boys could fly high over Rome and still locate their targets. And so off they went, every plane American-made, every pilot, bombardier, navigator and wireless operator American-trained. Most of these boys had been brought up in the belief that Rome was a holy city. But they had seen the photographs and knew they did not lie. They forgot that this was Rome, home of the representatives on earth of the Prince of Peace. If there was any sacrilege it had been committed by Mussolini and the German High Command when they made an arsenal of a city never intended to be dedicated to war.

Rome was bombed on Monday, July 19th. On the morning of Sunday, July 18th, most of the men who were to go on the raid attended church services. They knew where they were to go the next day, and so did the priests who conducted the services. Many of these Army chaplains had been educated in Rome. They venerated the old city and yet, during Mass, without exception they offered special prayers for the safe return of the boys and prayers for the success of their mission. On the morning of the raid the chaplains had given, in case the lads needed it, a friendly pat on the shoulder or perhaps spiritual consolation in the form of confession. When a raid is finished the boys laugh and tell you it was a cinch, but it's different during that long hour before take-off. They know they may not all come back, and even though you have never been to church in your life, it's nice to have a priest or a minister around during that last hour. I know, because I was there.

The Pope? He would understand why the raid was necessary. It is hard to escape the conclusion that Pope Pius XII was anything but a prisoner. For months his voice had not been raised in protest against Nazi atrocities and yet, before he was silenced, he was never backward about castigating the forces which had destroyed Catholic Poland and Belgium. On January 28, 1940, the Pope made a fearless and vitriolic attack on the Germans. He issued the text of a memorandum received from August Cardinal Hlond, Primate to Poland, in which it charged the Germans with the murder of dozens of priests. Between the time war broke out and January, 1931, His Holiness delivered more than thirty speeches, radio talks, sermons and pastoral letters, all of which indicated that his attitude was consistent with what one would expect from the head of the Church. There is no doubt that His Holiness still believed in the principles expressed in his magnificent First Encyclical, when he said: "To consider the state as something ultimate to which everything else should be subordinated and directed cannot fail to harm the true and lasting prosperity of nations." The man who said that so forcefully and who later, in a speech, blamed the outbreak of the war on "the cult of force" would not remain silent had he the chance to speak. I have often heard Catholics criticize the Pope for not using his office to alleviate the sufferings of the victims of Nazi power.

"Is he," they have asked bitterly, "just another Italian diplomat?"

Two men whose judgment I regard above all others on matters pertaining to Italy are Reynolds Packard of the United Press and Herbert Matthews of the *New York Times*. Both are convinced that the Pope has been silenced by German orders, and that when the true story comes out it will be shown that the Pope had no opportunity to protest or to influence either Mussolini or Hitler. Incidentally, neither Packard nor Matthews is a Catholic.

All of us at advanced air headquarters chuckled over the last words shouted to the crew of a B-26 as it taxied away for the take-off to Rome. They were shouted by one of the Catholic chaplains. He knew these boys well; had lived with them, eaten with them, played cards with them and, when they suffered as they do suffer before take-off, he suffered with them. A pilot stuck his head out of the cockpit to wave a friendly good-bye to the padre. "Give them hell over there!" the priest shouted fervently. His words reached the crew even over the noise of the motors. These chaplains of ours do not allow their calling to interfere with their honest Americanism and hatred of our enemies.

Then the bombers were off and now North Africa seemed silenced with expectancy. There was no breeze and the Mediterranean, incredible in its changing blues and greens, quietly lapped the white sands of the shore. Waiting for men to return from a bombing mission, especially from such a one as this, is a terrific strain. General Spaatz and his staff, waiting in their white house by the sea, envied Jimmy Doolittle, who was leading the raid. The pilots always felt good when the "Old Man" personally led the raid. They worship Doolittle, not only because he is a great pilot, but because he is a great human being.

I went to the airdrome where the B-26s were based, to await the boys' return. It was tensely quiet there, and now that the sun was high it was unbearably hot. The heat arose from the sand in shimmering waves and then a breeze ruffled the sand. It was a sirocco which only intensified the blistering heat and filled your lungs with sand. The commanding officer and his staff sat in a tent. They dripped with sweat and nervousness. Occasionally they drank water from the little bag which hung by the side of the tent, but even the rubber lining of the bag was no proof against the sun, and the water, sickening with its taste of chlorine, was warm and brackish.

It seemed an eternity, waiting there, and then suddenly

[189]

where there hadn't been even a cloud in the sky there was a squadron of P-38s. They dived and climbed and rolled their wings in ecstasy. They were in no known formation. Their work was done, and we sensed from watching their antics that it had been well done. Behind them in formation came the B-26s. They circled twice and then, one by one, swooped down to land at that terrific landing speed of theirs. Glenn Martin gave our Air Force a lovely airplane in that B-26 —a plane that has proved itself one of the greatest of medium bombers.

The first crew to land hopped out of the plane, got into a waiting jeep and dashed over to our hot tent. The Colonel, gray-haired veteran of the Philippine fighting, threw off his Mae West and smiled contentedly. He had been flight commander of this group. His pilot, slim young Captain Jack Simms, a veteran of the raid on Tokyo, smiled too as he made his report. Their target had been one of the airports of Ciampino; they had dropped their bombs smack on the target, they said. When they finished their job they had a chance to look around.

"The Vatican? Yes. We saw it and we saw St. Peter's and St. John Lateran," the Colonel laughed. "Not a bomb fell within four miles of the Vatican. We saw the marshaling yards that the Fortresses hit. They were on fire, but there wasn't a sign of smoke outside the yards. The heavies didn't waste an egg."

Jack Simms smiled agreement. So did big Captain Jack Perrin, the bombardier. The weeks of planning and briefing had been well worth while. They had hit what they had been told to hit and nothing else. I hurried to another airport. The heavies were coming in here now—Liberators and Fortresses. The crew tumbled out of the big aircraft, laughing happily. The anticipated heavy opposition hadn't materialized. The flak had been bad, but they had seen only seven enemy fighters over Rome and these had refused to give battle. I talked to a dozen of the boys. Second Lieutenant Anthony Mastropalo of Pennsylvania was grinning broadly. He was a bombardier on one of the Fortresses that had slapped the Lorenzo yards silly. Incidentally, he was born in Sicily and is a devout Catholic.

"Feel bad about bombing Rome?" I asked him.

He said, in surprise, "Of course not, I consider Rome as much a military target as any other place we've been kicking around. But look at our target map."

The target maps carried by all crew members were enlarged aerial views of Rome. The targets were marked clearly and circles drawn around Vatican City, St. Peter's, St. John Lateran and the San Paolo Basilica. In large capital letters was printed, "MUST ON NO ACCOUNT BE DAMAGED."

Visions of a night in May 10, 1942 came to mind: I saw a dozen churches in flames in London that night, but perhaps the Luftwaffe doesn't have the same type of target maps our lads carry.

Back at General Spaatz's headquarters the pictures were coming in. First there were the pictures taken by the bombers as they dropped their eggs. There were dozens of pictures taken of each target, and in no case could you see a burst (the rose-petal cluster young pilot Vittorio Mussolini once said looked so beautiful) outside the target area. Then Colonel Roosevelt walked in with his pictures, taken by high-flying photo-reconnaissance planes two hours after the bombing. The smoke had cleared and the damage done could be ascertained and weighed by Spaatz and his staff. These pictures were amazingly clear even without the aid of the magnifying stereopticon glass. Roosevelt had done a great job here from the beginning, but this was his masterpiece.

Late that night the reports were all in. We had lost five aircraft out of the more than 500 that had participated in the raid. The bombers had completely destroyed the targets assigned to them. For some time, no more material of war would flow through the Littorio yards from industrial Italy to Naples and the southwest coast. No war materials would be sent to the San Lorenzo yards to be loaded on freight cars and transported to the south. It would be many weeks before the two airdromes at Ciampino would be serviceable again, and the Italian Macchi 202s and the Junkers 88s destroyed on those airdromes by our bombers would never again be used to shoot down American pilots in American planes, nor would they ever again do any ground strafing of American troops. Nine correspondents accompanied our bombers on the raid and their opinion was unanimous that it had been an unqualified success.

But there is a significant story behind the raid that is not so well known. When General Spaatz arrived in London a little over a year ago he held a press conference. The unassuming, slightly built Spaatz talked quietly, but nevertheless he threw the press conference into a furor. At that time we had very few pilots or aircraft in Britain beyond those sent under Lend-Lease. But American planes and pilots were on their way and we asked Spaatz what their job would be. "Daylight bombing," he snapped. "Pinprick bombing. That's what their job will be."

We gasped at that. During the autumn of 1941 we had seen the Luftwaffe send as many as 500 aircraft over Britain in daylight. We remembered the havoc wrought by the Spitfires and the Hurricanes. We remembered that unforgettable September 15th when 186 Nazi planes were destroyed in daylight. Never again did the Luftwaffe attempt daylight bombing on anything but a very small scale.

We called the General's attention to these significant facts.

"Our Fortresses and our Liberators can take care of themselves," he said. "A time will come when we will bomb by day, and the RAF, with its heavy Wellingtons, Stirlings and Lancasters, can bomb the same targets by night."

This was a completely revolutionary theory to us. We hurried to the Air Ministry to get the opinion of the RAF chiefs. They shook their heads dubiously. "It will be suicide," they told us. "You can't send heavy bombers over enemy territory in daylight unless you give them the kind of fighter protection we just can't afford to give. Even then the losses would be out of proportion to the results obtained." We knew that Spaatz and Air Chief Marshal Harris, head of the RAF Bomber Command, did not see eye to eye on the subject. Harris was a great believer in night bombing.

But back home General Arnold felt as Spaatz did. So did pilots like Jimmy Doolittle and the others who ran our heavies. They said they hated to drop bombs on targets they couldn't see. They had plenty of guns on their Liberators and Fortresses, and they knew how to take care of themselves.

Finally, Spaatz began his daylight operations. He bombed France almost daily and his casualties were few. Of course, in those days the Fortresses were given a very heavy cover of Spitfires. Spaatz insisted that the day would come when his bombers could dispense with fighter protection. You could only have fighter protection on short-range raids anyhow, and the big heavies were designed for long-range bombing. The Rome raid proved finally and conclusively that Spaatz was right all along. It is true that about 200 fighters went along with the B-25s and B-26s. Medium bombers do need protection, but the Liberators and the Fortresses went off proudly alone and they returned as proudly alone. Their casualties were too slight to consider. They were sighted by enemy fighters, all right, but in every case the enemy fighters veered off.

This was the first time in the history of air warfare that

a very large force of big bombers ever went over enemy territory unescorted in daylight. Our air force heads had proved their point. The significance of this cannot be over-estimated. The result of the raid may change a great many preconceived ideas about daylight bombing. It may mean the beginning of an era in which fighter planes will not be considered a threat to bombers flying in large force. It may mean that even now engineers and designers are bending over drawing boards planning bigger and better armored Fort-resses and Liberators—planes which ultimately will be im-mune to everything except flak but which may have a high enough ceiling to take them out of range of flak.

The raid also proved, as no other raid has done, the im-mense value of our bombsight and the value of those long months spent in training our bombardiers and pilots in its use. This was the perfectly planned, perfectly executed raid. It's one they'll be studying in the classrooms of military academies fifty years from now. However, that day in North Africa, the significance of the raid was more localized. We knew that because of the damage done by our bombers men would sleep in Sicily; men who otherwise might have spent the night hiding from the dive bombers which were destroyed at Ciampino—dive bombers using ammunition which twelve hours ago lay in freight cars on the siding at San Lorenzo. Because of that we rejoiced.

Tunis, July, 1943

****

Chapter XI

MEDITERRANEAN CRUISE

THINGS BECAME dull around Tunis after the Rome raid. Our Press Relations Officers were a fine group and every afternoon Major Max Boyd, Captain Phil Porter and I would take a swim in the Mediterranean. There was a good beach at La Marsa and an Officers' Club conveniently near by. This was a combined RAF-American mess and the food was excellent. The boys had a cook who was a genius at disguising the American C rations. And there was always ice-cold lemonade, made, of course, from powdered lemons, but the cook knew how to get the most out of it. Preparing for a swim was a simple matter. We walked to the edge of the sea, dropped our uniforms on the sand and waded in. The Mediterranean is so salty that you can almost walk on it. We would lie there, watching the P-38s on constant patrol overhead, and we'd think this wasn't such a bad war after all. Then, when the sun had dried us, we'd dress and walk back to the Officers' Club to drink a beautiful concoction called, very appropriately, a Blockbuster. It had everything in it but Sloan's Liniment. But it was ice cold and, in lieu of a civilized drink, we found it palatable. There was whisky, but we were rationed to fourteen drinks a month. I managed to get over that hurdle by buying the bartender a few of his own Blockbusters. After he'd drunk three, I'd go outside, put on a tie and my army hat, walk in, tell him my name was Joe Doakes and that I'd just arrived and could I please have a whisky ration card. The bartender, by now living in a delightful dream world of his own, would hand me one of the precious books. When I left I had accumulated five books which I left with my pals who were less adroit in the matter of deception.

The Officers' Club was one of the most delightful spots in this otherwise miserable, arid section of North Africa. The RAF men and our air force officers got along like blood brothers, and the only argument I ever heard between them occurred when the bills for drinks came. Everyone wanted to buy. I was there for a week and was never allowed to buy even a meal. I was a transient, a guest, and they refused to allow me to join the club officially, so I could never pay for my own meals.

Carthage, down the road from La Marsa, like most historic monuments, was a disappointing place. It looked like what it was, a pleasant summer resort with some lovely villas, all built by the Italians. It was hard to believe that this was once a nation mighty enough to battle Rome and attempt a conquest of Spain. It was not the Carthage that Aristotle wrote of, whose power seemed so alarming that Cato the Elder always ended his speeches in the Roman Senate with the ominous warning, *"Delenda est Carthago."* There were still a few old ruins in the city, but only the fifty-mile aqueduct, stretching from the base of Mt. Huthna to the city, gave any hint of the grandeur that once dwelt there. There were also some modern ruins caused by our bombers. Carthage and La Marsa housed our air force headquarters. Here Air Marshal Tedder and General Carl Spaatz worked in beautiful harmony—a relationship based on mutual respect and liking. Jimmy Doolittle and Elliott Roosevelt were in and out of air force headquarters, a beautiful villa right on the sea.

One day I was sitting at press headquarters trying to badger Colonel Joe Phillips, in charge of Press Relations, into getting me on a plane to Sicily, when the phone rang. It was for me.

"This is Tedder speaking," a voice said. "Will you have lunch with me today?"

"I'm sorry, I'm lunching with General Eisenhower," I said airily, wondering which of my colleagues was putting on this act for me.

"Oh, really? I thought that Ike was in Algiers," the voice said. "That is odd, I was only talking to him an hour ago."

Then I felt a cold chill of apprehension and realized that this indeed was Air Marshal Tedder. I sputtered out apologies and he laughed them away. It was an understandable mistake. Air marshals don't, as a rule, phone correspondents and ask them to lunch. I had known Tedder fairly well in Cairo, when he was stationed there in 1941, but I had only known him as correspondents know sources of information. Anyhow, I went to his headquarters. His villa was about a mile from headquarters.

"You don't mind riding in a jeep, do you?" he asked, laughing.

"I love jeeps," I told him.

"Oh, you haven't been told about my driving, I see," he said. "It's become a legend around here. But you were at Dieppe, weren't you? You shouldn't mind my driving too much."

We got into the jeep and he perched himself behind the wheel. He had no driver, no aide, no insignia on his car, no flags—and yet Tedder was just about the most important man in this part of the world. We whirled out of the driveway, swerved sharply to the left, avoided a ten-ton half truck by two feet, and then shot down the road at eighty miles an hour. I saw what he meant. I hung on desperately as we bounced over the uneven road and then we turned sharply into a driveway. The driveway led almost vertically upward to his villa.

"Dieppe was nothing, sir," I said, wiping the perspiration off my forehead.

"I've had this jeep souped up a bit," he said cheerfully. "A wonderful discovery, the jeep."

"I think Ernie Pyle, the jeep and the American Red Cross girl are the only three really great discoveries of the war," I told him.

He agreed. Like everyone else in North Africa, Tedder had a great admiration for little Ernie Pyle. Ernie's column appeared every day in the Algiers edition of *The Stars and Stripes* and the GIs had made Ernie their voice. He lived with them and, better than anyone else, expressed their feelings and their reactions. I suppose hundreds of GIs have asked me, "Do you know Ernie Pyle?" I not only admire Ernie Pyle, but I love the little guy. So does everyone who ever met him.

Tedder lived in one of the most beautiful villas in North Africa. Perched high on a hill, it commanded the Mediterranean. It was nice to sit down in a lovely drawing room and drink real martinis. The meal was standard. Even air marshals dine on ordinary army rations. Tedder talked brilliantly about past successes and about the current Sicily show. He talked of his admiration for Tooey Spaatz, and it gave you a warm feeling to hear a British air marshal (a rank equivalent to that of lieutenant general) pour out unstinted praise for our own pilots. There was nothing half-hearted about the way he spoke of our Fortress and Liberator crews.

When I got back to press headquarters, Herbert Matthews of the *New York Times*, Al Newman of *Newsweek* and Farnsworth Fowle of CBS were there. They, too, were anxious to get to Sicily. Our best bet, we were told, was to get to Bizerte. Planes were leaving every day from Bizerte and we could probably hitch-hike to Sicily. They gave us a command car (a grown-up jeep) with a trailer attached, and the next morning we set off for a five-hour trip in a holiday mood. Our baggage, which included three bottles of Algerian wine and our cigarette rations, were safely tucked into the trailer. We drove on and noticed that we were getting a lot of attention from passing jeeps, trucks and command cars. We couldn't figure it out until we drew up to a sentry post to show our identification cards.

"We could see you coming a mile off," the M.P. said. "In case you don't know it, your trailer is on fire."

So it was. Our driver grabbed for his fire extinguisher. We hurriedly threw our half-burned musette bags out of the trailer. Matthews lost everything, including his typewriter. He grabbed his brief case. The leather was smoldering. In the brief case was the manuscript of a book he had been working on for three years. It was the only copy he had. Fortunately, most of it was untouched. I lost every piece of clothing I had, but saved my typewriter. Newman lost everything, including his typewriter. The fire continued to blaze until Newman thought of the three bottles of wine. We uncorked them and, when we dumped the wine on the fire, it died instantly. We shuddered at that. What manner of wine was this that was so good a fire extinguisher?

We went on to Bizerte, our holiday mood completely gone. Bizerte looked lopsided. Our boys had really hurt this place. Most of the damage had come from shelling. There weren't many houses intact. Headquarters were what had once been the French barracks. They looked very Foreign Legion. The officers in charge were sympathetic about the loss of our clothing and immediately opened their storehouse and outfitted us completely. They replaced everything but our typewriters. They put us up in a large room and apologized because there were no beds. We didn't mind the lack of beds once we had bed rolls, but we did mind the lack of windows. The rooms were filled with flies, and North African flies are the most persistent insects on earth. You can't brush them off; you have to pick them off.

There seemed little chance of getting to Sicily by plane immediately, but there was another way. I met an old friend, a naval officer, Lieutenant Henry (Bud) North, brother of John Ringling North, and, with John, co-owner of the Ringling Brothers Circus. North told us that there was a squadron of P.T. boats in the harbor and that it was leaving for Sicily the next night. If we wanted to go along he'd fix it. The P.T. boats might run into trouble and, if they did, we'd all get ourselves a nice story. We sat around talking of old times and then North said that he had a bottle of anisette. He'd contribute it and we'd have a party. Matthews and Farnsworth went to sleep, but Newman, Bud and I stayed up with the bottle of anisette, a drink which combines the worst features of vodka and absinthe.

Not wanting to wake Herbert and Farnsworth, we took a canteen of water, a tin cup and the bottle and parked ourselves in a command car outside.

"Notice how this stuff scares the flies away?" North said optimistically.

"That's all you can say for it," I grumbled.

We sat there for hours, talking of home; talking of the circus; talking of the wonderful days of the past when Heywood Broun and I used to visit the winter circus quarters at

Sarasota, Florida. We talked of everything except the war. Bud told us stories of the circus and Newman and I listened, entranced.

The next afternoon we took our new gear down to the P.T. base. We had dinner with the group of young naval officers who manned the motor-torpedo boats. Lieutenant Richard O'Brien commanded the squadron. We might be able to get away a bit later, O'Brien said. He was waiting for a weather report. Meanwhile, how about a little poker? The cards were brought out. We used small iron washers for chips. It was a nice game and these youngsters needed no lessons from anyone. We played for an hour or so and then a sailor came in and handed O'Brien a note. Instead of reading it, he looked at his cards. I had two small pairs and I had just bet a dime and now it was up to him.

O'Brien said, "I'll raise you a dime," and then I took a look at him and said to myself, "This is not a kid who bluffs." O'Brien had celebrated his twenty-third birthday the week before. He was an Annapolis graduate, with a snub nose and a freckled face, and he looked like anybody's kid brother. I told him he could have it all, and he pulled in the pot. It wasn't a bad pot—about two bucks—and in that part of the world two bucks was not two bucks at all but one hundred francs if you were in North Africa or two hundred lira if you were in Sicily. Then O'Brien looked at the note and he said calmly, "The weather isn't too bad. Let's try it."

The seven young lieutenants who commanded the P.T.'s in O'Brien's squadron looked delighted. They were Fred Rosen of Dalton, Georgia, who once played football for Georgia; Jack "Doc" Oswald, who had a doctor's degree from the University of California; Norm Devol of Oroville, Illinois; Bob Boebel, a golfer from the University of Wisconsin; Paige Tullock, of California; and George Steele, who went to Bowdoin College in Maine, and Lieutenant Larry Sinclair.

They threw in their cards and said, "Let's go!" We piled our gear into jeeps and hurried to the docks where the boats that Higgins of New Orleans built were waiting. I went along with O'Brien and "Doc" Oswald, who was technically skipper of the craft.

The narrow channel of Bizerte was fringed with broken hulks sunk by our bombers. Our P.T. boats picked their way daintily through the debris, and then we were out of the harbor. A cool breeze fanned us, which was good after a few weeks of that stupefying heat in North Africa. We all put on oilskins and with our boat in the lead, our flotilla of little ships put out to sea.

"The weather isn't too good," O'Brien said. "There's a wind out there and some sea, so it may be a rough trip. Still, anything is better than just hanging around Bizerte. The hunting may be good off Sicily and we'll head for Palermo."

The coast began to recede and the calm of the harbor gave way to choppy water. We were hitting knots now and everything seemed fine to me, but O'Brien and "Doc" Oswald stood on the deck looking a little worried. Darkness suddenly enveloped us. Spray broke over the bow and covered us. The boat began to slap-slap because the trough of the waves was wide and our bow couldn't quite make the top of the next wave.

"Watch that one, Okay!" O'Brien would yell to big Otis Kyle Cathey (Torpedoman), a full-blooded Cherokee Indian from Oklahoma, who was handling the wheel. Okay was clever at avoiding the big waves, but the weather had increased. O'Brien and "Doc" Oswald consulted and agreed to try to veer and sort of sneak up on Sicily that way. Then, when the waves got higher, they decided to anchor offshore for an hour or two in the hope that the weather might lighten. We threw over our anchors and headed into the wind. It was so dark that we couldn't see the other ships, but we knew they were there because they answered our blinker signal whenever we wanted to say anything to them. We were rolling a great deal and we had to cling to anything handy to keep from getting banged up and maybe breaking a rib or two because a P.T. doesn't roll gently. "We may not be able to make Palermo tonight," O'Brien said gloomily.

When dawn came to relieve the night, our little ships looked very forlorn against the jagged North African shore. We all felt a great sense of anti-climax crawling back into the harbor of Bizerte. It was as though we had arrived at the picnic ground only to find that someone had forgotten the food. We were all tired and knocked about and didn't like the kidding we got from the other navy lads who were just finishing breakfast. We sat down dejectedly to bacon and eggs and American coffee. A tall kid with cropped hair who looked like a basketball player from the University of North Dakota, came in, all excited, and O'Brien introduced me to him. He was Lieutenant Bob McLeod, and he really was a basketball player from the University of North Dakota. He had just returned with his P.T. boat. The hunting was good off the Italian coast, he told us. In fact, he added modestly, they had hit a nice fat lighter, a hundred-and-fifty-foot German boat carrying troops and oil. "We threw one fish into her and up she went," McLeod said gleefully. "Then they threw the works at us. Six-inch stuff and forties and God knows what else. So we got out of there fast."

"Any damage?" O'Brien asked.

"A little," McLeod said casually. "You ought to get over there, Dick. The hunting is good."

"We're going over tonight—or else," O'Brien growled, looking like a kid who dares you to knock that chip off his shoulder. "What say, 'Doc'?"

"What else?", chunky Dr. Jack Oswald said simply.

"Tell the boys to get some sleep," O'Brien said, and then we left the breakfast table.

There were some cots off the messroom and I tried to sleep, but someone kept playing an old, but good Vic Arden recording of "Kitten on the Keys," and there was a soft-ball game going on outside and every little while a P-38 would shriek low over the base—protecting it, I suppose, from bill collectors. And then people wandered in and out of the room, always saying, "Oh, I'm sorry! I didn't know anyone was trying to sleep." And it was a little like trying to sleep in Mr. Ford's Willow Run Plant. So I gave it up and instead read a six-month-old copy of *Reader's Digest*.

It was the same in the afternoon. And then, after an early meal, we tried it again. We were going out fast, O'Brien said, because he felt another storm coming on and he felt that we could beat it. We saw the sun go down and we saw a lovely North African afternoon turn into an ominous evening. We weren't fooling around this time, but heading directly for Palermo. For an hour things weren't too bad. If you were sailing in the *Queen Mary* you wouldn't even know you were in a storm, but in this P.T. you knew it, all right. O'Brien made us put on life jackets which, of course, is always good for the morale. He and "Doc" took hourly turns at running the boat while Okay, always smiling gently, as though he and the weather shared a secret joke, took hourly turns at the wheel with Quartermaster Whitey Burton and Seaman Bambi Perez. You could only hold that wheel an hour in weather like this or your wrists would break. The big Packard engines pounded rhythmically, as though to remind us that they wouldn't let us down. Pop Smith, Chief Engineer, and his two assistants, Struble and Kreyling, were down in the tiny engine room with the hatch secured over them. Dougherty and Berry, gunners, hung on at their posts. Dick Smith, who had a bad back from a previous rough trip, leaned over the map in the chart room. Each one knew what he was doing at all times and, in case of trouble, each one would know what to do and there would be no confusion.

"Tell the others to close in," "Doc" Oswald called down into the little chart room. The other P.T.'s were strung out behind us, but now heavy clouds were racing across the moon so that we couldn't see any of them. The heavy darkness of the night pressed down on us, and we had to cut our speed or risk breaking our ship in two. Time after time, we had been slapped down so heavily, thrown by one wave into the trough of the next, that everything movable in the boat, including us, was slammed against bulkheads, or, if we were on deck, against guns or ventilators or the ammunition boxes. "Doc" Oswald slumped into the chart room just under the bridge. He kept groping and I handed him a towel.

"That salt water gets in your eyes and blinds you," he said apologetically. "We'll have several hours of this, I'm afraid."

"I hope the boat can stand it," I said.

"Mr. Higgins builds sturdy boats," "Doc" Oswald laughed, and then he added soberly, "I'm afraid we have lost the boys. We can't raise them. You just can't hold a course in this stuff. How do you feel?" he asked unexpectedly.

"Just lovely. Oh, fine!" I told him. My arms were numb from hanging on, and I felt a dozen little-used muscles in my legs protesting that this was a hell of a Mediterranean cruise.

"Most people get sick in weather like this," he added. "Even those of us who are used to it. I don't mind saying that O'Brien and I aren't feeling too well. Now take Dave Morrison. He was executive officer on this boat, and he went out with us sixty times. He was seasick fifty-three times, and him a champion miler three years ago at the University of North Carolina. But game? He'd never quit until D Day on Sicily when we were escorting the invading troop ships, and he was so sick we decided to give him morphine. But he wouldn't take it. He couldn't walk for two days. They transferred him to shore duty and he's mad as hell."

"Why don't we slow down a bit? Wouldn't that ease things?" I gasped, as a slap hurled me against the stand that held the chart. I went on deck for no reason at all, except that it was stuffy in the chart room. I hung onto the rail alongside of O'Brien, and the kid grinned at me and winked, and I knew that it was all true what they said about these P.T. kids. O'Brien had been told to bring his ships to Palermo (at the moment their temporary base for action against E boats and German subs) as soon as possible. And now he and Doc and Okay and the others were deliberately fighting the weather to get through to Sicilian waters. We stood there, hanging on as the ship hurled itself into a wave and then twisted as though hurt. Then it would roll as a fighter rolls with a punch, and finally corkscrew into the next wave, so that the effect you got was that the boat was traveling in three directions at once. O'Brien nudged me and pointed to the side. Lightning streaked across the black horizon; it flashed again and again, but the noise of our engines and the waves breaking over us prevented us from hearing the thunder. There was something magnificent about the way these boys and this little ship were fighting against what appeared to be such high odds. And yet I knew that tomorrow, in the cold light of day, we would look back and say, "Oh, it wasn't so bad after all."

We had more hours of it, with the ship groaning and protesting loudly every time a large wave hit it, and then quivering as though in anger, and always gathering itself together, like the thoroughbred it was, to hurl itself forward again. Each hour O'Brien looked younger and more tired, and so did "Doc." But now they were smiling a little because they knew that the worst of it was over. We were getting close to Sicily and the weather was bound to be better near land. Finally the dawn, for which we had waited so long, put in an appearance. If you could call it a dawn. The night merely changed her blackness for a dull overcast of gray. O'Brien speeded up. The gray lightened slightly and there ahead of us loomed the mountains of Sicily, grim, forbidding, almost merging with the dawn. But they looked good to us. We changed course, and now the wind was with us and we laughed at the whitecaps because they were going our way, whether they liked it or not. O'Brien relaxed into a tired grin and called for more speed. The engines sang joyously and we leaped ahead. We passed a convoy and the boys recognized it as one which had left Bizerte three days ago.

Just as we entered the harbor of Palermo, the sun broke through the grayness of the early morning. Gradually, it began to dispel the ugly, low-hanging clouds and then it gleamed in golden shafts on the white houses. As we approached the docks, we saw an American flag waving in the wind and we remembered that this was American-occupied territory now and that was a good feeling. We tied up to a dock and some naval officers called out, "Where in hell did you come from?" When O'Brien told them, they looked shocked because they knew that P.T. boats have no right to make long trips in the kind of sea we'd been through. They asked if we had had any trouble, and O'Brien looked surprised and said, "No, the weather wasn't bad, was it 'Doc'?" "Doc" yawned and said, "Not at all."

Our other ships hadn't come in yet. Whitey yelled up from the depths of the cabin that he'd have coffee ready in two minutes.

We went down into the tiny, warm room and had steaming bowls of coffee. O'Brien and "Doc" told about missions they'd been on in these waters.

"About a month ago," O'Brien said, "we tried to sneak into this very harbor of Palermo. We got in pretty close and threw a fish into a German supply ship. We hadn't been spotted. Then the biggest darn searchlight you ever saw opened up and caught us in its beam. We couldn't shake it off. They threw the book at us from the shore batteries. We had a dozen near misses, but just did manage to get away. A week later we tried it again, and that same darn searchlight picked us up. We had to beat it—but fast. Every time we approached Palermo that one searchlight caught us, and how we hated that light."

"Yeah," "Doc" laughed. "We were offshore here the day our army marched into Palermo. As soon as the city was ours, we hurried in with just one thought. We wanted to get that German searchlight and smash it into a thousand pieces. So we tied up and ran to the dock where the searchlight was mounted. We looked it over, and what do you think? This German searchlight had a little metal disk screwed on the back of it saying that it had been made in Perth Amboy, New Jersey. So naturally, we couldn't smash it up."

"Sorry about the dull trip over from Africa," O'Brien said apologetically. "I hoped we could scare up some excitement for you, but it turned out to be just a routine trip after all."

"Sure," I said, feeling bruised in fifty places, "just a nice Mediterranean cruise."

Palermo, July, 1943

****

Chapter XII

SICILY WASN'T EASY

THE HILL was like a thousand other hills in Northeastern Sicily. The natives call it San Rosso Hill, but on the military map the colonel had spread before him it was called Hill No. 335. The troops themselves, swearing at it, called it simply Bloody Ridge. It was two miles ahead of us, and two companies of our 45th Division were trying desperately to hold it. They had lost it twice this day and now, as a blazing sun prepared to cool itself in the horizon of the Mediterranean to our left, our boys had regained it.

A mile back of us our 155-mm. guns (the boys call them the Long Toms) were walloping away at a hill just four hundred yards beyond San Rosso. The hill was higher than San Rosso by perhaps a hundred feet. The Germans had a lot of artillery there and were pouring it down on the crest of San Rosso. They were throwing 88s, machine-gun fire and that six-barrelled rocket gun they like so much. We could hear the firing and see the top of the hill crowned with white smoke. San Rosso had to be held at all costs, and tomorrow the hill beyond, where the Germans now were, would have to be taken.

"Over in North Africa," the colonel said bitterly, "they're probably saying we're having no trouble at all in clearing out Sicily. They're probably saying the same thing in Palermo and, for all I know, in New York as well."

"I don't know about New York," I told him, "but you're right about North Africa and Palermo." I'd just come from Palermo.

"I wish those who say that were out there on that ridge with my boys," the colonel said.

The Long Toms back of us roared, and even though you knew these were friendly shells, you couldn't help but wince at the devilish whine they made as they cleaved the protesting air over your head. Your mind knows those shells won't explode until they have traveled another two and a half miles, but your body instinctively tries to duck. That's how it was with me, anyway. But I may have been getting gunshy.

"We're going to try to close in on that farther hill tonight," the colonel said. "We've got to take that ridge before we can take San Stefano, before we can go on to Messina. And we'll have to fight every inch of the way. No, Sicily isn't quite as easy as some people think."

The boys had just brought in some prisoners. They were a tired lot, many of them wounded. All of them were Germans. This sector was too important to be defended by Italians, although, if you're up against a black-shirted Fascisti regiment, you've got a tough proposition on your hands, too.

These prisoners—some thirty of them—were questioned. Fifteen had belonged to Rommel's crack Afrika Korps. Ten others belonged to the Twenty-ninth Motorized Division, and they told us proudly that they had formerly belonged to the Seventy-first German Regiment, the regiment which was so valuable that the German High Command withdrew it from the Stalingrad front just before the Russians encircled the city. I had heard of that regiment in Moscow.

Well, that's what our boys were up against here. One surly Nazi soldier allowed his wound to be treated and then he volunteered the information that this was his fourth wound. He'd got it once in France and twice in Russia.

And our boys? Well, this 45th Division had originally been an Oklahoma National Guard outfit. When war came, men from New Mexico, Arizona, Colorado, the New England states and New York were attached to it. For the most part, they were tall, sun-tanned lads who a year ago were strumming guitars and punching cattle in the Southwest; they were working in filling stations in Albuquerque or in Worcester, Massachusetts; they were clerks in Wall Street or studying at New York University—hell, they were doing everything that normal, healthy Americans do. They weren't being trained for professional murder.

Yet today they were fighting against men who for years had been trained to be professional murderers. And these kids of ours were beating them at their own game. But they were being hurt doing it. The rows of fresh graves in the olive grove close to the shore of the Mediterranean showed that.

There was an advance battalion medical station and the wounded were brought here. It was well camouflaged by olive trees, and the trucks and operating tent were covered with green netting. Doctors were operating there calmly, unhurriedly, ignoring the roar of our own guns to the rear and the German guns ahead. These boys of ours received as careful surgical and medical attention there in that Sicilian olive grove as you'd get in your expensive city hospital.

The boys lay there after their wounds were dressed, smoking, usually, and not saying much, because they were still a bit dazed from the pounding they had taken at Bloody Ridge, and the noise of the guns still rang in their ears.

I asked one of them how he had got it.

"This morning," he drawled in his Colorado accent, "we took that damn ridge, and then they counter-attacked like they always do and kicked us out. We went back at them and they raised a white flag. Of course, we thought they were surrendering. We should have known better after Tunis, where they used their own dead as booby traps, so that when we went to bury them, we would get blown to pieces.

"Anyway, we went up the hill and we were halfway up when they pulled down the white flag and let us have it. They killed sixteen of us. Nice guys, these Nazis! The British are right about them. They say the only good German is a dead German. There's no rules in this war. Well, if they want to fight it like that, it's okay with us."

It was hard to sleep that night. Not because the ground was hard and we had no cots. Not because the flies and mosquitoes were bad. Not because two German planes circled above all night hoping to draw our flak so they could locate our anti-aircraft batteries, which were waiting for bigger game than two reconnaissance planes. Nor did the roar of the Long Toms or the sudden flashes which lighted the heavens when they fired bother you much.

It was hard to sleep because you kept thinking of those kids on San Rosso Hill just two miles ahead; you knew they were still taking it. It was hard to sleep because, looking at your watch and remembering the difference in time, you realized that people were just sitting down to dinner in New York.

You could almost hear the tablecloth strategists gathering in the bistros and saying complacently, "Now, my idea is that we'll clear out Sicily in another few days. It's just a matter of mopping up. Yes, sir, the whole operation was much easier than I anticipated. Sicily was a pushover. Now, when we finish with Sicily, my idea is . . . "

You don't really sleep at the front; you drop off into a sort of numbed stupor. But let's leave my small sector of the front for the moment. Let's take a look at the whole Sicilian operation and see just how much of a pushover it was.

It was undoubtedly one of the most daringly conceived and brilliantly executed military operations of all time, with Americans, British and Canadians working together. It was a textbook operation, with the Tactical Forces (Alexander in command) carrying out everything just as the Strategic Forces (Eisenhower in command) had planned. The success of the landing on D Day, which was July 10th, and the rapid advance through Sicily during the following days far exceeded the hopes of our military chiefs. But it was not all as easy as it looked.

Occasionally an Eyetie outfit laid down a red carpet and said, "We've been waiting for you." But this was not universally true.

Let's look at the whole operation from the beginning, consider some of the difficulties which had to be surmounted, and then perhaps the tablecloth strategists 6,000 miles away won't be so glib with their cracks about how easy it all was.

Our Intelligence told Eisenhower that there were about 335,000 German and Italian troops on Sicily. There was the 15th Panzer Division, called the Sicily Division by the Germans. This had been formed to replace the original 15th destroyed in Tunisia. There was the famous Hermann Goering Division, composed of air force, ground troops, infantry and tanks. Part of this outfit was the remnant of the original Goering Division, which, for the most part, was captured in Tunisia. There was the crack 29th Motorized Division, made up of Afrika Korps and veterans of Russian fighting and there was the Italian Ariete Division. Eisenhower decided to land about 95,000 men on D Day and then gradually increase his force as needed.

The First Division was given one of the toughest jobs in the Sicilian landing. But the Fighting First had proven itself in one war and was now most emphatically proving itself in another. It was a colorful division. Kids from the sidewalks of New York—wiry Jewish youngsters, swarthy Italian-Americans, big, laughing-eyed Irish boys—formed the nucleus of the First.

General Terry Allen was as colorful as his division and so, of course, was Brigadier General Teddy Roosevelt. Once during the campaign I lost a bet on Roosevelt. I bet one of the First Division aides that Teddy would be killed within two weeks. I gave ten to one odds—bet him ten dollars to a dollar. He took the bet not because he thought he would win it but because he said he'd take any ten-to-one bet. During dive-bombing attacks the men (under order) huddled in small slit trenches (foxhole is strictly a Pacific term; I've never heard it used in the European theatre of war). General Roosevelt would stalk about, his helmet under his arm, barking encouragement to the men. They honestly thought he bore a charmed life. Anyhow, I lost my ten dollars and was never happier about losing a bet in my life. When I told Teddy about it later in Palermo he bought me a ten-dollar meal and gave me a lecture on the evils of reckless gambling. Teddy only gambled with his life. I think Ted Roosevelt is perhaps the only man I've ever met who was born to combat.

Terry Allen was a smiling, good-looking, charming man; small, wiry, tough, he gave the impression of immense strength. His division had gone through some bad times in the Tunisian campaign and had absorbed one or two bad beatings. One of its toughest jobs was to take Hill 609 (hills are named for their height in meters), some fifteen miles from Bizerte. The fine 34th Division was given the equally

nasty job of taking Hill 523. The Germans were firmly en-
trenched on the top and slope of Hill 609. Their 88s were
well dug in, and the casualties of the First were heavy. Terry
Allen likes to fight at night. He will talk analytically about
the advantage of night attack and will discourse on the
elements of surprise, etc., that can be utilized at night but,
when you press him, hard-boiled Terry Allen will admit
that he can take an objective at night with fewer casualties.
Terry worried as much about the health of the men under
him as their parents at home. If I had a dozen sons I'd be
glad to know that they were serving under Terry Allen. I'd
know that their lives would never be wasted unnecessarily.
I can give no higher praise to a general than that.

Terry Allen had brilliant Major Ken Downs as his aide,
and he was full of praise for the former INS correspondent.
Ken spoke French perfectly and was often used as liaison
between the First and the French Army. Downs, Major
Robert Low (formerly of *Liberty Magazine*) and I sweated
out the first two and a half years of the war together in
France, London and Libya. Today they are both combat
officers and excellent ones.

The First took Hill 609, and Bizerte and Tunis fell shortly
thereafter. The division was then loaded into cattle cars and
headed for Oran to rest. They didn't get much rest because
the Sicilian campaign was due and General Patton asked that
the First be included in the Seventh Army. They trained on
the beaches between Oran and Algiers, learning the tricks of
amphibious landing. Finally they were ready, and they held
their dress rehearsal against the British 46th Division. Typical
of the thorough training our men get is the fact that beaches
were found which approximated the Sicilian beaches and live
ammunition was used by the "defending" 46th. The dress
rehearsal was beautifully done and the British general in
charge told Allen that his force had been able to hold out

only two theoretical hours. The First had a brief respite in Algiers then, and M.P.s still shudder when they think of that week when the First took over Algiers. They'd had months of intensive combat; weeks of grueling training and they wanted to play. They played all right, and Algiers will probably never be the same. Then they went off to Sicily.

Dick Tregaskis, Ernie Pyle, H. R. Knickerbocker, Clark Lee and several other correspondents with the First during most of the difficult twenty-eight-days' campaign, which culminated in the capture of Troina, were all filled with praise of Terry Allen's leadership. They noticed that each evening, after studying the maps and deciding on the attack for that night, Allen would walk off by himself into the darkness for a few moments. Then he would return and give crisp, decisive orders. They wondered what Terry did on those solitary walks. One night one of them found out. He had found Terry Allen alone—praying.

Just before the attack on Troina, nasty because Troina was on high ground, Allen was very obviously worried. He knew the attack had to be made. He was concerned about the casualties, and he took every precaution against unnecessary loss of life. His worry was so obvious that the men noticed it. Just before one company was to advance, an old regular army sergeant blurted out, "Hell, Terry, stop worrying. We'll take the Goddam town for you."

I asked Allen about that afterwards and he said that the story was true.

"Did you discipline him, Terry?" I asked curiously.

"Discipline him?" Terry exploded. "Good Lord, no! I felt like decorating him."

Allen was not the stickler for formal discipline that his boss, General Patton, was, but in combat the First didn't need to be goaded by any disciplinary methods—they had terrific pride in their division and in their general. They felt a bit unhappy after a month in Sicily. They'd had enough, they felt, and they were homesick. They did a lot of "grousing" about conditions. They were feeling sorry for themselves, but Allen let them "grouse" (a word borrowed from the British and now in common use in our army).

"An army that doesn't grouse can't fight," Allen said once, and there is no doubt that he was right.

The First had one sustaining interest in life beyond fighting—the fate of the Brooklyn Dodgers. *The Stars and Stripes* reported all baseball scores daily. They were sure the Dodgers would win the 1943 National League race, and it wasn't long before they were saying, "We got to get home for the World Series." In August the Dodgers were trailing and were finally out of the race. One of Allen's aides sighed with relief. "Thank God, the Dodgers are out of it," he said. "Now our men can stop mooning about how nice it would be to be home for the World Series. Now they'll get on with the war."

The First Division landed at Gela on the southwestern coast. Their performance won even Montgomery's admiration, and Monty is not one to toss bouquets around—even to his own troops. The weather when they landed was what the navy boys call "force five," which meant that a thirty-mile wind was ablowin'.

However, Terry landed his men on time. Gela is a historic old city. It was here that the poet Aeschylus met his death. According to tradition, the old gentleman was wandering about the fields, minding his own business, when an eagle, mistaking his bald dome for a stone, dropped a tortoise on it and fractured his skull. But no one thought about that legend on D Day. They landed and advanced rapidly against pillbox opposition which they soon smothered.

Then the Hermann Goering Division came at them, hell-bent with tanks. The First had to fall back to the beach where they would have fought it out to the end, and, against tanks, there could have been only one end. The two American cruisers, the *Savannah* and the *Boise*, offshore, got word of what was going on, and opened up with their big guns against the tanks. It was probably the first time in military history that an engagement between tanks and cruisers took place. Anyhow, they paid off on the cruisers.

Then the First went on again. Our Rangers helped, and before the enemy knew what had hit them, the First was in possession of the airdrome at Ponte Olivo. The Second Armored had landed by now, with its medium tanks, and everything was just ducky. But they had a very tough few hours, and please don't ever say to a member of Terry Allen's mob, "That Sicily operation was a cinch, wasn't it?" Or, believe me, you're apt to get hit in the head with the nearest blunt instrument.

The original plan called for General Matt Ridgway's 82d Airborne to work with the First. However, on D Day there was a hell of a wind blowing, and the lads who took to the silk were blown all over the island from Canicatti to Noto on the east coast. Instead of being able to consolidate according to plan, the airborne lads ganged up in groups of six to ten and just improvised as they went along.

The beauty of our army, as I see it, is its infinite capacity to improvise. If the scheduled plan goes awry, the boys can dream something up on the spur of the moment. Mentally, our kids are elastic. That night the airborne boys just went wandering all over the landscape, popping off at anything they saw alive, and this considerably baffled the orthodox Eyetie and German defenses, which didn't think it quite sporting.

They tell a story of one of our airborne men whose name should go down in history. I have done my best to get his name, but although I talked to a dozen men who saw what he did, it was dark early that morning, and no one who witnessed it was able to identify him. He was standing there with his tommy gun when a Tiger tank rumbled down a road that he and his mates were guarding.

This kid thought he might put the enormous tank out of action by some sharpshooting. If he could send a flow of tommy-gun bullets through the slit in front of the tank, he might get the driver. He held his fire until the tank was eighty yards away, then let go. The tank approached steadily, throwing its small stuff. A stream of bullets blew the boy's right arm off and knocked him down.

A dozen witnesses say that he got up, grabbed the tommy gun with his left hand and kept on firing at the tank until it hit him and rolled over him. Oh, sure Sicily was a cinch! Nothing to it!

Let's go back and see what the 45th Division had to contend with. They landed all right, against only nominal opposition—which meant mortars, machine guns and a spot of air bombing. They proceeded to take the airfield at Comiso, which was their first objective. This wasn't exactly knocking off clay pigeons at a Coney Island shooting gallery.

Tanks defended the airdrome, and the 45th had to knock them out with what they had. Well, they had mortars and anti-tank weapons, and somehow they did the trick. The 45th knocked out six tanks of ten which defended Comiso, and then headed for the important city of Vizzini—important because it was on high ground commanding the adjacent territory. The Canadians had taken the city once and then been tossed out by the inevitable counter-attack. The Germans always counter-attack.

The Canadians attacked again from the west while the 45th continued on north, where it was given the difficult job of starting to clear out the northeastern section of the island. During the later stages of the campaign, the Third Division, which had now had some rest, relieved it.

Now let's see what part the Third Division played in this dogfight. After it landed, it had the job of scurrying northwest to take the airport and city of Canicatti. From there, the Third headed west again to take Agrigento. They fell on the old city like a ton of bricks, which didn't bother the old city at all, because people have been falling on it like a ton of bricks these past 3,000 years.

Back in 406 B.C., the Carthaginian General Himilco conquered the city, and 200 years later, the Romans took it and changed its name to Agrigentum, which a waiter at the local hotel told me means City of Many Temples. In 827, the Saracens stormed it and changed its name to Girenti. It remained Girenti until 1928 when Mussolini changed it to Agrigento.

It is still known as the City of Many Temples, but when the Third Division got through with it, the city fathers met and decided to name it the City of Many Headaches. Anyhow, on July 13th, when the Third moved in, the boys really didn't give a damn about the history of the old city.

Now the Third, together with the Second Armored, the 82d Airborne, and a regiment combat team, proceeded to pull off one of the great military feats of all time. They marched from Ribera to Palermo, a distance of seventy-two miles, in two days. If you don't believe it, look at your map. This would have been a commendable achievement in maneuvers without any enemy opposition.

General Geoffrey Keyes headed this walking marathon. The terrain was difficult; sometimes hills as high as 3,000 feet barred their march, but they got there. They moved so fast that often the German and Italian anti-tank 88s, which they captured en route, hadn't been pointed around or set up to shoot against them.

"They'll be studying that one in the textbooks when we're

all dead," General George Patton chuckled when he told me about it.

They had some opposition not furnished by the terrain, which is hilly in some places and marshy in others, but they did something the Italians have never done—they marched by night. The Eyeties fight strict union hours—from nine to five. When the sun goes down, they quit. They thought it not quite sporting for hordes of Americans to barge into their camps just when they'd got to sleep. General Keyes accepted the surrender of Palermo. If the city hadn't surrendered, Keyes would have blasted it right into its lovely harbor. This was done a full week earlier than the General Staff had anticipated.

Very sketchily, that is the story of the American campaign in Sicily. If you think that I am blindly, hopelessly impressed by and devoted to these kids of ours; if you think that I am prejudiced and completely lopsided on the subject of our American troops—why, you're absolutely right. For three years I've been with every army but our own, and it is pretty exciting to see our kids in action and realize that they are as good or better than any other army you've ever seen, and this includes the Russian Army as well as Montgomery's admittedly great Eighth Army. I have traveled with both.

Any American who isn't deliriously proud of our army should have his head examined. I am just trying to say that they took Sicily (I know the British and Canadians had important parts, but we're not considering them for the moment) against great odds. But let one far better qualified than I have the floor. Alex Clifford is the war correspondents' war correspondent. This brilliant young Englishman, who writes for the *London Daily Mail*, has made a thorough, scientific study of warfare. I knew him in France, and from there he went to Libya. He was at Crete and he was with the great victorious drive of the Eighth Army. In our profession, we rate Clifford right up there. He forsook the Eighth Army to follow along with our First Division on the Sicily operation. He was with the First throughout its campaign (and still is).

"You know, I got the surprise of my life, Quent," he said to me. "I have been with the veteran Eighth Army for a long time and naturally I didn't expect much from a comparatively green outfit like the First Division. Yet in action they were absolutely cool, and they acted like veterans. When tough artillery fire came at them, they didn't bunch up as green troops always do. They fanned out beautifully. Oh, they're good fighters, and cruel fighters, too, and, in an odd way, they are the best-disciplined outfit I ever saw. They storm a town and have a tough time with casualties and then they walk in. Instead of getting tough with the local inhabitants or with prisoners, what do they do? They share their chocolate, their cigarettes, when all their instincts must be to slaughter them, as they think of their own casualties. That's what I call great discipline." Well, that's what a very expert British observer thinks of our army. Who am I to disagree with him?

On the island, we occasionally heard American and British radio commentators talk smoothly of "Rapid progress and lack of opposition."

That kind of talk hardly endeared the prophets of the air to the men who had to take Sicily foot by foot, stopping only long enough to bury their dead.

The next time you hear someone say that the taking of Sicily was a cinch, think of that obscure ridge in the northeastern part of this island which the natives call San Rosso and think of a white flag held up treacherously by the Germans.

When Messina was finally captured and the whole island was ours, General Eisenhower held a press conference. He went over the whole campaign with us. He was especially pleased with the magnificent work of General Omar Bradley who commanded the Second Corps. Unassuming, quiet, brainy General Bradley earned the respect of all of us during the Sicilian campaign. He is a great general. Eisenhower praised the Engineering Corps, and we all heartily agreed. Sicily was, to a great degree, an engineers' war; especially in the northeastern part of the island, where there was only one road and that had long stretches clinging to cliffs two hundred feet above the sea.

"I can only say this," Eisenhower told us. "Today, the Seventh Army is worthy to fight alongside the Eighth. I can offer no higher praise. From now on General Alexander has a one-two punch. He can hit equally hard with either army."

The brilliant work done by General Patton was completely obscured by his unfortunate behavior to a shell-shocked man in the Evacuation Hospital at Sant Agatha di Militello near Cape Orlando during the last days of the campaign. That story has been told and there is no use rehashing it here. Patton is an impulsive man whose emotions are always bubbling over. This is his weakness—and his strength. "Patton discipline" was a phrase often heard in Sicily. He laid down a few rules, and they had to be obeyed. Even at the most advanced front, men had to wear ties. At all times they had to wear their helmets and their leggings (a sensible precaution against mosquito and flea bites). I remember driving to the front from Palermo with Al Newman of *Newsweek*. It was very warm and we had tossed our helmets on the floor of the jeep. We were stopped five times between Palermo and Cefalu, a distance of about forty miles, by M.P.s. Each time the shocked M.P.s told us to put on our helmets.

"Things are quiet today around here," I protested. "Why helmets today?"

"General Patton's orders," he said stolidly. "Must wear helmets at all times in combat zones. If the provost catches you without your helmet you're liable to a forty-dollar fine."

In Sicily we also had to wear the hated "woolens" instead of our cool light-weight uniforms. We were under army discipline to a great extent, although I never heard of an incident where the discipline was irksome. As soon as men or officers saw the War Correspondent tab on our shoulders they left us pretty much alone and treated us magnificently. We went from mess to mess and were always treated as fellow officers by the real officers. But when you were with Patton's army you had to put up with his regulations. When Patton visited the front the men would be nervous. He would notice if they hadn't shaved; he would notice a dirty gun or a tie that was askew. But leggings were his fetish.

Actually, there is only one real proof of a general: was he successful? And Patton was definitely a successful general. To us he was pleasant, genial and affable. Demaree Bess and I went to see him once at his Palermo headquarters, and he kept us for an hour chatting informally, answering every question we asked him with frankness. Patton had a touch of the theatrical about him. Sometimes he was like a kid playing soldiers. He liked to be called "Blood and Guts" Patton, but the GIs didn't like it much.

"Yeah," they'd grumble. "His guts and our blood."

Patton favored the armored forces above all. His dashing, flamboyant personality impressed itself on the men of the tank corps, and today all armored corps men have an intense pride in their branch of the service.

Patton likes to have a lot of personal transport available. In Sicily he had kept for his personal use a big Douglas transport plane, a small Piper Cub for short trips, a tank, a command car, a scout car, a jeep and his sedan which flew two large flags—the American flag and the flag of the Seventh Army. When he roared around Palermo he would always be escorted by M.P.'s on motorcycles. Eisenhower would drop into a town and he'd be there an hour before anyone was aware of his presence. Fanfare and display only bored General Eisenhower. They wasted time. But the fanfare was all part of Patton's system. It is true that the Seventh Army was well disciplined; that disease was held down to a minimum; that it was beautifully equipped—and that it won battles. No one can take the credit for that away from Patton. If an army flops, its general immediately gets the ax. If it wins, the general should get the credit.

Merrill (Red) Mueller of NBC and Demaree Bess happened to visit the hospital near Cape Orlando where Patton had struck the shell-shocked boy the day after the incident occurred. They heard the whole story from men in the same ward, from nurses who had been present and from the doctors.

Both in London and in Africa General Eisenhower had emphasized at press conferences that we could be helpful to the army if we wished. He had often said that we were able to get closer to the ordinary GI than officers could. If we heard any complaints from them that seemed well founded he would appreciate it if we would forward those complaints to him. Once, after spending a month with our American troops in Ireland, General Eisenhower called me to his office in London and asked me about conditions there. He wanted to know about the little things that officers might overlook or ignore. I had often heard the men grumbling because they were getting ice cream only once a week. They weren't getting enough cigarettes. Such small items loom large in the life of a GI. General Eisenhower took notes when I told of these complaints and when I saw him a week later he told me that he had taken action and now the ice cream and cigarette ration had been increased. I believe a mark of Eisenhower's greatness is the fact that no small detail is too unimportant for him to consider if that detail involves the comfort, health or morale of a GI.

So it was natural that when Mueller and Bess returned to Algiers a few days after the Patton incident that they bring the story to General Eisenhower's attention. They had written the story in the form of an affidavit and had the signatures of fourteen witnesses to it. Eisenhower was deeply shocked. He told them that he had a similar report which coincided exactly with theirs from the Colonel in charge of the hospital.

Three days later I had dinner with Commander Harry Butcher, Naval Aide to Eisenhower, and he told me that Eisenhower hadn't slept in two nights. He was trying to find the right solution to the problem. Demaree Bess went back to America. Before he went he said that when he reached home he would not mention the incident. It would only give Goebbels food for propaganda, he said. And he had every confidence in the ability of General Eisenhower to handle the situation. A few days later Mueller, Clark Lee and I went to see General Eisenhower. He talked freely about the Patton incident. He told us what he had done, and it seemed to us then (and does now) that he had come to a Solomon-like decision.

He had written to Patton. He ordered Patton to apologize to the shell-shocked man in the presence of the same witnesses who were there when the offense occurred. Eisenhower went further. He ordered Patton to visit his various staff headquarters and to apologize to the officers and to have them communicate this apology to the men. By now a dozen versions of the story were common gossip all over Sicily and in Algiers.

"It's a difficult situation," Eisenhower said to us, and he was obviously worried. "General Patton made a great record in the Tunisian campaign. He did fine work in Sicily. It would be dreadful to have this one incident undo all of that work and nullify his excellent record. On the other hand, there is the boy to be considered and the other men. I have asked General Patton to apologize. The army needs General Patton. If he apologizes in the right spirit and demonstrates, what I believe, that the strain of sustained combat had made him lose control merely for the moment, the incident, as far as I am concerned, is closed."

"This would be a nasty story to get out," I suggested. "Goebbels could do a lot with it. Every mother in America would think that her son was being subjected to this sort of treatment."

"I know. I know," Eisenhower said, wearily passing his hand across his forehead. "But I will not impose any censorship on the story. No security is involved."

We assured General Eisenhower that we believed it was up to the army to handle the story as it saw fit.

"I appreciate that, boys," Eisenhower said, "but I still won't order any censorship ban."

We left, completely satisfied with Eisenhower's decision. He had taught Patton a lesson and had humbled the proud general, and yet he had not lost his services to the Allied cause which a court-martial or an "official" reprimand might have done.

Every correspondent in Algiers (there were about sixty of us there) agreed with us that it would be only playing into the hands of Goebbels to use the story. Neither Eisenhower nor General McClure, in charge of Press Relations, put any pressure, direct or indirect, on any of us. And yet not one word went out on the story. It was broken by Drew Pearson, a radio commentator, on Sunday, November 21st, nearly four months after the incident occurred.

It was the only regrettable incident in the whole Sicilian campaign. In Sicily we saw an army come of age. Our men who had gone into Sicily gaily, in the spirit of adventure, now knew what they were fighting for. The white flag and the booby-trapped dead had taught them that the Germans were as bad as people at home thought the Japs were. This was worth knowing. From now on our men would know how to fight them.

Palermo, August, 1943

✳✳✳✳✳✳✳✳✳✳✳✳✳✳✳✳✳✳✳✳✳✳✳✳✳

Chapter XIII

THE *MIGHTY MAY*

THE TUG GAVE two blasts of her futile little whistle, the heavy towline straightened, and then the *Mighty May* crept away from her dock. It is not usually the fate of an American destroyer to be towed away from her dock by a miserable little tug, but somehow the *Mighty May* was proof against this indignity. There was something magnificently arrogant about the way the ship looked; something in her bearing that seemed to say, "I'll be back soon. If any of you guys make a nasty crack about me, I'll get rid of this tug and slug it out with you right now." That's the message she gave me, standing there on the dock at Palermo.

I was glad to see the *Mighty May* get out of Palermo. We'd been having a lot of air raids lately, and this can was tied up to a dock, with thirty mattresses stuffed into three gaping holes in her hull. She couldn't even fire her five-inch guns during the air raids, for fear the mattresses would be jarred loose and she'd fill with water. She pulled out at dusk for a North African port where her wounds could be properly taken care of. I stood there, watching the last rays of a sultry Mediterranean sun bathe her with soft crimson tints as she pulled away in tow. I saw the skipper on the bridge and I waved to him and to Big Pancho, his executive officer, who stood beside him, and I waved to Little Pancho who was on the port side. I looked up and waved to the Indian, Travis Curtis, who was stroking his beloved 20 mm. guns.

I knew just about everyone on this ship and, in a way, I hated to be left behind. I am not saying that the *Mighty May* (her real name is the *S. S. Mayrand*) is more worthy of mention than any one of perhaps fifty other American destroyers. It just happens that I got to know the can and her crew very well.

Perhaps the story of the *Mayrand* typifies the whole destroyer service, and let that be the excuse for the telling of it.

There is a bronze plaque just outside the wardroom which says: "*U.S.S. Mayrand*, Destroyer, named for Capt. John Mayrand, USN, built in Boston. Authorized—March 27, 1934. Keel laid—April 15, 1937. Launched—May 14, 1938. Commissioned—Sept. 19, 1939." That is the genealogy of the ship which her crew, without exception, calls either the *Old Can* or the *Mighty May*. She was named for a captain who served under John Paul Jones. Instead of discussing her early career, which differed little from that of any other destroyer, suppose we consider how it was that the *Mighty May* and I came to know each other, and then let us consider the five days which almost cost the ship her life and did cost many of her crew theirs.

The front had moved away from Palermo. The real fighting was going on some fifty miles to the northeast in the region of San Stefano. I had returned from the front to file a story and was in no hurry to return. Someone in Palermo told me that there was a story in a destroyer that had just limped into the harbor—a destroyer which had been bombed heavily and which had survived by a miracle. The great Commodore William Sullivan, best of all salvage experts, was trying to save her, but there appeared little chance.

I went down to the dock to visit the stricken ship, partly out of curiosity and partly because there is always good American coffee on a destroyer and American coffee was something that Palermo did not have. The destroyer was listing in toward its dock, and a group of men were working very busily up forward. Winches were screaming and riveting machines were hammering, and authoritative voices were giving orders. I have always found that it is better to ask for the executive officer when you board a navy ship than it is to ask for the captain. I asked a young seaman standing on the dock if the executive officer was around.

"Big Pancho? Yeah, he's forward, directing the work," he said. "That big guy in dungarees."

I walked forward and there, incredibly dirty, was a familiar figure giving crisp orders. This was the executive officer whom they called Big Pancho but whom I had known for some fifteen years under another name. He gave me a double take and then, in the manner of old friends who haven't seen one another for more than a year, we began cursing each other affectionately. It wasn't long before executive officer, Lieutenant Franklin D. Roosevelt, Jr., his skipper, Commander Edward Walker, and I were sitting in the messroom, drinking very hot and very wonderful coffee. After that, of course, I went to the *Mighty May* every morning to drink eight or ten cups of coffee.

When bombers came over Palermo at night I would wake in a cold sweat, hoping that they wouldn't hit the ship, and then at dawn I'd hurry to the harbor to see if she was still there. One morning Big Pancho and Skipper Walker told me the story of D plus sixteen. Everything on the island of

Sicily figured from D Day (July 10th), the day we landed, and so D plus sixteen was July 26th.

"It's Frank's job to keep up the log," Captain Walker said. "Here's the log for that day. I'll read it to you.

"Now, remember we were about ten miles off Palermo. We were patrolling, and I suppose the nearest ship to us was the minesweeper *Strive*, which was some five miles to starboard. The log reads: '09.31—Enemy aircraft sighted port bow. Three planes. General quarters. Changed speed to 25 knots, gave right full rudder. 09.34—bombs falling close aboard ship. 09.35 near miss three to six feet port beam.' That's the language we use in writing the log," Walker explained apologetically.

"Get away from navy language," I pleaded. "What happened then?"

"Well," Walker nodded to his executive officer to take it up, and Frank went on. "That bomb hurt us badly. All of our guns were going, of course, but even above them you were deafened by the sound of that bomb. It was a lucky hit they made because the bomb exploded maybe three feet under the surface of the water. Our hull got the full blast of it."

"We listed badly to port," Walker interrupted. "We had lost all auxiliary steam power. We shifted to the emergency electric power, but the log says that we lost all steerage way at 09:38. We found that the after fire room and engine room were flooding rapidly. We ordered all available pumps to work. By 09:42 our power was all gone and our port deck was only four inches above the water. Then we began to jettison all topside weights. I'll never forget the look on Frank's face when I gave the order to jettison those torpedoes. Remember, Frank?"

"Yes, sir." The executive officer's face clouded. "I hated to see them go. Eight beautiful torpedoes, each weighing a ton, each costing $8,000. When you take torpedoes away from a destroyer, you've practically left her defenseless. Then we jettisoned our depth charges and 900 rounds of ammunition. I've been with this ship two and a half years, and it hurt to toss stuff overboard—stuff you knew would leave the ship helpless."

Other officers had drifted into the wardroom. There was Lieutenant Donald Craggs, who once played football for Whittier College before joining the pro ranks. He was about half an inch shorter than six-foot-three Frank Roosevelt, so they called him Little Pancho. There was Lieutenant Larry Savadkin, with his head swathed in bandages, a memento of that morning. There was the medical officer, Lieutenant Commander Victor Canforti. Each contributed to the story as we drank coffee served by a Filipino mess steward. You could feel the horror of that morning when all were convinced that their ship was doomed. You could almost hear the horrible hissing of the steam from the half-flooded fire room.

"Craggs heard cries from the fire room," Walker said suddenly. "It was full of live steam, but he put on an asbestos suit and went down there. He found machinist's mate Fred Decker down there with both legs broken. He carried him out and then he collapsed on deck. Decker died two days later. Machinist's mate Harold Steeves of Quincy, Mass., went down and brought Roy Peterson up. Pete had become entangled in the machinery. He was burned badly but, hell, he was back on duty in three days."

"How did you get yours, Larry?" I asked Savadkin. He shrugged his shoulders and touched his bandaged head.

"I'll tell you," Medico Canforti said. "When the bomb exploded, Larry was blown twenty feet away. His head was badly cut, but he kept running around closing hatches with the blood streaming down his face and neck. Then I grabbed him and made him quit."

"This crew didn't need any orders that day," Captain Walker said proudly. "Everybody knew what to do. A skipper couldn't help but feel proud. In all, we lost five men: Decker, Strong, Losey, Kelley and Hiatte. Hiatte was a fireman way over the draft age, but he came in all right.

"Meanwhile the mine sweeper *Strive* had come up on the port beam and had her pumps going, trying to get the water out of the stricken ship faster than it was coming in. She also gave the *Mighty May* electric power to run some of her own pumps."

"Funny thing," the executive officer laughed. "I looked over on the deck of the *Strive* and saw an old pal of mine, Buzz Knowlton. He was the executive officer of the sweeper. We'd gone to school together. That seems a long while ago —when we went to school."

Meanwhile, two destroyers had come close. It's like that in the navy. You get into trouble and you think you're alone and then all of a sudden you look up and there you see a couple of pals. A small sub chaser had come alongside too.

"Earlier that morning," Captain Walker laughed, "the chaser had signaled us, asking if we could spare some fresh bread. We gave them six loaves and now two hours later they were returning the favor. The mine sweeper towed us to Palermo and the chaser stuck along and helped to maneuver us to the dock."

"Didn't the planes come back after you?" I asked.

"No," Walker said. "Why, I don't know. Maybe our flak scared them off. We think we got one of them. If they had come back we were a sitting pigeon, all right."

"Anyhow, you made Palermo," I said.

"Just," Executive Officer Roosevelt said grimly. "We had three holes on our port side you could have walked through. We tied up here in twenty-three feet of water."

"Then we got lucky," Walker said. "Only that morning

Commodore Sullivan had arrived in Palermo from North Africa. We were awfully glad to see him. He took one look at the holes in our hull and yelled for mattresses. We've got the hole plugged with mattresses now."

"What's with your hand?" I noticed that Roosevelt was wearing a bandage.*

"I scratched it," he said shortly. "Can you stand another cup of coffee?"

I looked at him reproachfully. "I've only had five cups, Frank. What kind of a host are you? Get it up."

Well, that's how I got the story of the *Mighty May*, just sitting around, listening to the officers and the men talking. Meanwhile they were working frantically trying to get the ship ready to be towed to a port where there was a dry dock. The filling of mattresses was the kind a dentist would give you for temporary relief. Actually, a large section of the hull would have to be taken out and new plates put in. This was a major repair job and Palermo had no facilities for such work.

"I guess the first excitement we ever had came in August, 1941," Captain Walker told me over one of our morning coffee klatches. "Frank had the gunnery control watch then. Late one afternoon he sighted an unidentified convoy on the horizon. We had no knowledge of any convoy being in the vicinity. We were off Newfoundland. Well, Frank got real excited when he saw two cruisers and five destroyers ahead of us, and he immediately trained the guns and the torpedoes on them. However, they identified themselves as friendly, so we didn't fire. Tell the rest of it, Frank."

The executive officer smiled sheepishly. "I was an ensign then. I didn't know any better. When you're new at it you're kind of trigger crazy—you just want to shoot something.

*Four months later, when the New York newspapers announced that Roosevelt had received the Silver Star for conspicuous bravery, they added that he had been wounded in the hand during the bombing of July 26th. Until then I hadn't known it.

Many a whale has been killed in the North Atlantic because some ensign thought he'd sighted a sub. Anyhow, one of these ships had an awning rigged up on her deck, which was strange. We couldn't figure it out at all, but we stuck around and then we got a signal from it which read, 'Ensign Roosevelt report to the Commander in Chief when off duty.' Well, naturally, I was scared stiff. I couldn't figure out what Admiral King wanted to see an ensign for. Anyhow, when I was off duty I put on my only clean uniform and believe me I polished those buttons. Then I went over to the ship.

"An ensign was officer of the deck when I went aboard, and I said, 'I got orders to report to Admiral King.'

"He said, 'It isn't Admiral King who called for you. It's your old man.'

"And sure enough it was. I was the most surprised guy in the world when I saw Pop there. That was the Atlantic Charter meeting."

"Tell about the Prime Minister's cigars," Walker laughed.

"Well, Captain Walker let me ashore one day when Churchill was inspecting some troops in Newfoundland. I straggled along with his party. I knew some of them. Well, there were a dozen Scotland Yard men guarding the Prime Minister and taking care of his baggage, and what do you think happened? They mislaid his box of cigars. You never saw anyone so unhappy as the Prime Minister. Those Scotland Yard men just went pale. They started chasing all over, looking for the missing box of cigars. The whole inspection tour stopped. And then, just when things were reaching a crisis, a Scotland Yard man came racing up on a motorcycle holding up that precious box. The Prime Minister looked at it to be sure it was the same box. He smiled gratefully, and the inspection went on."

The *Mighty May* found herself two days off Capetown when war came to us on December 7th. It just happened that there was a large British troop convoy in the neighborhood and the *Mighty May*, chuckling perhaps at the coincidence, promptly joined it. Since then the can (all destroyers are called cans by our navy) has really been traveling. She spent some time at Scapa Flow and then did a few North Atlantic convoys. She dropped depth charges on or near subs in the Caribbean and then was assigned to convoy duty on the Murmansk or Suicide Run. She made two trips to "north of Spitzbergen" which were, as Captain Walker says, "not without incident."

Then came the invasion of North Africa. Needless to say, the *Mighty May* was in on that show. What else? Within eight hours the *Mighty May* had sunk one Vichy French destroyer and had assisted in the sinking of a cruiser off Casablanca.

"We threw 600 rounds into that ship," Captain Walker chuckled. "And I'm sure the crew was sore at me because I didn't claim it for ourselves alone. This is a great crew I got—cocky as hell, but they got a right to be cocky."

After Casablanca, the *Mighty May* convoyed around the Mediterranean—just looking for trouble. To hear the crew talk, you'd think they sunk a submarine every other day and maybe they did. But you can't actually claim a sub unless you have absolute, direct evidence that it has sunk. Only rarely does a submerged sub that has received its death blow come to the surface to be counted as dead. An oil patch on the surface is only presumptive evidence. In the navy they say that to get credit for sinking a sub you've got to bring back the skipper's pants for proof. So the *Mighty May*, a relatively tiny fighter, roamed over the usually placid waters of the Mediterranean.

Then came the famous Casablanca meeting between the President and the Prime Minister and their military leaders. The *Mighty May* didn't know anything about the meeting, although she was in and out of the harbor all the time. One of the President's party told me this story and Frank says it's probably true, though he never checked up on it. Even Prime Ministers worry about such mundane things as laundry and Churchill interrupted one of the conferences to tell his colleagues that he didn't like the way his shirts were coming back from the Casablanca laundry. An American Admiral said, "Let me have your laundry. We have a destroyer, the *Mayrand*, in the harbor and I'll have them do it for you."

"The *Mayrand*?" the President looked up, surprised. "I know a boy on that ship. I hear he's the exec now. Perhaps I could see him."

And so for the second time Frank received a summons to report to his Commander in Chief. It was quite a family gathering, because Colonel Elliott Roosevelt was there too. He was there on business, as a member of the staff of General Carl Spaatz. Harry Hopkins and Averell Harriman, two old family friends, were there too. It was a pleasant change after more than a year at sea with virtually no leave at all. But it ended soon enough and the *Mighty May* went back to work.

There were long stretches at sea and then the ship would go into Bizerte or Algiers to stock up with ammunition and food. Captain Walker believed that a well-fed ship was a contented ship. The *Mighty May* ate well.

"Commissary Officer Robert Fry is a genius at scrounging food," Roosevelt laughed. "Every time we hit port he goes ashore and somehow manages to get fresh vegetables and meat. He's a wonder. How does he get it? You don't think I'd be foolish enough to ask him, do you?"

Now that brings us to the invasion of Sicily. The *Mighty May* acted as part of the "screen" to protect the invasion ships from subs. The subs didn't give much trouble. The invasion proceeded satisfactorily, but the supply line had to be maintained from the mainland. Day and night, supply ships lumbered out of Casa, Bizerte, Tunis, Algiers—all bound for Sicily—and the *Mighty May*, among others, had to take care of these precious cargoes. In between times she prowled up and down the coast of Sicily looking for trouble and then she found it. That was July 26th when those three Ju-88s slapped her around.

You might have thought that the fates which rule the sea would have given the *Mighty May* and her crew a rest. She lay there, leaning against the dock in Palermo harbor, a mighty tired young lady. She wore her upper structure the way a tipsy lady would wear a hat, but withal there was a strange dignity about her.

Then came that nasty night in Palermo when they came over. They came over about midnight and stayed until dawn. It was clever, accurate bombing they did, too.

They dropped their flares and then went to work on the harbor; so accurate was their bombing that they didn't drop a thing in the city itself. All of their bombs hit either the docks or in the harbor area. The noise was terrific. We were sending up shells and, going up, they sound much like a bomb screaming down, so we kept ducking instinctively. Then came a series of sharp, quick explosions. Our hotel, the Sole, was half a mile from the docks. The all clear sounded about six but the sharp explosions kept on and we knew that an ammunition ship was hit—or perhaps an ammunition train. As soon as it was light I hurried down to the *Mayrand* to see how she had done. By now, of course, I felt as though I were one of the crew. I knew them all. She was there all right, still looking like a tipsy lady who has successfully negotiated a flight of stairs. An ammunition ship had been hit and an ammunition train had been destroyed. Shells and bullets from the long, burning, freight train were still popping all over. The train was on a dock about one hundred yards from the *Mighty May*. All night those shells had been whizzing over her. The sides

[239]

and bridge were pockmarked where shell fragments had landed. There were forty scars on the bridge itself. Big Pancho was busy directing the work of clearing up. He looked tired, but there was nothing tired about his voice as he barked orders. The men were all grimy and some wore bandages, but they were working as though they'd just finished ten hours of sleep.

"G'wan down to the wardroom. The Skipper is there," Roosevelt said. "There's coffee on the fire. I'll see you later."

"Did you get hit last night?"

"No," he said shortly, "but it was a bad time. Some of the boys got it."

There was a hulk sunk months before just off the starboard side. That had received a direct hit during the bombing. Roosevelt pointed mutely to two large bomb craters on the dock, each about twenty yards from the *Mayrand*.

"Couldn't have come much closer," he said casually.

"Well, I'm glad you didn't get it, sucker," I said fervently.

"Oh, I don't know," he said slowly. "Probably be good if one of us got killed. Jimmy or Elliott or John or me. It might stop some of those enemies of Pop's from shooting off their mouths so much. They seem to think all of us have soft jobs or that Pop used influence to help us. Believe me, nobody uses influence in this navy. That's why it's the best damn navy in the world. . . . Well, I got work to do."

Captain Walker was drinking coffee in the wardroom. Lines of fatigue streaked his cheeks and obviously he hadn't changed his clothes or slept.

"It was a bad night," he admitted. "But the old can stood up fine. She can take a lot of beating. Well, she's used to it now. Young Frank did a good job. He's asleep now. I sent him to bed."

"The hell he is. He's on deck now."

Walker shook his head. "He ought to be in bed. Did he tell you about saving that young seaman?"

"No, he didn't."

"He wouldn't," Walker said. "Well, we couldn't use our big guns at all last night. The vibration might have jarred those mattresses loose and we'd have dropped twenty-three feet to the bottom. We had our smaller stuff going all right though, and the boys are sure they got one—a Junkers-88. They saw it crash on that mountain off the port side. Frank was on the bridge when he noticed that this kid, his name is Nuncio Cammaratta, had his pants legs rolled up and Frank bawled him out. You're liable to get flash burns from our own guns if your legs aren't covered. Then Frank bent down to roll one of the kid's trouser legs down and at that moment a bomb hit the dock and a big hunk of shrapnel hit the kid's other leg and tore it right off."

"It didn't hit Frank?"

He shook his head. "Just one of those things. It should have killed them both, but it just tore the kid's leg off. So Frank climbed down off the bridge and went to that ship anchored forward of us. He told the doctor there to come back with him to fix Cammaratta up, but the medico was busy with other wounded men who had been brought to him. He couldn't leave, so Frank borrowed a hypo of morphine and a tourniquet from him and then went back to the bridge. Stuff was dropping all over then and shells from that ammo train were whizzing around. It was no time to be walking along a dock or to be on an open deck. Anyhow, Frank got back."

Just then Roosevelt came in. He poured himself a cup of coffee, drank it at a gulp and then poured another. "Things are all right, Captain," he said, sinking into a chair. "The pumps are doing fine and at least we're holding our own."

"Good," Walker nodded. "I was telling Quent about that kid you helped last night."

"Didn't help him much." Roosevelt shrugged his shoulders.

"Just put a tourniquet on his leg and gave him a hypo. Funny thing about that kid. There he was, lying there with his leg shot off, but when I started to put the needle into his arm he winced and asked, 'This won't hurt much, will it, Lieutenant?'"

"Then Frank put the kid over his shoulder," Walker said, "and carried him down from the bridge and along the dock to the ship where there was a doctor. No, he didn't do much for the kid. Only saved his life."

"He's going to be all right," Roosevelt said wearily. "I just saw the doctor. You mentioned that we ought to get most of the crew off here tonight, sir. Shall I go ashore and find a place for them?"

"You better do that. Get a place with running water and close enough to the docks so they can walk back and forth. Transportation is pretty scarce."

We walked along the waterfront and then saw a nice-looking street and turned into it. Meanwhile, Frank was talking about members of the crew—about John Scanlon, the Quartermaster. "He'll be Mayor of Boston some day—wait and see." About Clarence Davis, ship fitter, who had received a thigh wound the night before. "Never whimpered once."

About Don Craggs (Little Pancho) and about the Indian, Travis Curtis, gunner's mate. "When things were tough last night I asked Curtis how he was doing. He was throwing lead up into the sky from his twenty millimeter. He never looked down—kept looking up. He said, 'They don't bother me none. I'm happy as long as I can feel this gun.'"

"I've been on the can now for two and a half years," Roosevelt said. "Naturally I love it."

We found a house finally. It was big and completely deserted. There was running water and bathrooms. People who had lived in Palermo were trickling back slowly, but most of them still remained in the hills and in villages around. They were taking no chances and you couldn't blame them. The owner of the house was there and Frank did quite a job with his pidgin French and Italian, convincing him that the U. S. Navy was confiscating his house.

"Take this note to the commanding officer of the port," Frank told him. "You'll get paid while our men live here. Sure, you'll get more rent than you're getting now with the place vacant." Then Roosevelt chuckled, "I don't know how the army missed this house. They've got every other decent place in town. But if we're not careful, they'll try to grab it."

He found a large piece of cardboard and on it he wrote: "Barracks for men of the *U.S.S. Mayrand.*" He signed it in large letters Franklin D. Roosevelt, Jr., and underneath wrote "Executive Officer." Then he stuck it on the outside of the door.

"You made that 'Jr.' very small," I said.

He laughed. "Yeah. I guess that's the first time in my life I ever used Pop's name. I hope they miss seeing the Jr. on that sign. That army is awfully good at confiscating the best houses."

That night all of the men except a skeleton crew to man the guns stayed on shore. But the skipper and the executive officer remained aboard. You couldn't pry them off the ship. However, there was no raid that night, nor the next night and then the *Mighty May* was deemed fit to proceed to Malta. She'd have to be towed, of course, but she'd be away from the harbor of Palermo. The German airfields of Sardinia and Foggia were too close for comfort. So I said good-bye to the Skipper and to Big Pancho and to the rest of them and watched the little ship slip away from her dock.

You'll hear from her again, I'm sure. I know the Germans will.

Palermo, August, 1943

****

Chapter XIV

THIS IS SICILY

IT WAS CALLED the Café of the Two Palms and it was in an alley knee-deep in debris, for Palermo had been bombed heavily by our air force, and not even the narrow alleys of the city had escaped. Herbert Matthews had heard a rumor that one might get a steak at this dingy bistro and, to my surprise, he was right. It was not a very good steak, but if you haven't tasted steak for a long time you are not too particular. It may well have been that this particular steak had been pulling a plow in the pasture land outside the city a week before, but in the war zone, when you are lucky enough to get a steak, you do not ask questions about its family tree. Even if I knew that this steak had won the third race at Pimlico in 1928 I wouldn't have minded. I've bet on horses often enough. Why not eat one for a change?

I finished most of the steak, washing it down with a well-watered and evil-tasting Sicilian wine, and then I noticed two gaunt cats looking at me hopefully. One cat was white and orange, the other coal black. The charm of the black cat was marred by the fact that he had lost an eye and part of an ear. But I like cats—even filthy alley cats—and I tossed a piece of my steak to them. I was hardly prepared for what followed.

With angry snarls, both leaped for the piece of meat. For a moment, the room seemed filled with furry masses of white, orange and black cat, and they fought desperately for undisputed possession of the bit of meat. They screamed in pain, and their howls only ceased when the black cat nabbed the steak and scurried out into the alley with it.

"I am sorry"—the swarthy proprietor shrugged eloquent shoulders—"but we have had no food for our cats for many months. We were all right, but our cats and our babies suffered a great deal."

When our troops marched into Sicily, they were greeted by people who looked reasonably well fed. There was always plenty of fruit—watermelon, grapes, pears—and there was some wheat, even though most of it had to be shipped to the mainland for the use of German and Italian troops. But there was no food for cats, and the cats of Palermo, once accustomed to nocturnal meals at the fat garbage pails of the city, grew gaunt and starved.

Now what is true of cats is equally true of babies. Babies, like cats, need milk, and for a long time, there had been no milk in Palermo or any of the other large cities. During a month in Sicily I saw hundreds of babies, and every one bore the mark of malnutrition. Only the very old and the very young suffered in Sicily—but they suffered intensely. Due to the magnificent job that AMG (Allied Military Government) is doing in administering Sicily's economic and financial life, in supervising the rationing of food and in policing the island, this condition is being slowly corrected, but it will be a long time before the very old and the very young are really restored to health.

The AMG—which is half American, half British—took over the nine provinces of the island, all of which were in a hopeless state of chaos. By threatening, cajoling, by showing good faith and trust, it brought relative order to a land which was not only completely cowed by twenty-one years of fascism (which it always hated), but was, in addition, terrified and groggy after two months of intensive bombings.

This is the first time that we, as a nation, have occupied a foreign country since we took over Haiti in 1914. However, to watch our crowd operate, you'd think we'd been in the business for a thousand years. To begin with, most of our AMG men are Italian-speaking. Because so many individual problems not covered by the rule book arise each day, the head men in AMG keep dinning into the minds of their assistants: "Use your common sense." Common sense seems to be a good rule anywhere.

In Palermo, the largest city in Sicily, AMG has an especially tough job. Colonel Charles E. Poletti was in charge of Palermo all summer and a fine job the former New York Lieutenant Governor did. When the heavy bombings came to Palermo, virtually the entire population of 400,000 fled to the hills. As soon as we occupied the city, this enormous mass of people trooped out of their caves and the outlying villages and returned to Palermo, confident that the Americans would feed them.

Unfortunately, ships which come from North Africa and from America to Sicilian ports are loaded with tanks, guns, ammunition, troops and food for the troops here. There is no room for excess food. Grain and wheat were the things most wanted. Sicily is as fertile as Iowa (except for the mountainous portions of the island) and wheat used to be shipped to the mainland at the rate of 600,000 tons a year.

There are two kinds of wheat—the kind used for bread and the wheat used for spaghetti and macaroni. Sicily has always specialized in the latter type. In exchange for this 600,000 tons per year, Rome paid Sicily partly in lire (at what was virtually a confiscatory rate) and partly in the kind of wheat used in making bread. This type of wheat was sadly lacking when we marched into such cities as Syracuse, Ragusa, Vittoria, Caltagirone and, of course, Palermo. People cried out piteously for bread.

Our AMG leaders suspected that wheat was hidden in the country, in mills and granaries and farmhouses. They issued a proclamation ordering the wheat hoarders to disgorge. When this didn't work, they sent men out searching. They found plenty of wheat which the canny Sicilian farmers had hidden and were holding until the shortage would result in higher prices. Our AMG leaders, who have the status, the power and, incidentally, the guns of our army behind them, wasted no time in grabbing the wheat, paying a fair price for it and distributing it where it would do the most good.

In Palermo each morning, long lines of citizens form in front of the office building which serves as AMG headquarters. Each citizen has a different problem. A twenty-year-old youngster from Brooklyn, Corporal Caesar Catti, was borrowed from the army by AMG. He acted as the initial buffer. He heard the stories they had to tell and then he would send them on to the man in charge of that particular problem. I sat with him one morning, listening to the complaints and admiring the common sense used in handling them.

One quite attractive Sicilian girl with dark, flashing eyes sat down to tell her story. She told Corporal Catti that she was very pregnant indeed. The corporal showed interest but no embarrassment. The man who had been her lover was now one of our prisoners of war. He was a Sicilian who had been drafted by the Italian army. Her hostage to fortune was due to make its appearance within three months, and she thought it would be very nice if the United States Army would release her dream prince, so he could legalize their union. He was, she added, quite willing to marry her; they just never got around to it, what with the bombings and the war and everything. If he were released and they were married, they could live on her father's farm, and her husband could help with the harvest.

Corporal Catti wrote a note explaining her story and sent her along to the boss man.

"Get the guy out of the clink and get them married!" ordered the boss.

The corporal said, "The boss don't want to punish anyone. He's a very fair man and he uses a lot of common sense."

The next customer was a dark-looking gent in khaki without insignia, who explained that he was a war correspondent. He was good-looking in an unwholesome sort of way. He explained that he had an automobile but wanted a license to run it. In Sicily, people could only use automobiles on official or necessary business. The corporal looked at me. There were many things about this theatre of war I didn't know, but I did know every war correspondent in Europe.

I questioned the man, and he answered glibly that he was an Egyptian war correspondent. I rolled my head with that punch because being an Egyptian war correspondent is like being a Swiss sailor. There just isn't such a thing. Then the gentleman in khaki made a bad mistake. He lowered his voice to a confidential tone and told the corporal there'd be fifteen dollars in it for him if he could arrange the necessary permit.

Being from Brooklyn myself, I know how Brooklyn characters react. I was immensely surprised, therefore, when Corporal Catti did not put the slug on the jerk, as we would say around Ebbets Field. Instead, he merely asked him his name and address and said that he would hear from him later.

"We are not allowed to slug anybody," the corporal said apologetically to me. "Instead, we report him. So I will report that phony bum, and he will get into plenty of trouble. I would like to have had my pal Terry here. Terry," he added wistfully, "was a prize fighter in civilian life and he can hit very good, too."

One day a buxom Sicilian woman, with fire in her eye, came charging into AMG headquarters. Her place of business had been bombed by our air force some weeks earlier and she wanted restitution made. Her place of business, she insisted, housed an essential industry—she ran a brothel. She insisted that AMG repair her building so that she could reopen. She was told politely (the patience of Poletti and his assistants was inexhaustible) that labor gangs were trying to repair as many bombed houses as possible and that her establishment would be reached in due course.

To say that the Sicilians were head over heels in love with America and our American troops is to put it mildly. One day Demaree Bess and I borrowed a jeep and a driver and went touring. In three days we covered some 600 miles and we saw and learned a great deal more about Sicily than we had learned either in Palermo or at the front. We also had a lot of fun because Demaree was a great traveling companion, and our driver, a pleasant GI who, like ourselves, was a tourist at heart. Never once did we see an unfriendly act or even an unfriendly glance on the part of the local citizenry. This was true even in heavily bombed cities like Trapani. Trapani, on the northwest coast, had once been a fairly wealthy town because of its extensive salt beds; but after two days of bombing by Tooey Spaatz and his air force, Trapani went out of circulation. Yet, when the people returned

[249]

to their ruined homes, they showed no resentment. They showed nothing but hatred of Germany, Italy and fascism.

I met an old friend from London in Trapani. He was Chief Inspector Bartlett of Scotland Yard, now in charge of policing Trapani. We went with him and the head of the local *carabinieri* to look over the police force. As we met a policeman, he would salute in our style. One unfortunate *carabinere* forgot and absent-mindedly snapped to attention with his right hand upraised in the fascist salute. The huge, mustached chief of the *carabinieri* let out a howl of rage and tossed as pretty a left hook as I ever did see right to the point of the unhappy copper's jaw.

"We've had enough of that nonsense," the chief of the *carabinieri* roared, while my friend and I just stared. "There'll be no more of that on this island—ever!"

Bartlett was a good cop. One of the first citizens of Trapani to return to the city after we occupied it was a lass whose business it was to provide relaxation for tired business men. She was a free lance, and she returned to her old office and hung a sign outside. She had picked up some English words useful in her trade. The sign read: "Short Time—Five Lira." A lira was established at two cents by AMG, so this young lady was really running a cut-rate shop. McDonald summarily closed her place.

"Any girl who only charges ten cents for a job," he said quite seriously, "can't have any pride in her work or herself. If she isn't diseased now she would be soon. So out she goes." And out she went.

The genuineness of the Sicilians' hatred is too apparent to be an act. They have always been the goats. They had to accept the responsibility of being citizens of Rome without receiving any of the benefits. Each of the nine provinces was ruled over by a Rome appointee who received a very small salary. But he was allowed to feather his own nest—and he did. He had the power of appointment, and any office could be bought from him. He fixed the prices of everything from watermelons to brothels, and he took a cut on everything.

Mussolini thought so little of Sicily that he never even visited it until 1938, when he arrived and made a lovely speech, promising Sicily everything. When he returned to Rome, he did nothing but decrease the prices which Rome paid for Sicilian wheat.

There is an island off Trapani called Favignano. While I was in Trapani, my friend the Inspector went to visit the island. I was in the AMG office when he reported on his return.

"There are 6,000 people on that island," he said, "and about a third of them have typhus. They have nothing to eat except the fruit that grows on the island and the fish they catch. The Eyeties used the island as a naval base, and we bombed it pretty heavily. We ruined the mills that ground their grain. These must be repaired and petrol sent over to run their machinery. They need doctors and medical supplies."

Within eight hours, a gang was on its way to repair the machinery; doctors and drugs were en route; grain and wheat taken from inland farms were being hurried to the stricken people. Those six thousand people can hardly be blamed for loving America. Nor were these Sicilians backward about showing their appreciation. Our hospital at Palermo was woefully understaffed, so an appeal was issued for voluntary workers. The next morning, a crowd gathered in front of the hospital, asking to help. Today the orderlies, mess attendants and laborers at the hospital are all Italian volunteers.

Driving through Sicily these days is an amazing experience. There are towns here of 2,000 population which will boast ten or twelve *saloni*, or barbershops. The Sicilians were quick to learn the English word, and today, all over the island, you see English signs, hastily penciled on cardboard, over their barbershop doors.

You drive through remote towns like Carina, perched high on a mountain peak two miles inland from the northwest coast, and you'll find that the American spirit has even infiltrated here. You have to drive slowly in your jeep through the narrow, winding streets, and a hundred children run after you, yelling joyously "Good-bye"—the only English they know.

Whenever a jeep stops, kids swarm all over it, asking the driver for "*una caramella*," which means the kids want candy. The soldiers oblige if they have any. The kids too have learned the "V" sign and they never miss a chance to display it. Our troops have no defense against the warm, eager welcome these youngsters give them, and in towns which have opened up to the extent of having ice-cream stores, you'll always find a dozen kids chaperoned by a few soldiers who are buying them *gelati*. This genuine, honest friendship of the children is merely a reflection of how their elders feel.

The old fascist signs were still up all over, and our civil and military leaders were smart enough not to take them down. Let the people take them down or paint over them, if they wished. Insofar as is consistent with public health and security, no discipline beyond an eight-o'clock curfew was imposed on the people of the island.

The most surprising aspect of it all is the lack of resentment felt by the people of even the most badly bombed cities. Demaree and I visited Marsala. Only in Russia have I ever seen such destruction. Marsala was a peaceful city on the west coast which did nothing but make Marsala wine. Unfortunately, the Germans used it as a base for their E-boats and, after Tunis fell, Rommel used it as his headquarters.

Marsala is proud of one date—May 11, 1860—when the great Garibaldi landed on the shore at Marsala to liberate

Sicily. They do say Marsala was really born that day. But it died on May 11, 1943, when Spaatz and Tedder sent their Liberators and Forts over the town. Within two hours, Marsala was a shambles; Rommel's aide was killed and Rommel himself was wounded. All the shipping in the harbor was destroyed, and more than a thousand Germans were killed.

Marsala can never be rebuilt. Today it is a ghost city and, walking through it (you can't drive for the debris), you unconsciously lower your voice. The people fled from Marsala and have not returned. We talked to the venerable mayor—*podesta* in Italian. His name is Antonio Spano Grignano. He talked of his city with sadness, yet without resentment.

"The Americans were right in bombing our city," he said. "It was filled with Germans, and they were using it as a naval base. But that was a pitiful day, May eleventh. The people were frantic, of course, and they cried up to the American planes, 'He isn't here—he is in Rome. Go and bomb him in Rome.' They thought the Americans were after Mussolini."

Perhaps the attitude of the Sicilians toward the Germans can best be summed up by what the maitre d'hotel of the Excelsior in Palermo had to say. This was the only good hotel functioning in Palermo. I asked white-haired Alfredo Ferrari how his waiters and himself liked the Germans.

"No good," he said, rolling eloquent eyes ceilingward. "We did not like them. You know what they tip? They tip one lira, two liras, never more."

Our army boys had a lot of strange experiences here and a lot of laughs. I think the strangest experience of all fell to the lot of Captain Charles Rosenbaum of the 82d Airborne Division. When he and his mates were dropped from their plane, they found themselves in a peaceful part of the island. Rosenbaum found an Eyetie colonel sleeping blissfully underneath an olive tree. He woke him gently and told him that he was a prisoner. He demanded the colonel's gun. The colonel handed over his Baretti. The Baretti is a beautiful weapon, much prized by our troops. Rosenbaum, a lover of fine weapons, was horrified that the colonel's gun was filthy.

"You don't deserve a lovely gun like that," the young American raged. "Look into that barrel. It's dirty."

"My orderly was killed last week," the colonel said. "That's why the gun was dirty. I had no one to clean it."

As Rosenbaum marched his prisoner off, he kept telling the colonel how ashamed he should be to have a dirty gun. Two days later, a message came to Rosenbaum. The Italian colonel, after thinking it over, had come to the conclusion that he had been insulted by the American officer, and he demanded satisfaction on the field of honor.

I asked Rosenbaum if he would accept the challenge.

"But the guy is in the hoosegow," Captain Rosenbaum said plaintively. "How can you fight a duel with a man who is in jail?"

Press headquarters in Palermo was at the Sole Hotel. It was not exactly a luxury hotel, although we did have a bathtub on each floor. There was a bar which sold only lemonade and Marsala wine. Because the army officers' mess was a mile and a half away and because you had to depend on hitch-hiking to get there, we usually had breakfast at the Sole. Our breakfast consisted of three or four glasses of lemonade. The big, juicy Sicilian lemons were marvelously sweet.

When we entered Palermo we found the city a sad shambles. Our daylight bombers had completely wrecked the harbor and there wasn't a dock intact. But the night bombing had been, like all night bombing, a haphazard affair. It was cruel surgery the British and Americans did to the lovely city of Palermo, but it was necessary. It was terror bombing and it did drive the civilians out, did make them realize that

[254]

we were the masters, and did demoralize that part of the German Army which had been stationed in Palermo. In one day our bombers killed 9,000 people in Palermo. The estimate given by local civilians who were in the city that day was that about 4,000 of the dead were German soldiers and officers. The intensive bombing of Sicilian centers like Palermo hastened the fall of the island by months and, regrettable as it was, the fact remains that thousands of American lives were saved by this blitz of Tedder's and Spaatz's. The bombing showed the Sicilians that the much vaunted Luftwaffe was impotent when confronted by the combined strength of the American and British air forces. So they hopped off the fence and hurried to our side. All of their instincts were to come on our side to begin with, but the Sicilian never had the courage to do it while his country was under the domination of Germany. It is difficult to have much respect for either the Sicilians or the Italians (Sicilians themselves make the distinction). They never helped us when we needed help. They waited until we had done the hard, grueling work of invasion. Then they liked us all right—we were their deliverers. But they never fought with whatever poor weapons they had, the way the Dutch and the Czechs and the Poles and the Norwegians and the Belgians are fighting right now.

Although our bombers had hit every one of the thirty-nine churches in Palermo (not by design) they hadn't hit several book shops. They were open when we entered the city. We were surprised to find so many English books there—Tauchnitz editions of American and British novels. The Red Cross swooped down on the book stores, buying everything in sight to send to hospitals in Sicily and back on the mainland. The Red Cross, magnificent as always, never misses a bet. However, Al Newman made two great discoveries which he shared with me. He found a very small book store and an ice-cream shop. We told only a few trusted friends about both. As soon as it was known that an ice-cream store had opened the GIs descended like locusts upon it. We each bought about thirty books and holed up in the Sole Hotel for a few days with them. It was as pleasant a way as any to combat dysentery. No one escaped it. Ernie Pyle, who only weighs about 100 pounds with a family Bible in his lap, took a bad beating from dysentery. He lost another twenty pounds, and we were all afraid that a stiff breeze would blow him right out into the Mediterranean. Demaree Bess lost thirty pounds from what the troops merely called the "GIs." Red-headed Knickerbocker, just to be difficult, caught dysentery and malaria at the same time. That was considered par for the Sicilian course. The army had a marvelous thirteen-day cure for malaria, but there wasn't much they could do about dysentery except give you pills. And there was absolutely no way to prevent dysentery.

One of the books I had picked up was *The Letters of D. H. Lawrence*. Lawrence had lived for some years at Taomania and his letters touching on Sicily came alive there in the hotel room in Sicily. One night we were bombed. It was a bad bombing, although they concentrated on the harbor. There was a lot of ack-ack close to the Sole Hotel, and some of our shells were going up near by. Al Newman and I went down into the lobby. It was crowded with officers, GIs and civilians. It was the first time many of the uniformed men had ever been in a bombing. When a shell went off they'd drop to the floor and then rise and say, "Boy, that one hit close." Women stood in the small lobby, clutching babies. After two hours of it everyone was tired of the suspense. No bombs had hit near our hotel, but we could hear big ones landing in the harbor only half a mile away.

One elderly Sicilian woman stood there praying. I recognized her as a woman who worked in the laundry. Her husband had been killed, she had told me a few days before, when our bombers came. Now she repeated over and over, "Gianni, unne si? Gianni, unne si?" I remembered what D. H. Lawrence had written in one of his letters. "The Sicilians always cry for help from their dead." She was crying, "Giovanni, where are you?"

At daybreak, Newman and I went to the top floor. Through a window facing the sea, we could see three huge pyres of smoke ascending from the harbor. The ack-ack was still barking furiously. Then came the scream of a bomb, and it sounded as though it were coming through the window. We dropped to the floor and huddled there. But there was no explosion.

"My God, we're getting jittery," Newman said.

It ended at about 6:30 in the morning. Newman thought that Demaree Bess might have some army rations in his room. If so, we could get some coffee or cocoa. We banged on Demaree's door and in a moment the sleepy-eyed Bess poked his head out. He had been asleep all during the raid. Newman and I felt very ashamed of ourselves.

Well, that was Sicily—an interesting prelude to the real invasion of Italy. General Terry Allen and General Theodore Roosevelt were going back to Algiers. Demaree and I hitchhiked a ride on their plane. The Sicilian show was over. What would be next?

Trapani, August, 1943

****

Chapter XV

ALGIERS HOLIDAY

To PUT IT inelegantly but quite accurately, there was a lull in the joint. Messina had fallen and the Sicilian campaign was over. Now the staff was making plans for the next big show. We felt that it would be Italy, but we weren't interested enough to speculate. Speculating and Monday-morning quarterbacking is a pastime peculiarly suited to people at home. We didn't do much of either. It might be Sardinia or Corsica or Crete; we didn't care as long as we went along. Meanwhile, there wasn't a story in North Africa worth the writing; certainly not worth the six-cent-a-word cable tolls we had to pay a benevolent cable company to transmit our stories Newyorkwards (as we say in cablese).

The benevolent cable company in question was the Mackay Radio and Telegraph Company which, for some strange reason, was given a monopoly by the Federal Communications Commission to operate from Algiers on the understanding that it "would give satisfactory service." The service was distinctly not satisfactory to us and often during the Sicilian campaign the already overburdened United States Army Signal Corps had to handle newspaper stories for the correspondents. Last Christmas, as an example, 10,000 messages from service men to their families were either hopelessly delayed or failed entirely to be transmitted due to lack of communications. Our complaints fell on the sympathetic ears of our army chiefs but they could do nothing. In vain we screamed that Press Wireless, Inc., an international communication carrier for American newspapers, magazines and news services organized as a co-operative outfit in 1929, be allowed to operate in Algiers. Press Wireless had leaped into the breach during the collapse of France and had handled not only our news stories but had handled embassy messages as well. All of us knew how excellent the Press Wireless service was and we knew too that the organization was willing to set up shop in Algiers. We had used it constantly in London and even during the worst days it never broke down. But the FCC had granted a monopoly, and we were stuck with Mackay and Mackay alone. Their rates for sending a message "urgent" (giving it priority over messages at ordinary press rates) were so exorbitant that we got together and agreed collectively not to use the "urgent" service at all. We never did, and we saved our various organizations thousands of dollars. Beyond this, we had few complaints about press arrangements in Algiers. We had a large room in the Maison d'Agricole, where communiques were read at stated periods. General Robert McClure, an old friend of ours from London, was in charge, and we all felt that he handled the difficult job as well as could be expected. We had regular press conferences with General Eisenhower and Admiral Sir Andrew Cunningham. Eisenhower was the soul of frankness at his conferences. He trusted us completely and no one ever violated that trust. The rest of us would have murdered anyone who did.

In the beginning, General Eisenhower had given us the choice of two alternatives: he would answer questions "on the record" or he would talk freely to us with the understanding that everything was "off the record." We chose the latter. That is why we didn't bother with speculation among ourselves. Eisenhower never gave us a bad steer, never indulged in the custom of sending up trial balloons. But everything he said was completely dead once we left his conference room.

There wasn't much work to do in Algiers, so we indulged in a North African holiday. Having a vacation in Algiers was like spending a vacation in the New York subway during the rush hour. Algiers was bulging at the seams with American, British and French officers and correspondents. Transportation was at a premium, for there were virtually no civilian cars or taxicabs. We hitch-hiked around town in jeeps or command cars, but mostly we walked. Most of us were at the Aletti Hotel which commanded the waterfront. When I arrived there were no rooms available, so I slept on the floor in the room shared by Reynolds Packard and hard-working Don Coe of the United Press. That wasn't a pleasant prospect for a long spell, so the next day I scouted around. Al Shacht, who combines the restaurant business with the business of being a very funny comedian, had a room all to himself. He was in Algiers to entertain the troops. His room had two beds, so I moved in even before Al had a chance to invite me. I told him all big shots in Algiers had aides; I would be his aide. This was fine, but Al left two days later. I had the room to myself for one night, but early the next morning I was awakened by small noises. A very apologetic and worried-looking man was unpacking his bag. His name was William Parisian, and he was a British Vice-

Consul. This room had been assigned to him, he explained, but he didn't mind if I stayed there until I could get a room. He was a very nice chap, that Vice-Consul.

That afternoon John Steinbeck, writing for the *New York Herald Tribune*, H. R. Knickerbocker of the *Chicago Sun*, Clark Lee of INS, and Jack Belden of *Time* and *Life* arrived from Sicily. There were no rooms for them in the Aletti. Obviously they couldn't sleep in the hall, so I invited them to spend the night with me. The Vice-Consul was surprised when he returned that night to find his room populated with correspondents and their gear. Musette bags, tin hats, sleeping bags, bed rolls, typewriters, emergency rations and various trophies of the hunt picked up on Sicilian battlefields completely filled every corner of the room.

"This is John Steinbeck, America's greatest writer," I introduced him to the Vice-Consul, "and this is H. R. Knickerbocker, our greatest newspaper war correspondent, and Jack Belden, our greatest magazine correspondent—he wrote *Retreat with Stillwell*—and this is Clark Lee of INS who just arrived from the Pacific—he wrote *They Call It Pacific*. They all wanted to meet you," I ended lamely.

"It's damn nice of you to put us up like this," Steinbeck said, practically wringing the poor man's hand off.

"Well I . . ." his voice faltered.

"You know," Knickerbocker said in an admiring tone, "people say that the British are cold and reserved. That's not true. Here you hardly know us and you take us in like we were your brothers. . . ."

Belden and Clark Lee contributed their quota of admiration. The Vice-Consul was bewildered but game. Knick and Belden had bed rolls which they spread out on the balcony. John had stolen (requisitioned is a better word) a broken-down army cot and Clark Lee threw two blankets on the floor. When we awoke the next morning the Vice-Consul's bed was empty. Knick made a leap for it and was asleep within two minutes. Then the Vice-Consul came walking out of the bathroom. He blinked when he saw that his bed was taken.

"I've only been gone a minute," he said plaintively.

"You said you had to be at the office at nine," I defended Knick. "It's almost that now."

"True enough," he said amiably. "True enough."

We lived there very happily for three weeks. Never once did our host complain. Steinbeck had promoted him to the position of British Consul and, because his own name was so difficult to pronounce, we never called him anything but the British Consul. He became a legend in Algiers. His routine differed a bit from ours. He worked from nine until five, but he had two hours off for lunch. It was Steinbeck who suggested that we allow him to sleep during those two hours. We generously cleared out of the room between one and three and let him sleep. Of course he had to answer phone calls for us and take down messages, but that was all. The British Consul fell into the spirit of the thing; he liked us and he knew that we liked him and appreciated his generosity. He even became accustomed to sleeping through our long nocturnal sessions with the miserable Algerian wine we drank. It was awful, but it was the only wine in town. In addition to our regular contingent we often had such transients as John Lardner of *Newsweek*, Red Mueller of NBC and Lieutenant Douglas Fairbanks, Jr., of Hollywood and the Navy staying with us. After a week or so Steinbeck became worried.

"You know the British Consul isn't looking well," he said. "It's that bad food he gets. Let's fix it up for him to eat at the American officers' mess downstairs. We don't want anything to happen to him."

We were so proud of our host that we always brought distinguished visitors in to meet him. His appreciation of these visits was somewhat lacking in warmth, but perhaps it was difficult to get used to being awakened at 4 A.M. to meet Douglas Fairbanks or Bob Hope or one of our generals. One day Lieutenant Douglas Fairbanks, Jr. and Lieutenant Commander John Kramer dropped in for a visit. I introduced them to the boys.

"Are you Steinbeck the writer?" Commander Kramer asked sharply.

Steinbeck admitted the indictment.

"I just wanted to let you know I thought your play *The Moon Is Down* was lousy," Kramer said coldly.

Steinbeck arose (all six-foot-two of him) from his chair and I shuddered. We had been so peaceful in our little home by the sea. Steinbeck stuck out that enormous right hand of his and then he laughed, shook hands with Kramer and said gratefully, "You know, I'm glad to find someone who agrees with me on that play. I never liked it. It didn't play well. No, it was a bad play."

From then on Steinbeck and Kramer were firm friends. Kramer, a tall, nervous, fast-talking son of New Jersey was one of the most brilliant experts on mines our navy had. He knew contact, magnetic and vibration mines the way he knew chamber music, and chamber music was his life. He and Steinbeck often argued for hours about which was the most important instrument in an orchestra. Kramer held out for the violin; Steinbeck was a firm believer in the piano. Kramer talked of warfare in terms of music.

"A Naval engagement now," he'd say, "is fought in terms of chamber music. The tactics are the same. You send your destroyers out—that would be the statement of the theme. The firing begins. The thirty calibres start firing at attacking aircraft—those are the violins. The fifties fire; those are the violas and the six-inch guns are perfect cellos. I've never," he said sadly, "had a chance to compose with the bass of the sixteen-inch guns."

"If he wasn't a genius with mines we'd think he was a little off the beam," Fairbanks laughed. "He always talks like that, planning operations in terms of music."

Bob Hope had nearly gotten it in Bizerte; he went to Sicily to entertain troops and he was bombed there. Then he came to peaceful Algiers which hadn't been bombed for weeks. Seeing Bob Hope was like getting a letter from home. He and Frances Langford looked tired. They'd been on the go for weeks now doing three and four shows a day.

"You ought to get some rest tonight," I told Hope. "They've stopped bombing Algiers."

"That's good," Hope said. "We've got three shows to do tomorrow and I can stand a night's sleep."

He got to sleep all right and was asleep for five minutes when the sirens wailed and almost simultaneously our ack-ack guns began to roar. They were after the ships in Algiers harbor, of course, and the docks and waterfront were filled with ack-ack guns. So were the eighty or more ships in the harbor. When they let go, the hotel pulsed with sound; it seemed to tremble with fright. It was a noisy, uncomfortable night and neither Hope nor anyone else got any sleep.

"Get out of town, Hope," I told him the next morning. "Wherever you go there's trouble. You're a nice guy but you're unlucky."

The real bright spot in our Algerian interlude was the visit of a mystery man, Mr. Charles Lytle. I had known Mr. Lytle very slightly in London. He had been introduced to me once as London's biggest backer of plays and an owner of six West End theatres; another time he was introduced as the head of a big advertising agency; a third time he was the representative of the whisky trust—actually he was all three. I met him one day in Algiers, and he looked like a gremlin. He was chubby and smiling and he wore regulation GI pants and shirt, but his military appearance was slightly marred by the battered gray slouch hat he wore and the tan-and-white sport shoes on his feet. Within a week he, like our British Consul, had become a legend. Steinbeck wrote the story of our British Consul and Charles Lytle for the *Herald Tribune* and it explains far better than I could how Lytle's visit affected our lives. Without permission from John, but merely to testify to the truth of what he wrote, I reproduce that portion of his story which applies to Lytle.

. . . It was during one of the all-night discussions of things in general that someone, perhaps Clark Lee, perhaps dour Jack Belden, suggested that we were getting very tired of Algerian wine and wouldn't it be nice if we had some Scotch. From that point on this is our story and we intend to stick to it.

Someone must have rubbed something, a ring or a lamp or perhaps the utterly exhausted British Consul. At any rate, there was a puff of blue smoke and standing in the room was a small man with pointed ears and a very jolly stomach. He wore a suit of green leather and his cap and the toes of his shoes ended in sharp points and they were green, too.

"Saints of Galway," said Reynolds. "Do you see what I see?"

"Yes," said Clark Lee.

"Well, do you believe it?"

"No," said Lee, who is, after all, a realist and was at Corregidor.

Jack Belden has lived in China for many years and he knows about such things. "Who are you?" he asked sternly.

"I'm Little Charley Lytle," the elf said.

"Well, what do you want, popping in on us?" Belden cried.

The British Consul groaned and turned over and pulled the covers over his head. Knickerbocker has since admitted that his first impulse was to kill the elf and stuff him to go beside the sailfish in his den. In fact, he was creeping up when Charley Lytle held up his hand.

"When war broke out I tried to enlist," he said. "But I was rejected on political grounds. It isn't that I have any politics," he explained. "But the Army's position is that if I did have, heaven knows what they would be. There hasn't been a Republican leprechaun since Coolidge. So I was rejected, pending the formation of an Elves in Exile Battalion. I decided then that I would just make people happy, soldiers and war correspondents and things like that."

Reynolds' eyes narrowed dangerously. He is very loyal. "Are you insinuating that we aren't happy?" he gritted. "That my friends aren't happy?"

"I'm not happy," said the British Consul, but no one paid any attention to him.

Little Charley Lytle said, "I heard some mention made of Scotch whisky. Now it just happens that I have . . ."

"How much?" said Clark Lee, who is a realist.

"Why, all you want!"

"I mean how much money?" Lee demanded.

"You don't understand," said Little Charley. "There is no money involved. It is my contribution to the war—I believe you call it EFFORT."

"I'm going to kill him," cried Knickerbocker. "Nobody can sneer at my war and get away with it."

Reynolds said, "Could we get a case?"

"Surely," said Little Charley.

"Three cases?" Reynolds added.

"Certainly."

Jack Belden broke in: "Now, Quent, don't you strain him. You don't know what his breaking point is."

"When can you deliver?" Reynolds asked.

Instead of answering, Little Charley Lytle made a dramatic and slightly ribald gesture. There was one puff of smoke and he had disappeared. There followed three small explosions, like a series of tiny depth charges, and there on the floor of Room 140 of the Aletti Hotel in Algiers were three cases of Haig & Haig pinch bottle.

That night there was an air raid, and even the British Consul enjoyed it.

Any one who doesn't believe this story can ask any of the people involved.

Now the funny part of it is that Mr. Lytle did produce three cases of Scotch whisky for us. We insisted upon paying and, after considerable argument, he accepted the huge price of eighteen dollars a case for the whisky. Scotch, when you could buy it in Algiers, was worth twenty-five dollars a bottle. We considered Mr. Lytle the private property of our room, so we shared the Scotch. We persuaded the British Consul to accept a couple of bottles; it was the only gift he would accept from us in return for his hospitality. John Lardner and Reynolds Packard had heard of our windfall and refused to leave our room until they got their share. We were the most popular men in town while it lasted. We made it last too, knowing we'd never get any more.

Ernie Pyle hit Algiers about then, looking like something that had been drawn through a wringing machine. Pyle heard that Steinbeck was in town and he asked me to fix up a meeting with John.

"I'd rather meet John Steinbeck than anyone in the world," Ernie said reverently.

That night I said to Steinbeck, "John, Ernie Pyle is in town . . ." That's as far as I got.

"Quent, there's one favor I want to ask you," Steinbeck said. "I want to meet Ernie Pyle. Will you fix it up? He is the only one of us who has captured the thoughts and the voice of the GI. His stuff is so magnificent, so much better than the stuff the rest of us write. Please, Quent . . ."

"We must allow the Miracle Man to give us a party," I said. I called Mr. Lytle and told him I wanted to bring Ernie and John to dinner. Mr. Lytle had a villa in the hills beyond the city. He said to bring them along tonight. Transportation? Oh, he'd send a car for us. Mr. Lytle made the most extravagant claims, but he always came through. A command car drove up for us at 5:30. I sat in the front with the driver while Steinbeck and Ernie Pyle held hands in the back. They formed the damnedest mutual-admiration league I had ever seen. And both were right.

"Why don't you guys swap autographs?" I suggested.

"Why don't you go to hell?" Steinbeck said contentedly.

"I hope you two will be very happy," I told them, feeling pretty happy myself to be with them.

Our Miracle Man was not at home but two U.S. Army corporals were. It was a small but lovely villa on top of a hill overlooking Algiers. From here the filthy city looked pleasant and clean. The corporals explained that Mr. Lytle had a staff of five taking care of him.

"Who is he?" one of them asked. "He must be an important guy. He's always got a couple of generals in here and he's got a bigger staff than General Eisenhower. He's got two jeeps—one American, one RAF. Would you like some Canadian ale?"

We said that we only knew him as the Miracle Man and yes, we all wanted Canadian ale. It came from the icebox, sweating cold, and we sat on Mr. Lytle's terrace and sipped it contentedly. Steinbeck was embarrassed when Ernie told him how he loved *Grapes of Wrath* and *Of Mice and Men* and then Ernie would blush when John recalled stories Pyle had written. Finally Mr. Lytle arrived and put an end to their billing and cooing, and he vetoed the Canadian ale and insisted on making martinis. We had a good dinner cooked by the army corporals and afterwards we sat on the terrace in the half light, hoping that Algiers would get it tonight so we could see it without hearing it. Pyle said that he was going back home. He was sick and he'd had enough. He was tired and written out and he wanted a little bit of his farm in Albuquerque for a change.

"But of course with the priority we have," Ernie said, "it'll take a week or two maybe to get off."

"I wish you could get off tomorrow," I said to Ernie. "You're one sick mouse."

"I'll arrange that," Mr. Lytle said confidently. "Forget it, forget it."

By now we had learned not to laugh at any promise Mr. Lytle made. We talked for hours there on the terrace, and then Mr. Lytle suggested that we stay with him. Why not? So we draped Ernie on a couch and Mr. Lytle had his staff toss mattresses on the floor for John and me. They were comfortable mattresses, and we were asleep in no time. A few minutes later, it seemed, a shrill chirping awoke me. I tried to ignore it, but the sound persisted. It was daylight now and a rooster was crowing proudly in back of the villa just because he'd probably made a hit with some scrawny Arab chicken. But it was the chirping that woke me. I pulled the pillow over my head, but that didn't help. I heard Ernie swearing in the next room. I heard Steinbeck getting up.

"What the hell is that noise?" I asked.

"It's a chicken, a baby chicken, country-bred," Pyle said.

It sounded like a very frightened chicken. By now Mr. Lytle too had been aroused. He appeared in rosy-hued pajamas and sleepy eyes. We located the baby chicken in the kitchen. It squealed horribly as we tried to catch it. We threw hats at it but it kept side-stepping. It ran into the living room shrilling loudly with fright. The three of us tried to gang up on it. Mr. Lytle sat on the couch, his cherubic face beaming. He laughed and laughed and shook and shook.

"Three grown men," he gasped, "defeated by a chicken that weighs about four ounces. I'll never forget this picture."

Finally the chicken found the door and slipped out. Its frightened whimpers lowered an octave and now the little brat just chirruped with relief but we knew there was no use trying to sleep again.

Our Miracle Man suddenly became practical. "It's going to be a warm day," he said, looking at the sun. "Now the best way to start off a warm day is by having ice-cold beer for breakfast."

[269]

"That's an old custom we have in Albuquerque," Pyle said admiringly.

"Beer is a nice breakfast any place," John said gently. Who was I to disagree?

We drank cold beer sitting on the terrace sans clothes. The stone terrace was cool on our feet. Then the two corporals woke up and before we knew what was happening we were having bacon, fried eggs, hashed brown potatoes and American coffee. Put it all together and it made as tasty a breakfast as I'd ever seen in any country. The Miracle Man just sat smiling gently at us and we thought that any minute he'd disappear in a cloud of smoke and we'd find ourselves back at the Aletti.

"Is there anything you can't do, Mr. Lytle?" Steinbeck asked.

"I just like to help you boys along," Mr. Lytle said blandly. "Now I'm worried about Ernie Pyle here. He doesn't look well. He should get home quickly. I'm going to phone Ike this morning . . ."

"Not that," I protested. "That would be too much. Do you really call General Eisenhower 'Ike'?"

"I've met the general once or twice," Mr. Lytle said modestly.

"Who are you anyhow, Mr. Lytle?" Ernie asked. "We know you act as sort of liaison between Ensa and the USO. We know you produce all the food and drinks in the world just by waving a hand. We know you got the guest villa reserved for cabinet ministers and real big shots. Quent lived in London a long time and even he can't figure you out."

"I don't believe you're a person, Mr. Lytle," John Steinbeck said seriously. "You're something that James Stevens invented. You're out of the *Crock of Gold* or you're out of something one of those Irish poets wrote. I had a grandmother like that. I'm Irish, you know. My grandfather used to take a nip now and then. On his deathbed he looked at my grand-mother and said, 'Please, one little glass of brandy before I go,' and she became very indignant and she said, 'Ah, now shame on you. Wanting to go before the throne of God with the smell of liquor on your breath.' "

"Did she give him the drink, John?" I asked.

"She did not," John said. "She was a very God-fearing woman. But in after years when she began to fail herself the doctor recommended that she drink a little port after each meal. The doctor néver told her how much port to drink, so she would fill herself a water glass of it after each meal and during the last years of her life she just lived in a wonderful rosy dream world of port. Yet, if you ever told her that she was drinking she would have been horrified."

"You know, another bottle of that Canadian ale . . ." Ernie Pyle had no sooner said it than the corporal appeared with three more bottles.

Oh, it was mighty pleasant sitting there, talking. Steinbeck is as good a talker as he is a writer, and so is little Ernie. The sun was above the hills now, and it was nine o'clock and Steinbeck thought we should go to the Aletti to be sure the British Consul was up and at the office. Our Miracle Man waved a wand or something and a jeep was at the gate. We said good-bye to him and got in the jeep. As we drove off, the driver, most unaccountably an RAF man, said, "There's a package there for you men. Mr. Lytle told me to wrap up a few bottles of bourbon for you. By the way, what is bourbon?"

"You don't know what bourbon is?" Ernie asked in shocked tones.

"No, sir," the driver said. "I come from Lancaster. I never heard of bourbon."

"You haven't lived," Ernie said reproachfully. "You just haven't lived."

[271]

Back at the Aletti we were a little hurt to see that in our absence the British Consul had overslept.

"We leave you alone for one night and look what happens," Steinbeck said sternly. "You might lose your job and that would be on our conscience."

"I couldn't sleep," the British Consul admitted. "It was so lonely here last night. Only Knick and Jack Belden and a couple of friends of Quent's named Major Charles MacArthur and Colonel Rex Smith popped in."

"They didn't keep you awake, did they?" Steinbeck asked in threatening tones. By now we all were sincerely fond of our roommate. The British Consul had a quiet sense of humor that captivated us all. Half the time he was kidding us, but he did it so subtly that you didn't catch the point until much later.

Three hours after our return Ernie Pyle got a phone message informing him that he was off for America that afternoon. He waited while we wrote letters for him to take along.

"How about that Miracle Man?" Ernie said in awe. "He gets things done, all right. I didn't expect to get off for two weeks."

"Maybe he really does know Eisenhower," I said. We never found out anything more about him. But, as Steinbeck said, it was better that way. He remains a mystery to us, one of the nicest mysteries we ever knew.

I had a refuge when I wanted to get away from the Aletti. A fighter wing was stationed some twenty-five miles from Algiers and I spent many a night there. This was a combined British-American group flying P-39s by day and Beaufighters by night. My friends there were Major "K" Mills (formerly of *Time* and *Life*); Captain George Davis (one-time New York broker); big, genial Major Gerald Hayes, the medical officer (a Notre Dame graduate); good-looking Captain William

Bowan (head of a Boston trucking firm and fish business); and Wing Commander William Moresby, D.F.C., one of the few RAF pilots who survived France, the Battle of Britain and months of Mediterranean combat. At least once a week I'd phone "K" Mills to tell him I wanted to get out of town and a jeep would be around to pick me up. One night, Moresby, C.O. of the night fighter group, sent me up in a Beaufighter. It was a pleasant experience. The weather was perfect and a big Mediterranean moon gave us plenty of light. We were flying in the neighborhood of Algiers. The hunting was poor but ground control told us that there was a show on at Bizerte. Unfortunately, it was over before we could get up there. We returned to the base to find the officers' club in an uproar. Bill Moresby had gotten two Jerry planes over Bizerte and everyone was celebrating. The barmen had made a special drink in Bill's honor, something which used "American grog" as a base. This North African version of rye was sheer dynamite. The barman, an RAF lad, had gotten some lemon juice and a few other ingredients to hide its rawness. Everyone was excited about Bill's feat except Bill himself. Knocking down Jerry planes was an old story to handsome Moresby. His American colleagues were much more excited than he was.

This was an important airfield because it protected the coast all the way from Algiers to Tunis. The Germans came over nearly every night somewhere along the coast but they never got very far. The Beaufighters invariably got to them before they reached the coast and the Beaus never missed. The Germans have no defense for the Beaus and, because they haven't as yet captured one intact, they know little about them. That meant that I couldn't write about my flight. Anything you'd write concerning a Beau would be giving information to the Germans.

Occasionally Moresby, Mills, Hayes, Davis and the others would come to Algiers. They had located an apartment high above the city where a Viennese woman served food. She could only handle about fifteen customers a night, and you had to make reservations a week in advance; but it was worth it. When my windfall from Mr. Lytle came, I was able to contribute some Scotch and Moresby always came through with a bottle of gin. We'd sit in the immaculately clean apartment, sipping martinis and then we'd have civilized food and try to cure our homesickness with talk of baseball and of people we knew in London or New York. I'd usually go back with the men to camp and enjoy the experience of watching them get up at six while I would dive back into the sack for a couple more hours of sleep. Watching other people get up when you don't have to, is one of the pleasantest experiences I know. When you return from a long trip to the war, you don't have many pleasant memories, but I'll never forget the kindness and good fellowship I enjoyed with "K" Mills, Bill Moresby and the others.

Time passed like that in Algiers. We knew the big show was only a few days away. Colonel Joe Phillips had allotted us all to different parts of the show. The press associations were given priority positions. The big newspapers and the radio reporters came next. The rest of us so-called "specials" were last on the list. This was reasonable because we were feature writers and not interested in spot news, valueless to us because of the time lag between the sending of our stories and the publication of our magazines. Lieutenant Commander Charles Duffy, naval P.R.O., had made me the naval correspondent, which meant that I'd go along on the *Ancon*, the command ship. I couldn't ask for a better spot than that.

Barry Faris, INS editor back in New York, who always had that seventh sense which enabled him to anticipate news, cabled his man, Clark Lee, to stick close to General Eisenhower in case of a big operation. It was a smart move.

"But I never met Eisenhower," Clark Lee moaned. "I've been in the Pacific. How can I go to him and say, 'General, I got orders to sleep with you all during the next big show?'"

"There is a man named Butch," I told him. I phoned Commander Harry Butcher, Naval Aide to General Eisenhower, and explained Clark's difficulty.

"Bring Clark Lee up right away," Butch said. "The General has a few minutes and Clark can tell him about it."

Clark Lee and I hotfooted it to GHQ. Clark was understandably nervous. He'd never met the Boss before and his request was a rather embarrassing one. Butch brought us in. General Eisenhower was sitting behind a big desk. He got up from his chair and walked over to us. He smiled and said, "Quent, is this that Clark Lee who wants to trail me around during the next operation?"

Clark gulped and choked. "I'm sorry, sir, my office . . ."

Eisenhower slapped him on the back. "Listen, Clark, I've been wanting to meet you ever since I read your book. That was a fine job. Butch tells me you want to stick around with us during the next show. Well, why not? You'll hear a lot of things you'll have to forget, but I'm sure your judgment will tell you what can't be used. Butch will let you know when we move and you move right along with us. Are you coming along with us?" he asked me.

"No, sir, I'm assigned to the navy this time," I said.

"A fine thing," he growled in mock anger. "Deserting us like that for the navy."

"Well, after all, they are our allies," I said.

"You don't know Tooey Spaatz or Tedder or Jimmy Doolittle, do you?" he asked Clark. "No? Well, you will. We'll be spending a few days with them just before D Day. You'll like them. Butch will let you know when we're leaving. I hope you can find some stories with us, but it's apt to be dull."

[275]

We went out with Clark muttering, "What a guy . . . ! What a guy!" Later, during the Italian show, Clark Lee got some magnificent stories. He was with Eisenhower and the staff at North African GHQ during the Salerno invasion and during the surrender of the Italian fleet. Eisenhower treated us like grown-ups; some generals treated us like bothersome children. Eisenhower felt that the parents of the boys in the army had a right to know everything that was going on at the front (consistent with security), and he looked upon us as a link between the battle front and the home front.

On the way home, Lee and I stopped at the Red Cross to get some ice cream. The girls who worked in the Algiers Red Cross Headquarters worked long hours. They performed miracles every day. On this day we saw one of them. A GI had come to the Red Cross desk. Charming Molly Ford of New York City was in charge that afternoon. The GI explained that he had been married eight months before to a WAC. That was back home. Shortly afterwards he had been shipped overseas and now he wondered if it were possible for Molly to find out where his wife was stationed. She might be at Fort Knox or Dallas, Texas or London or Cairo or Timbuctoo; he had no idea. Molly got on a phone and in a couple of hours found that the girl was stationed in none of these places—but was working (honest, Mr. Ripley) in Algiers. Within an hour Molly had arranged for the girl to have a furlough and, as we entered the lobby, the shy, good-looking GI and the radiant WAC had just been reunited. That was typical of the things Molly Ford and her colleagues were doing all the time in Algiers. The Red Cross was run efficiently and so humanely there by Bill Stevenson and his lovely wife Bumpy Stevenson.

Back at the hotel there was a cable for me from *Collier's*. It read: "Better come home at once and have a rest. Then suggest going Londonwards." There was also a telephone message from Commander Duffy which merely said, "Stay close to your hotel. You may be getting off soon." All my instincts were to rush to PRO headquarters and ask to be sent home on the next plane. But could I pass up the big show that was due any minute? I wrestled with my conscience, trying to overcome it, but for once it won out. I decided to go along on this one show and then head for home. I'd been away six months—a long and, for the most part, dreary six months. You can stay away from home just so long before you go nuts. There is no known inoculation for loneliness.

Dick Tregaskis of INS, the author of the best seller, *Guadalcanal Diary*, was off that night, which meant that the big push was close. Dick is a very sweet and brave man who never bothered to duck. Dick is six-foot-six. When he left that night to join an unknown ship at an unknown port bound for an unknown destination, I said, "So long, Dick, and, for God's sake, don't forget to duck."

"I'll duck, all right," he grinned. "This ought to be easy anyhow, after Sicily and Guadal. Anything ought to be easy after those places."

Tregaskis did forget to duck. At this writing he is in a hospital outside of Naples in a serious condition. Twelve pieces of shrapnel pierced his helmet and entered his brain.

That night Jack Belden found an empty room which held two beds. We decided to commandeer it and let the British Consul have a real night's sleep. Belden had received a letter from *Time* suggesting that he return too, but he was going to sweat it out. Neither of us slept well that night. I woke a dozen times to hear Jack muttering in his sleep. In the morning both of us received our orders. He was to take off from Oran; I was to leave from Algiers.

"So long, sucker," Jack said, grinning. "Take care of yourself. Here we go, trying to beat the law of averages again."

Algiers, September, 1943

****

Chapter XVI

D DAY—ITALY

It was a nice, large ship, and so full of apparatus for detection and communication that I felt if I sat down in any given chair I'd be electrocuted. It was the headquarters and flagship in the previous two invasions and there was some reason to believe that the Germans had spotted it. However, that was a chance we had to take. We were going to take a lot of chances in this operation right from the beginning but, as the ball players say, "You can't get a base hit if you don't take your bat off your shoulder."

Lieutenant John Mason Brown, former drama critic of the *New York World-Telegram*, has told the story of the *S. S. Ancon* in his exciting book, *To All Hands*. It was Lieutenant Brown's unique task to broadcast over the ship's public-address system a play-by-play description of the action in which the ship was engaged. Four of us had been assigned to the *Ancon*: Lionel Shapiro of the *Montreal Gazette*, Reynolds Packard of the United Press and my old pal, the irresistible

Sammy Schulman, the International News Service photographer who wrote *Where's Sammy?* I was put into a large cabin with two of the ship's officers, young Lieutenant Howard Schink and Lieutenant Van Alstyne. There were three bunks in the cabin and young Schink insisted that I take his commodious lower. That was typical of the way the navy treated Shapiro, Packard, Schulman and myself. We were fortunate, too, in the army and navy press relations officers who were to take care of us. Commander Charles Duffy, an old Hearst editor, handled the press for the navy, while Lieutenant Colonel Kenneth Clark, another distinguished Hearst alumnus, handled army press relations. We talked of our old bosses, for I, too, am a graduate of the Hearst organization. It would have made Barry Faris and Joe Connolly, who run International News Service and King Features, feel good, I am sure, to hear three of their old pupils talking about them on a ship in Algiers harbor—and talking nothing but praise. Connolly and Faris ran a hard but good school, and you learned your trade from them or you didn't last. I'll always be grateful to both of them.

We spent the night tied up to our dock in Algiers, and I didn't like that. The night before I'd had dinner with my pals of the Second Fighter Wing, and they had told me they expected a raid on Algiers the following night. This was the night. When they raid Algiers they ignore the city and concentrate on the harbor. We had a couple of pretty good sluggers alongside of us: H. M. S. *King George V* and H. M. S. *Howe*, Britain's newest fashions in battleships. They could throw up a tremendous amount of flak, but I've never had much confidence in even the excellent Algiers brand of flak. The odd plane or two can always get through. But nothing happened.

We slipped out so quietly at 7 A.M. that I never woke up. I did get up at ten, had a salt then a fresh shower and decided that the U. S. Navy was all right. I went to the wardroom for breakfast and was shocked to find that the navy stopped serving breakfast at 8:30. This was indeed a blow to a person who believes that nothing worth while ever happens before 10 A.M., whether on land or sea. But there was always coffee, the Negro mess attendants told me. There was beautiful, strong American coffee, and I went into the galley and clowned with the mess boys, hoping they wouldn't notice that I was drinking six cups. They didn't know about that coffee made of acorns I'd been living on in Russia, or the miserable chickory coffee we'd had in Sicily or the Godawful imitation French coffee they gave us in Algiers. The longer I stay abroad the more provincial I become. I begin to think that everything American is better than its European counterpart. In some cases I may be wrong—but not about coffee. Any resemblance between French, Russian, or British coffee and our own real coffee is entirely accidental.

After breakfast I investigated the ship's library and, to my delight, found it filled with detective stories. It would, I decided, be a good trip after all. Then we were called to the operations room forward and briefed. Until now we didn't know where we were headed. We thought Italy, but it might be Sardinia or Corsica. If it were Italy it might be Taranto or Naples or most anywhere else. We were told the whole story of the operation by Commander Richard English, one of the naval planners, and a G-2 officer, and an air force colonel. It was to be Salerno, thirty-five miles south of Naples. It was the logical spot. We were told that, undoubtedly, the Germans knew we were on our way. The audacity of the plan subdued us considerably, especially when we realized the problem of air cover. Our fighters would all have to come from Sicily, 180 miles away. That meant about a forty-minute flight for a Spit or a P-38. We realized that

[280]

the Spitfire, because of its lower fuel capacity, could stay over us for only a short time. The P-38s, with their longer range, could stick around for about an hour. However, we were to have four British converted aircraft carriers carrying Seafires—Spits modified to land on carrier decks. But still our air protection was going to be mighty thin.

Then General Mark Clark called for us. We went to his cabin just off the bridge. Lanky, likable, Mark Clark grinned when he told us to sit down.

"How do you like our plan?" he asked.

"My God, it's daring!" I blurted out.

"My God, it *is* daring," he laughed. "Sure, we're spitting right into the lion's mouth. We know it. But we have to do that. We had several alternate plans and we studied them all carefully. This seemed to be the only real answer."

"Do you expect either strategic or tactical surprise?" I asked him.

"Certainly not strategic surprise." He stretched out his long legs and made himself comfortable in his chair. "And I doubt if we get any tactical surprise. German G-2 is good. They have studied these maps of Italy as we have studied them. They know we want and need a port in Italy. Naples is the obvious port for us to go after. We could go after it from the beaches north of Naples or go into Salerno as we are doing. They know, as we know, that the coastline north of Naples isn't good for landing an assault force. They know that landing there would stretch our air cover to the breaking point. There is no doubt that they figure us to land on the Salerno beaches." He looked serious, and added, "We may get hurt, but you can't play with fire without the risk of burning your fingers.

"By the way," he said, turning to me, "I have a message for you from Butch. I had dinner with him last night."

"Butch" was Commander Harry Butcher, Naval Aide to General Eisenhower.

"The message was," General Clark quoted, " 'Tell Quent not to get my watch wet.' "

I looked guiltily at the wrist watch I was wearing. My own watch had broken the week before and Butch had lent me his. "I don't even want to get my feet wet, much less Butch's watch," I said fervently to Clark. "But I hope Butch isn't sucker enough to think he's ever going to get this watch back?"

"He has vague hopes—that's all," Clark said.

Clark sat there talking easily, and I marveled at his composure. He was leading the first real invasion of the continent. He was, he told us, "Making the longest end run in history." General Montgomery's slash across the Straits of Messina was merely a quick quarterback thrust. Our end run was the play designed to be the pay-off; the touchdown play. Or, in terms of the ring, Montgomery's attack was the left jab; ours was the Sunday punch. We were going to throw everything we had into it.

And if it missed? Clark, as Commanding General of the Fifth Army would be the goat. A general has to win battles —or else. No excuses are accepted. This was Clark's first big chance, and he sat there relaxed, smiling, confident.

"Are you apprehensive about what their air will do?" I asked him.

"Apprehensive?" he exploded. "I'm scared stiff of what their air will do, but we hope to have two of their airfields by D plus 2 and then our fighters won't have that long pull from Sicily."

"When do you expect to establish headquarters ashore?"

He shrugged his shoulders. "Who knows? If everything goes according to plan—and it never does—I may get ashore on D plus 2. We want to get this ship out of the harbor as soon as possible. It is far too vulnerable. Yet I can't establish headquarters ashore until our communications are set up."

When we left General Clark we felt a little better because of his quiet air of confidence. Clark at forty-six looks thirty-six—if that. He had never commanded large units in combat, but Eisenhower had picked him. General Eisenhower didn't make mistakes—and he was sold on Mark Clark.

I went back to the wardroom to get a couple of detective stories from the library. Looking over the books I found an old friend, *Personal History*, Vincent Sheean's great book written ten years ago. I remembered that he had a chapter on Palestine in the book and I wanted to reread it. I thumbed through the book, looking for it, and then one of those things that can't happen did happen. I know it's difficult to believe, but one really can't invent such coincidences. I found the chapter and was quite engrossed in it when I felt a slap on my back and, turning, looked into the smiling face of nobody else but Lieutenant Colonel Vincent (Jimmy) Sheean.

"You'll never let me live this down, Jimmy," I groaned. "Look what I'm reading."

"I admire your taste in literature," Sheean said with mock modesty. Sheean had done a great job as aide to General Cannon in the Tunisia and Sicily campaigns. He had been especially fortunate and efficient in his dealings with the French. His knowledge of the language as well as the people had done a great deal to smooth over some rough passages. Now in Italy he would act as liaison between our technical men and the Italian technical men. I admire Sheean not only because he has always been one of the shining lights in our trade; not only because when he is hot he can write like an angel—but because he was wearing the combat uniform of his country. Not the synthetic uniform I was wearing, with the insignia War Correspondent on his shoulders, but with the silver leaf of a lieutenant colonel and with campaign ribbons over his heart.

We sat and talked of many things not connected with the operation and so smoothly did our ship glide through the water and so muted was the music of our engines that it was hard to believe that we were at sea.

"You've been briefed?" Sheean asked.

When I nodded, he said, "Pray that it doesn't rain in Sicily the next few days."

"Why, Jimmy?" It seemed a strange thing to pray for.

"We have no all-weather airfields in Sicily," Sheean said. "You've landed on them—you know what they're like. No concrete runways. They're full of thick dust and sand from the summer, and rain will turn them into mudfields. If that happens, the Spits and the 38s won't be able to take off or land. That Sicilian mud is really something. So, baby, pray for sunny skies and dry weather."

That noon at dinner (the navy has dinner at noon) I sat opposite the Catholic chaplain, Lieutenant Ballinger. He said Mass on the gun deck at four-thirty every afternoon. I suppose one of the last official acts the Pope ever did for America was to give our army and navy chaplains permission to say Mass any time up to 7 P.M. I told Father Ballinger what Jimmy Sheean had said, and I suggested that he incorporate a special prayer for good weather in his Mass that day. Had any one of his Jersey City parishioners ever suggested that to Father Ballinger in pre-war days, he probably would have laughed. But he didn't laugh this time. Gradually, a thin gauze of tension was wrapping itself around the ship and around each one of us. We were creeping up on Salerno, and we all knew that this was a fight for keeps. Father Ballinger nodded and said quietly, "Not a bad idea."

The weather was real Mediterranean weather at its best. The sun tinted the sea with gold and, because of the varying depths of the water, it took on hues of blue, aquamarine and indigo and, where the water was very deep, emerald green. We had kept a rendezvous, and now ships were all around us.

Our convoy moved smoothly in parallel lines, each ship perhaps three hundred yards from the one in front and a little further from those on either side. Most of the ships were large troop ships and some could be identified as former luxury liners. We were hugging the coast, for our next rendezvous was off Bizerte. We had roast turkey for dinner that night and peach pie and all the coffee a man could drink. I figured that no matter what happened from now on I was ahead of the game. It was the best food I'd had in nearly seven months. Our navy is good to travel with, except for the childish rule made by former Secretary of the Navy, Josephus Daniels, the prohibitionist (some twenty-five years ago), that no alcoholic drinks could be served on any American naval vessel. I think that to be one of the most un-American orders ever enforced on our armed forces. There is absolutely no reason for it, beyond the fanaticism of our former Secretary of the Navy. The navy of every other country in the world serves drinks, and I never recall a battle being lost because the ships' officers happened to be drunk. Drinks are served in the wardrooms of all British warships, from little gunboats up to battle wagons, and in three and a half years of frequent traveling with the Royal Navy I have never seen any officer or man the worse for drink. A drink tastes mighty good when you come off a bitter-cold, eight-hour watch. It would have been pleasant to sit around our wardroom on the *S. S. Ancon*, having a cocktail before dinner and a Scotch and soda afterwards.

I resent the implication that it is all right for British officers to drink on board their ships because they handle liquor well, but it isn't all right for our own naval officers to drink on board because they might run their ship on a rock. American naval officers have too much pride in their ships and their uniform ever to disgrace either. Our naval officers feel rather ashamed of the absurd rule, but they obey it implicitly. In many ports our sailors have made bad names for themselves because when they do get ashore they go to town on that grog as though they were never going to get another drink. In British wardrooms (and RAF stations) no money is passed. Men must sign chits for every drink they buy. Each week the commanding officer looks over the chits. If an officer's bill shows that he has been buying too many drinks, he will be hauled up very quickly before the C.O. and measures taken. But this doesn't happen often. However, it gives the commanding officer a perfect check.

We lay about twenty miles off Bizerte that night. During the early evening I was on the bridge talking to Admiral Hewitt, in command of the whole amphibious part of the show. Hewitt told me that Bizerte was having an air raid.

"Twenty plus are reported en route," he said. "I hope they don't spot us on the way home. By the way, have you heard the news from Italy?"

"Not all of it," I said cautiously, just fishing, of course. I hadn't had any news of Italy.

"Well," Hewitt said, smiling, "it's strictly hush-hush, but we may have some good news soon."

"Italy might fold?" I was surprised, because there hadn't even been a rumor in Algiers about any capitulation. Only smart Herbert Matthews had believed that Italy would surrender. I recalled his remark of a few days before. "I have every confidence in the Italians," Herbert had said. "Yes, I am confident that they will double-cross the Germans just as they've double-crossed everyone else."

The night and the next day passed pleasantly. By now I was completely sold on my two cabin mates. Big Van Alstyne, nearing fifty, was one of the friendliest men I've ever met. We sat around and talked of the two previous invasions. The *Ancon* had been the command ship in those operations, too, and had two very narrow escapes. "But she's a lucky ship," Van laughed, "and we have a lucky skipper."

We passed Sicily and then headed north. By now, of course, we had been spotted by reconnaissance planes. You can't hide a fleet of hundreds of ships in the Mediterranean. It was, in the language of invasion, D minus one. The landing would take place at 3:30 A.M. In that other war it was called Zero Hour. Now it is merely H Hour. We had a magnificent meal that night: cream of celery soup, steak, onions, mashed potatoes and apple pie. You couldn't help but think of the old cliché, "The condemned man ate a hearty meal." The men were greatly disappointed, however.

"In the other two invasions," I heard one of them grumble on deck, "we had apple pie and ice cream the night before. Yeah, and on the Sicily show we each had two lumps of ice cream."

Each member of the crew was given a mimeographed sheet during dinner.

U. S. S. ANCON (AGC4)
PLAN OF THE DAY FOR THURSDAY 9 SEPTEMBER 1943

During Thursday, 9 September it is expected that the *Ancon* will be in the transport area, operating its landing boats, as directed, to debark certain army personnel and equipment; the crew will be at General Quarters to repel enemy attack by air and sea. It is expected that the ship will be hove to for a while and then anchored, with the anchor at short stay ready to slip at a moment's notice, with a full steaming watch on and full steam at the throttles. During the time the crew is at General Quarters it is proposed to feed all hands at their stations. To accomplish this, ship's cooks and bakers will be excused from ammunition details and will occupy themselves with the preparation and serving of food under the direct supervision of the Supply Officer. Food will be brought to General Quarters stations in food carriers by men detailed from ammunition parties. Troops going ashore on Thursday will be fed an early breakfast at 0100, in the crew's messing compartment.

In general, boats will be loaded by details from damage control parties under the supervision of the First Lieutenant and Boatswain.

Subsequent employment of the crew will depend upon developments and the local situation. In general, boats' crews from the 2-A Division will man the boats and will lower their boats as directed.

All hands are directed to have with them, throughout the day and night, helmets and gas masks. Boat crews will have with them such uniform and equipment as has been furnished them.

D. H. SWINSON, Comdr., USNR.
Executive Officer

NOTE: When this vessel is in the combat zone and all hands are at General Quarters, it is expected that for several meals mess tables will not be set up for the service of meals. In lieu thereof the Army Field Ration K will be served to both officers and men at their stations. Paper cups will be provided for the hot coffee.

Sufficient cooks and stewards, stewards' mates and commissary personnel will be secured when directed by the Commanding Officer to act as runners for serving the rations. Lt. jg Knowles will supervise the service forward of the crews messing compartment and Lt. Comdr. Nicol aft. Runners will wear helmets and dungarees, keeping the body covered at all times.

Gun platform crews will provide three fathoms of manila line for hoisting and lowering 10-gallon Aervoid coffee containers.

After dinner the Captain of our ship asked me to "brief" the whole crew on the ship's public-address system. The crew had no idea where we were going and they were getting slightly jittery.

"Give them the whole works," the Captain said. "Where we're landing, how many divisions, and so on. And you might stress the fact," he added casually, "that our air cover is going to be excellent."

"I hope you're right, sir," I couldn't help saying.

"So do I," he answered grimly.

I spoke from the bridge and loudspeakers all over the ship carried the story to the crew. I drew slightly on my imagination and dwelt cheerfully on the 200 Beaufighters which would be over us all night and the 500 Spits and Lightnings which would cover us by day. I became so enthusiastic I almost believed it myself. Later, Reynolds Packard gave a fascinating talk on Italy. He explained that the Italians were a very unpredictable people; we might be able to walk right in without opposition from them; we might, on the other hand, find them to be very tough. Pack went on:

"There were two stories which used to go the rounds of Anglo-American newspaper circles in Rome before this war began. They help as much as anything else to explain the weird makeup of the Italian people.

"One of these stories concerns an American tourist who walked into a spaghetti joint in Naples. He sat down at a table and looked around for a waiter. There were signs in big block letters on the wall, saying: GUERRA CONTRA LA MOSCA—WAR AGAINST FLIES. The tourist finally ordered some *zuppe pavesa* which is a popular soup made with chunks of bread and two raw eggs in it, sprinkled with grated cheese.

"The waiter shuffled out to the kitchen and returned twenty minutes later with the soup. The plate was rimmed with flies. There were even a few of the flies struggling in the soup.

"The tourist, in disgust, told the waiter: 'Look at those flies around here. What's the meaning of those signs: War Against Flies?'

" 'Well,' answered the waiter, 'there was a war against flies here once, but the flies won.'

"The other story is about an Italian anti-fascist in Rome who daily went to the Café Aragno on the main drag—the Corso Umberto—for his afternoon drinks. As soon as he came in he would immediately ask to have all the newspapers for that day brought to him. It's an old Italian custom, I must explain, that you transact business, write letters, make phone calls, get your shoes shined and meet strange women in cafés. In fact, you do almost everything in an Italian café, except bring your wife in with you. It's the poor man's club. To get back to the story. The anti-fascist would glance through one front-page after another, without ever looking at the inside pages. This procedure, occurring day after day, intrigued his waiter. One day the waiter asked him what he was looking for in the newspapers.

" 'I am looking for a death notice,' he said.

"The waiter pointed out that death notices in Italian newspapers are always on the inside pages.

"The man replied, 'Not this one. The one I'm looking for would be on the front page, all right.'

"What I am trying to get at in these stories is this: The Italian is indifferent to his surroundings in a lazy, even talkative sort of way—whether it be flies or fascism. Although almost all the Italian people disapproved of Mussolini when he declared war against the United States, in December, 1941, they did nothing to oppose his declaration. In fact, the Duce was not bounced out of power until just a few weeks ago, when the great Allied victories in Sicily sawed off the balcony of Venice Palace right out from under this baloney Caesar.

"As far as the Italian people are concerned, 95 percent of them are for breaking away from Nazi Germany and doing some sort of diplomatic somersault which will land them on the bandwagon of Allied victory. How to do it? They are looking for a formula. Bagdolio is looking for a formula.

"Maybe this very convoy may be the solution. If this particular attack is struck hard enough, then all sorts of things may happen. I believe that the impact of this well-organized invasion will shake the Italians out of their Latin laziness and indifference and cause them to rise up against the Germans and come over to our side. But the impact must be strong enough to crack the back of the Roman wolf.

"It must be a terrific crack. You must be prepared for tough fighting. Being the kind of people they are, the Italians will want to make sure first that when they do turn their somersault they will land on solid invasion ground and not just on an area held by commandos in a fleeting raid. That's a pretty lousy point of view the Italians have, and I don't think they will profit by it other than to get off the losing side.

"In this connection, I suspect even the care the Italians are giving their fleet is not an effort to hold it for attack, as it is to hold it for bargaining purposes over a green-baize peace table somewhere."

After his talk, Pack and I strolled into the wardroom. The radio had just been turned on and a calm voice was saying, "General Eisenhower announced tonight that Italy had unconditionally surrendered. . . ." There was a stunned silence for a moment and then a yell of delight from all over the ship. The news acted as a tonic. We all assured ourselves that it would be a walk-in now. We knew that two Eyetie divisions were in the vicinity of Paestum, where our 36th Division was to land. If they were out of it our boys would have things easy. The British, who were to land near the town of Salerno on our left flank, would still be up against the 16th Panzer Division; but now the American Division could mop up quickly and strike north to help the British. Things looked wonderful. Everything seemed almost too good to be true—and of course they were too good to be true.

It was lovely on deck. The moon seemed friendly, although it was pouring down an awful lot of light. It was a real bombers' moon and, looking over the rail, I wondered why the

Germans hadn't come over. And then came the doleful sound of a bugle through the loudspeakers. I heard fast-running feet on the deck and cries of command and I realized that this was the alert, or, in naval language, "General Quarters." The bugle was followed by a sort of rasping buzzer, a monotonous sound. If the bugle didn't wake you, the buzzer would. Then came the flat tones of the Boatswain entirely unemotional, "General Quarters. General Quarters. Report to battle stations. Report to battle stations."

Then it was quiet, ominously quiet. That wait between the alert and the arrival of the planes is always a long wait. We were moving slowly and the throttled-down engines were hardly heard; the only sound was the soft lapping of the waves against the hull of the ship. Then, about five miles to port a flare blossomed in the night; a beautiful gold and crimson flare, that looked like a chandelier lighted with a thousand candles. These are usually dropped by fast Focke-Wulf 190's and serve as beacons for the bombers which follow within a minute or two. Another and yet another flare appeared and with the help of the moon our whole convoy was silhouetted beautifully. Our flak began to rise, but the Germans didn't get through to the center of the convoy; they remained on the outer fringes. Their attack lasted an hour. They hit three LST's (land-ship tanks), big 330-foot craft. This was hardly an auspicious beginning.

At 1:30 the moon disappeared and we felt more secure. "First light," would be at 6:30, though the real dawn wouldn't come until about 6:50. I stood on the starboard deck for a while and suddenly noticed huge, irregular shapes which almost merged into the night. Someone said quietly, "Well, there it is." We were off the coast of Italy and just south of our target objective. It was D Day and H Hour was fast approaching. For months, more than 150,000 men had been training for this moment. They'd be getting nervous now, and they'd be worrying a bit, too. All soldiers worry, especially before their first combat, and this would be the first combat for the 36th as well as for the 46th and 56th British. All men worry before H Hour, but their chief worry is that they may be weak at the decisive moment. They are all so afraid of being afraid, not knowing that fear is as universal as hunger and no one can escape it. I have never met a brave man in my life and never expect to meet one.

Down in the operations room men sat with earphones, listening and talking to other ships. General Mark Clark, tall, smiling, appearing unconcerned, sat with his aides, ready at any moment to change the plan, in case things ashore did not go according to schedule. The skipper of our ship stood bulkily on the bridge, his face tight with concentration. This was a big ship, with three admirals and a dozen generals aboard, a crew of more than a thousand, and he felt his responsibility. Nothing must happen to this command ship or the whole operation might fail.

We knew that a group of mine sweepers were ahead of us, and we hoped they were doing a good job. We knew where two mine fields were in the huge harbor. But had the Germans laid others during the past twenty-four hours? The weather seemed right, but would there be a large ground swell in close that would capsize the smaller landing craft? Lieutenant Commander Richard Steere, the navy's weather expert, had promised that the weather would be suitable, and he hadn't been wrong yet. But on this day a year ago there had been a gale; two years ago on this day there had been a forty-mile wind. But Steere had gone back over the records for fifty years, and in forty-eight cases the weather had been perfect on September 9th. A weather man bets on the law of averages. There was another question that would have to be answered. Hadn't it rained in Sicily tonight? If it had rained hard, God help us tomorrow. Those airfields were soft with the dust of the summer, but heavy rain would turn them into quagmires from which no planes could rise. Without good fighter protection, we would be sitting birds for the Luftwaffe, which had airfields in the Foggia region across Italy, airfields in Sardinia an hour away by air, and airfields in Southern France.

We crept into the harbor and took our place just off the mouth of the Sele River. The Rangers and the Commandos would strike north of us in the region near the city of Salerno. It was typical of the co-operation existing between the British and the Americans on the whole show. Also on the left flank (looking toward shore) and north of the river would be the two British divisions, the 46th and 56th. The naval force landing them and protecting them until their supplies and artillery were ashore, was led by a British officer, Commodore Oliver. Two weeks ago, Admiral Hewitt had wanted an American naval captain to assist Commodore Oliver. He asked Admiral Richard Connolly to recommend someone. Connolly recommended himself. It was pointed out to him that naval tradition forbade that an Admiral serve under a Commodore. Connolly used some very salty language to say that he didn't give a damn about rank, adding forcefully, "I only know one thing, by God, and that is that I'm not going to be kept out of this show!" He wasn't, and events proved that he and Oliver made a great team.

It was almost H Hour now, but no sound disturbed the dark, rather sinister quiet of the harbor. I knew that landing barges were being lowered all around us—that LCT (landing-craft tanks) and LCI's (landing-craft infantry) and all sorts of other craft were creeping in softly toward the beaches. I knew that the 36th Division, formerly the Texas National Guard, was in close now to the four beaches it was to land on. That was on the right flank, south of us some four miles. Faintly we could hear the sound of engines above, comforting, because we knew that these were Beaufighters, greatest of all night fighters. They were circling out beyond the limits of our convoy. Their job was to intercept enemy aircraft before it reached the convoy. If planes did get through, it was up to our anti-aircraft guns. We knew that there was a protecting screen of cruisers and destroyers around us, listening for submarines.

"As far as subs are concerned," Commander English, in charge of naval planning, had said earlier, "we're as safe as though we were home in our own beds."

It was 3:30 then, and we held our breaths and hoped for the best. But nothing happened—at first. Then from the north, where the British divisions were landing, came flashes of fierce light. No one had been surprised, after all. The enemy coastal guns were in action. In view of the fact that Italy had capitulated, our naval force had orders to hold its fire until the enemy coastal batteries fired. We had three cruisers, The *Boise*, *Philadelphia*, *Savannah*, and a dozen destroyers on the spot. Long golden fingers of flame reached out from their turrets. Shells went shoreward, screaming angrily. Within ten minutes the coastal batteries were quiet. The navy had done its job. The British divisions continued their landing operations.

Now to the south, where the 36th of Texas was landing, we saw disturbing lights. Red tracer bullets, firing low, scorched the black mystery of the night, and we knew that the 36th was catching hell. Men in the operations room sat looking at the three teletype screens which told them what was happening ashore. Every possible modern mode of communication was being used here, with our ship the nerve center of the whole show. There had been a miscalculation. The enemy had checkmated us on the right flank by laying a wide mine field in shallow water where we had expected a narrow one. It was well in-shore and it covered the red, green, yellow, blue beaches where the 36th was landing.

This large area had to be cleared before the big ships carrying the bulk of the 36th could move in. In the darkness the sweepers began their difficult job. Meanwhile, machine-gun fire blanketed the beaches. Men who had landed hurriedly scooped out slit trenches with their tin hats to get some cover.

News came that the Rangers had taken Maiori and that the Commandos had captured their objective—near-by Vietri. But in every message received in the operations room from shore there was the disturbing phrase, "Opposition strong." This was no walk-in, no pushover. We were against experienced German troops, and none of our men, except the Commandos, had ever been in serious combat before. Standing there on deck I looked toward the south or right flank, watching the gunfire and feeling bad about the 36th. We didn't have an army on that shore—we had a bunch of youngsters, that's all. When their artillery and their ammunition and their anti-aircraft stuff arrived—then they'd be an army. But that heavy stuff couldn't go through until the mines were swept clear. Suddenly the bugle sung its shrill note through the ship's loudspeakers. This was "General Quarters" again. Enemy planes had been spotted coming our way. We didn't hear them, but suddenly four lovely chandelier flares hung in the soft night air less than two thousand feet above us, and we cursed them because we were all a little afraid. Then to our port side and about two miles away our flak rose in brilliant red arcs. It rose from the right and from the left in symmetrical circles with the glowing chandelier flares trapped in the middle, so that the whole effect was of some gaily lit celestial Christmas tree. Then, high above the streaking tracers, the shells of the big guns exploded; but from where I watched they didn't explode—they were merely flickers of golden light. The line of ships parallel to ours began to fire tracers. For a mile there seemed to be a million red, golden, and occasional purple shafts stabbing the heavens.

The noise of the guns went almost unheard, so powerful was the visual effect of the scene.

Bombs dropped close brought one back to reality. Twice our ship shuddered under the impact of near misses. I walked to the starboard side and looked toward the beaches where I knew the kids from Texas had landed. There were flares over them and bombs falling, and I could visualize the kids there trying to keep their stomachs from tying into knots, for it is like that when fear grips you. I knew that on shore those boys were trying to strangle the ache of fear that rose in their throats—that threatened to choke them. Few of them had ever heard a gun fired in anger before. They were undoubtedly bewildered, too. They'd heard that Italy had capitulated. They knew that G-2 had reported two Italian divisions to be in this sector. Yet they were catching hell. From the Italians? They didn't know (we didn't until later) that only twenty-four hours before the two Eyetie divisions had been replaced by two German divisions. These boys on shore were not used to reckless uncertainties, unless it be the minor questions of what to throw a good hitter in a pinch or whether or not to try a pass in one's own territory, on third down. They had never been oriented to fear. No training can do that. Sometimes sustained and successful combat will, to some extent, immunize one against fear—and this helps to quell the physical manifestations of fear—the gray pallor, the hands that feel as though they clutched snowballs, the involuntary twitching of shoulder muscles. But this only comes with long experience. These boys on shore might have that in another month. Not today. They had been well trained; they were good gymnasium fighters, but even years of boxing in a gymnasium doesn't really prepare you for an actual fight. And so they reacted as all inexperienced troops always react. They cursed loudly and futilely into the dark mass of the night, and they shot their silly little tommy guns and pistols at enemy planes perhaps 15,000 feet above them. This, of course, did nothing but reveal their exact position, for even those small flashes could be seen by the German pilots.

There was an hour of this and then a sullen red glow crept over the tops of the jagged mountains back of the beaches and it was dawn.

We breathed more easily now. We knew that 36 P-38s had taken off from Sicilian airports at five o'clock. Seafires from our five carriers would be along as soon as the dawn strengthened, and we knew that our Spitfires and P-51s were now on the way. The Seafires would patrol at 3,000 feet; the P-38s at 10,000 feet and the Spits and P-51s at 20,000 feet. The dawn tumbled over the tops of the mountains and spilled into the harbor, and the whole field of operations was revealed. The 36th had landed on sandy beaches and behind the beaches stretched three miles of scrubby underbrush, good tank country. Then the slope rose at the base of the mountains, growing gradually sharper. The mountain range ended two miles north or to the left of us. That was where the Sele River flowed into the sea. North of that the country looked quite flat.

Reports began to come in from the various beaches. Small LCVI's (landing-craft vehicle infantry) darted all over the harbor acting as messengers. These shallow blunt-nosed craft were disdainful of mines. They only drew four or five feet of water. A message came from the 36th that a line of Mark IV tanks was approaching. Quick orders were given and soon we heard heavy gunfire. The *Savannah* was taking care of the enemy tanks just as she and the *Boise* had done at Gela, Sicily, on D morning when the First Division was so badly belabored by tanks. I stood on deck watching the *Savannah* fire. First a ball of orange fire would blossom on top of the gun turrets; then a puff of black smoke would cover it, and five seconds later our ship would shiver slightly and we'd hear the dull boom of the guns. Sound travels a mile in five seconds, which meant that we were one mile from the cruiser. The tanks turned back, leaving five in flames. A feature of both the Sicilian invasion and this one has been the remarkable accuracy of the naval gunfire, especially remarkable in view of the fact that they seldom saw their targets. The fire was actually directed from the shore by spotters.

After the Sicilian show we had a press conference with Admiral Cunningham. Cunningham, like Eisenhower, is always remarkably frank in press conferences. On this occasion someone asked him if he had been surprised by the accurate shooting of the American ships.

"Not at all," he said, his eyes twinkling. "I wasn't surprised —but the army was."

The Commandos sent back discouraging news. They had been dislodged from Vietri by the 16th Panzer Division. The tommy guns, the hand grenades, the knives carried by Commandos aren't of much use against tanks, and the artillery support which they had expected hadn't arrived.

Once again the alert sounded, but we didn't worry—we had faith in our air cover during daylight hours. We looked hopefully skyward and saw our Seafires patrolling sedately— there were thirteen of them at about 6,000 feet. Then, incredibly, came the scream of a bomb and then another. A half mile away we saw two huge fountains of water rise high on either side of a destroyer. The water hid the ship for a moment, and we wondered if it had been hit. We sighed with relief as it emerged from the spray intact. That shook our faith slightly in the invincibility of our air cover, and the events of the next few days shook that faith still more, and made us realize that a perfect air cover is absolutely impossible.

The sun was bright and it was warm here in the harbor. Too warm. We stripped off shirts but kept our life belts

buckled on and wore our tin hats. You couldn't look anywhere without seeing a hundred ships. They were waiting
for that mine field to be swept. There were huge troop ships,
cruisers, destroyers, flak ships, monitors, fat supply ships, and
LCT's and LCI's and small MTB's looking mighty pert alongside the big ships. I went down to the operations room again
and sat staring at the teletype. A message was coming in from
the beach where the 36th had its headquarters. In capital
letters the message clicked out: "LST 386 STRUCK MINE.
BEACHED. LARGE HOLE SIDE BUT SEAWORTHY. THREE DEAD
SEVEN WOUNDED. LST 375 HIT BY SHELL FIRE WHILE BEACHING.
TEN WOUNDED. LST 357 HIT BY SHELL FIRE WHILE BEACHING.
FOUR DEAD FORTY-EIGHT WOUNDED. MINOR STRUCTURAL DAM-
AGE. ON WHAT BEACH SHALL WE PUT OUR DEAD?"

The messages went on and the thought I'd been trying to
banish since H hour came back and now I couldn't ignore it.
Would this be another Dieppe or another Gallipoli? I had
been through one Dieppe and its tragedy, and hated the
thought of another. I kept my eyes on the teletype and then
started. The most amazing message was pecking its way
across the screen: "THERE ONCE WAS A YOUNG BULL NAMED
FERDINAND. FERDINAND LIKED TO SMELL FLOWERS . . ." Then
after a silence came the message, "ONLY PRACTICING. ONLY
PRACTICING." There was an operator I'd like to know!

I went on deck. For the moment no sounds of gunfire came
from shore. For the moment it was a peaceful scene. A cool
breeze was coming offshore. Most of the ships were anchored
now. A British monitor was moving half a mile off our port
bow. She was moving slowly and then suddenly her stern
lifted as though pushed up by some giant hand and a quick
bright flash hid her for a moment; then smoke billowed out,
covered her and hung there lazily. The breeze took it then,
and the ship pushed out of the smoke. Her stern was down,
but she moved steadily on as near-by craft hurried to her side.
She had struck one of the mines the sweepers hadn't picked

up. She was hurt but not fatally. Her two 15-inch guns still pointed toward the shore, and her ack-ack guns, her 40's and 20's stuck their black impudent noses skyward.

The ship's chaplain, Lieutenant Ballinger, said Mass at 4:30 in the afternoon on the gun deck, and his altar was flanked by open turrets which held the 40 millimeter guns. More than a hundred men stood and knelt on the steel deck. Four men received communion. One was a Negro mess boy still in his white coat; another was a sailor in blue denim; a third was a corporal in battle dress and the fourth was an American general with two stars on his shoulders. Everyone was pretty solemn.

At the end of the Mass, Lieutenant Ballinger said special prayers, part of a Novena to the Blessed Virgin. One of the prayers said by both priest and congregation seemed apropos.

Remember, O most compassionate Virgin Mary, that never was it known that anyone who fled to thy protection, implored thy assistance or sought thy intercession, was left unaided. Inspired with this confidence, we fly unto thee, O Virgin of Virgins, our Mother; to thee we come; before thee we kneel, sinful and sorrowful. O Mother of the Word Incarnate, despise not our petitions, but in thy clemency hear and answer them. Amen.

I think everyone there (more than half were non-Catholics) meant that prayer. Prayer is like a lifebelt we forget about until there is danger of drowning. Then we cling to it desperately. When danger threatens, prayers which you've forgotten come to mind. A few bombs drop close, a few shells scream overhead, and quite instinctively you find yourself praying and meaning it. It's like that with almost every man I know. Even complete unbelievers pray in tough spots. They laugh it off afterwards by saying, "It's just a little insurance I was taking out. I don't believe there's anything to it, but hell, maybe I could be wrong. And it doesn't do any harm does it?" The truth, of course, is that even the most rabid anti-Christ cannot fool himself when death is sending messengers to his particular front. All pretense and sham go then. You're alone with your fear.

Father Ballinger confirmed all this when I talked to him later. Many non-Catholics in the crew had gone to his cabin (which was always open) before the action began. Ballinger himself had been torpedoed during the North African invasion. He had been picked up by this ship of ours and because it had no chaplain the captain made him stay aboard. His first job was an odd one for a Catholic priest to perform. While the ship had been unloading at Casablanca it had been bombed and two Arabs working on the unloading had been injured. The ship finally pulled out with them aboard. One recovered but the other died. Admiral Kirk was on the ship then, and he told Chaplain Ballinger to hold funeral services over the dead man who would be buried at sea. In vain the chaplain protested that an Arab, being a Mohammedan, was, in the eyes of the church, a non-believer and the Catholic funeral service was not designed to send heathen Arabs heavenwards. Besides, the Arab himself would not have liked it.

But the Admiral was adamant and Lieutenant Ballinger had to obey orders. He solved the difficulty with ingenuity. He remembered that in the Good Friday Mass there was a special prayer (in Latin) for infidels. They wrapped the dead Arab in white sheets, draped an American flag around him and slid him into the Mediterranean while Chaplain Ballinger solemnly said the prayer for infidels. Everyone was happy. Everyone, that is, except the other Arab. His wounds had healed and he watched the sea burial of his pal with envy. He wasn't envying him his home in the Mediterranean depths. He was envying the white shroud which covered the dead man and he asked if he couldn't please have one like it.

Aboard U. S. S. Ancon, *September, 1943*

****

Chapter XVII

BLOODY SALERNO

WE KNEW NOW that we were going to be forced to fight for every bit of ground we took on shore. We reviewed the landings and tried to find out what mistakes had been made. The plan had been followed faithfully; the schedule had been closely adhered to. We learned that the airborne troops who were to have been dropped near Rome to grab two airports had not left Sicily. This part of the show had been called off forty minutes before it had been scheduled to begin. Evidently the High Command had felt that the Italians themselves might take over the airports near Rome and that the presence of the airborne troops would have been superfluous. However, the Eyeties evidently weren't doing much except sit on the fence and watch the performance.

We had been told that a naval bombardment would precede the actual landings, but no such bombardment had taken place. An hour of blasting by the cruisers and destroyers we had with us might have softened those defenses up a bit. Still, most of the German 88's were on high ground, hidden in stone or concrete emplacements hard to find and harder to hit. Even so, we wished that the naval guns had gone to work. Perhaps that part of the operation had been called off because of the new relationship with Italy. Apparently, we didn't want to run the risk of killing too many Italians. None of us felt very friendly toward the Eyeties at the moment. In Libya, in North Africa and in Sicily our men had found them to be treacherous, especially when taken prisoner. It will be a long time before we feel any brotherly love toward the Eyeties.

D Day was beautiful. The air was soft and the skies were clear, except when the raiders came, and then the sky was pockmarked with ugly black bursts where shells from our anti-aircraft guns exploded. Either our aim was very bad or the Germans were good at evasive tactics. They'd been over us five times during the day, but we hadn't been granted the welcome sight of a single one of them plunging seaward, trailing black plumes of smoke.

General Clark was anxious to get ashore, but with things in such an unsettled state he had to remain in the operations room where he could be in constant touch with his officers on the beach, with his air and naval commanders, with fighter headquarters in Sicily and with General Eisenhower and his staff back in North Africa.

Late in the afternoon the mine sweepers finally finished their job of clearing that mine field in front of the right flank beaches. Now the big LST's began moving and that made us feel better. Once those tanks were ashore our men would have something better than tommy guns in their hands. The portable hospitals would be set up and kitchens established. The men ashore had gone through a bad twelve hours, but now things would, we felt, be better.

It was a long day but finally the night fell over the Bay of

Salerno as suddenly as though someone had dropped a blanket from above.

We forgot the operation for one brief hour while we had a good dinner. The cheerful Negro mess boys, supremely unconscious of danger, joked among themselves and confidentially urged "seconds" on us. After dinner we listened to the news on the radio. We heard that the Italian fleet was surrendering. Then BBC came on with the news of our operation. The announcer hadn't said a dozen words when the alert screeched through the ship's loudspeakers. But we waited to hear the last of the news.

"On the whole," the smug voice from the loudspeaker said, "the operation in the Bay of Salerno is going according to plan. There is some opposition, but our men have landed and beachheads have been established. Our air cover is keeping the Luftwaffe away and . . ." The ship lurched as though some playful undersea giant had pushed it. She trembled, and your ears rang with the concussion of a bomb that had fallen close; then our guns spit angrily into the void of the night.

A British pilot, who had bailed out that afternoon and had been picked up by us, calmly took off his right shoe and deliberately threw it at the loudspeaker.

"Bloody nonsense," he said and then mimicked, "Our air cover is keeping the Luftwaffe away."

"Listen, chum," an American colonel put his arm around the youngster's shoulders, "take it easy. Just think what our American radio commentators are saying tonight. They're probably saying that the war is over. We're just naturally optimistic people. We know we're getting the hell beat out of us on all sides, but they don't know that at home."

We switched to the German radio. We turned it on loud. The excellent music the Nazi radio provides (mostly from American records) almost drowned the sound of the guns. When they put on a Bing Crosby recording of an old but lovely song, "Time on My Hands," I laughed and thought of how the Growler would feel if he knew that the German radio was broadcasting him. I know of no finer American than the Growler or anyone who has given more time to the war effort than he. Now the Germans were using him to attract audiences. This, I thought, would be one to tell Bob Hope whom I had left in Algiers a few days before. That is, if there was anything left of Hope when I returned. He'd been giving four and five shows a day now for a month in Sicily and North Africa. Hope and Crosby—it was good to think of genuine, down-to-earth men like that, here in this godforsaken Bay of Salerno.

Part of the wardroom had been taken over by the doctors and their assistants. Wire basket stretchers were piled high, grim reminders that this fight was for keeps. A table in front of the doctor held shiny scalpels, saws, bandages, gauze, tincture of Merthiolate, liquid green soap, sutures, morphine needles—loaded. Instinctively, when you passed you averted your eyes.

"No customers yet, Doc?" I asked, in rather bad taste.

"No," he said, and added slowly, "I hope to God I don't get any."

"Do you medicos really feel that way?" I asked him.

"Of course," he snapped. "I know every boy on this ship."

When there was an alert the Negro mess boys ran to their battle stations. Their job in combat was to pass the ammunition. But five stayed to act as stretcher bearers—in case. They sat at a table, playing rummy.

"Man, oh man, I got you murdered," the tall boy who waited on my table laughed. "Looka that hand."

They laughed and sometimes cursed at bad hands and sometimes the guns made so much noise that you couldn't hear them. I looked at them in amazement. This was a time for any sensible man to be frightened. These happy-go-lucky Negro boys either didn't realize how tough things were or they were impervious to fear.

"Don't you guys know those are bombs we hear?" I said to one of them.

"Ain't nothing we can do about it, Mister," one of them grinned.

They were over us five times that night. The whole crew was now on four-hour shifts, but during General Quarters all men had to be at battle stations so that no man on board got more than one hour of solid sleep at a time. One of the raids was bad. About 10 P.M. an LCT was taking on gasoline from a tanker. Suddenly the LCT burst into flames; somehow or other the gas had caught fire. The ship was only two hundred yards from us when this happened. Within two minutes the tanker had cast off and had put some distance between her and the burning craft, and had hoses directed on her. It was fast work, but it couldn't save the ship. Then the alert sounded. Bombers have a habit of aiming at flames. This flaming ship offered a beautiful target and the target was only two hundred yards from us. The bombers wasted no time. They dropped flares but they really didn't need the flares. Then came the bombs. Somehow or other two small craft had gotten lines onto the burning ship and they began to tow it out to sea where it wouldn't act as a beacon to guide the bombers. I stood at the rail with Reynolds Packard. We weren't saying much, just watching and involuntarily jerking when the bombs made the ship quiver. Our 20's and our 40's were in action now. The 20's fire very rapidly, like machine guns. They go rat-rat-rat-rat-rat—pause for a moment—and then repeat rat-rat-rat-rat. The 40's are heavier. They fire more deliberately with an interval of perhaps three seconds between shots. They have a dull sound. I found myself banging my fist on the rail, keeping time with the 40's.

"Hear that rhythm, Pack? It sounds just like a rumba."

"Sure, the devil's rumba," Packard said grimly.

"That's a good description of it. If we ever get off this crate I'm going to use it."

"Sure, if we ever get off," he said.

"I don't mind admitting I don't like this. I think it's worse than Dieppe. We were only at Dieppe nine hours. No matter how tough things got we knew we were heading for home at four that afternoon. We may be cooped here for days and days."

"I don't like it either," Packard admitted. "Anyone who does is a damn fool. And anyone who says he isn't scared is a damn liar."

But no one was saying anything like that. We breathed with relief as the burning ship receded into the distance. The flames had died down and then went out altogether. The fire hadn't lasted more than twenty minutes.

"I bet Sully was on the job there," I said to Packard.

"Sully never misses," Pack said. "The guy is a genius."

An hour later I sat in the wardroom with Sully. We had been right. Sully's men had put out the fire; he had undoubtedly saved us and the *Savannah* and *Philadelphia*, which flanked us, from getting hit. Like most naval officers, Sully hates to talk about himself. But I kept asking him questions about salvage work, and Sully is so wrapped up in salvage work that he opened up. We sat there drinking coffee in the wardroom, and I became so engrossed with Sully's talk of ships that had been raised and salvaged that two raids passed and neither of us left the wardroom.

When Casablanca harbor was found to be clogged with ships sunk by bombings, they sent a hurry call for Commodore William Aloysius Sullivan. He was working on the *Normandie* then, but he hotfooted it to North Africa with a bunch of divers he had trained.

"Best crap shooters I ever saw." Sully shook his head

admiringly. "We stopped at Natal for one night. When we took off the next day some of the boys asked me to take care of some money for them. I asked them where they got the money. They were embarrassed, but finally admitted that the army lads at Natal had inveigled them into a crap game. We got to West Africa and the same thing happened. The boys cleaned up there, too. Then we went to Gibraltar and spent a night there. They even got the British shooting craps. Sure my boys won. They couldn't miss. The first thing the boys did when they arrived at Casa was to send money orders home. It was a great trip for them."

These divers had been trained by Sullivan during the raising of the *Normandie*. We were lamentably short of divers and other salvage men, and most of the salvage operations for the navy were conducted by the old firm of Merritt-Chapman and Scott, "a very great organization," according to Sully.

"I used to get hundreds of letters of advice every day when we started work on the *Normandie*," Sully said. "And although most of them were from crackpots, a lot weren't. We read them all, too. The trouble is that each ship to be raised presents a different problem. There's a lot of desk work involved before you get down to the actual work. What kind of bottom is the ship resting on? What are the currents and the tide like? What condition is the hull in? How many portholes has the ship and how many of them are open? How strong is the deck itself because a lot of pressure has to be borne by the deck? These and fifty other factors have to be taken into consideration before you plan your campaign. We made our plans and went ahead. The boys from Merritt-Chapman and Scott did most of the work, and during the operation we trained a lot of divers. It takes time to train a diver, and the *Normandie* was a fine school for them."

Casablanca was in an awful mess when he and his men arrived, but within a week they had cleared enough of the harbor to permit a constant flow of ships to enter and leave. After that came the job of clearing Bizerte.

"That was a tough one," Sully smiled. "There was a rather narrow channel there and a couple of ships had been sunk in it. We couldn't raise them in a hurry, so we decided to really sink them. You can do that when there is a swift current, as there was at Bizerte. We cut the ships into three and then dynamited underneath them. The blast blew a lot of sand away from the bottom of the channel and the swift current washed more of it away and the ships kept on sinking. Yes, we just blew those ships—not up, but down."

He cleared Algiers harbor too, though that was comparatively easy. I'd met Sully first in Algiers. It was a big day for him. To begin with, it was his birthday. A letter and a box of presents had arrived from his wife. Then the official news of his promotion to Commodore had arrived. I remembered that day well because that night we'd had an air raid.

Later I met Sully in Palermo when he was saving the *Mayrand*. That was during an air raid, too. In all, he had a crew of 300 with him. He also had two small salvage ships along.

"When we get to Naples we'll bring a couple of big salvage ships over," he said. "I've got them waiting at Palermo now, but they're too valuable to let hang around this place. We can do any makeshift jobs with what we have here now."

We were joined by Lieutenant John Burns. He was in charge of Sullivan's fire fighters, and it was he who had put the fire out on the LCT. He'd smothered it out, he explained, with foam hoses. Young Burns was no amateur at the business of putting out fires. He had run a fireboat before the war for the New York City Fire Department.

"We've had a lot of casualties among John's men," Sullivan said, shaking his head. "We've been unlucky. We've had better luck with our divers. Haven't lost one yet. The British have lost several. When a diver is underneath, a bomb that drops in the water half a mile away will kill him. The concussion hits him like a ton of bricks."

"I've always felt like jumping overboard when we were being bombed," I told Sully. "Somehow it seemed safer to be in the water."

"You'll only jump overboard once," Sully said dryly. "The concussion will tear you to pieces. Hear that, now . . . Hear that!"

The ship bumped as though it had gone over a rock. Then it shuddered and the vibration made the spoons on the coffee saucers jingle.

"That bomb fell a quarter of a mile away," Sully said. "Maybe half a mile away, yet it made this big ship rock. If the concussion can do that to a huge ship with a steel hull, think what it would do to your body."

"I promise not to jump overboard," I told Sully.

"You better not," he said grimly.

I went down to my cabin. "There's no use trying to sleep," Van said. "Let's go into the petty officers' wardroom. They've always got coffee on the fire."

We went in there and two of the petty officers were arguing as to the relative merits of Frank Sinatra and Bing Crosby. They asked me what I thought.

"Who the hell is Frank Sinatra?" I'd never heard of him.

"Boy, you've been away from home too long. You've missed too many boats." He shook his head sadly. "Sinatra is the hottest thing there is at home right now. Listen to him give."

There was a portable gramophone in the small mess. We drank coffee and listened to the new dream voice. I tried to be fair.

"What do you think of him?" the petty officer said proudly.

[311]

"He's all right," I admitted, "but I'm a Crosby fan, that's all."

General alert sounded and they got to their feet wearily and went to the battle stations. I stayed and read a copy of *Time*. I was pleased to note that the Dodgers were leading the National League. Then I looked at the date. The magazine was two months old.

The night passed somehow, and then came the dawn of D plus one. Everyone was beginning to look a little tired now. It was a soft dawn tinted with crimson and the sea was as calm as cream in a saucer. I stood on deck with Jimmy Sheean for a while.

"There's a nice town called Paestum over there," Sheean said, pointing to the right, back of the beaches where the 36th Division was. "It has some beautiful Hellenic ruins and a lovely temple built in 420 B.C. It has a town wall about three miles around. The walls are nine feet thick. Outside the north gate is the Street of Tombs.

"Then, over to the left, there is a lovely little place called Cava Dei Tirreni," he went on. "It has a beautiful inn with fine food and the best Italian wine you ever tasted. You can get a bus from there to Naples—only takes about an hour."

"Look, Jimmy," I protested. "I know you're a smart guy. I know G-2 and A-2 are smart and have lots of information that the rest of us don't have, but how in hell do you know so much about an obscure little place like Cava Dei Tirreni which isn't even on the map?"

"That's easy," Jimmy said casually. "Eight years ago Diana and I spent our honeymoon there. . . . Look at that, back of the beaches."

About a mile in back of yellow beach a brief golden flash had appeared and then a burst of black smoke. A moment later there was a puff of smoke on the beach. The Germans had guns back there and were shelling the beach.

[312]

"The map shows that there's a railroad running parallel to the beach about a mile back," Sheean said. "I imagine those are railroad guns."

The cruiser *Philadelphia* was lying about two or three hundred yards off our port side. Suddenly her six-inch guns began to fire. One salvo after another went shoreward at those railroad guns—guns mounted probably on flat cars. The *Philadelphia* kept it up for fifteen minutes. Then the guns stopped. We looked toward shore and beyond. There were no further bright golden flashes from the railroad.

"What a navy we've got, Jimmy! What a navy!" I couldn't help yelling.

"It's a great navy," Jimmy said, and we both felt pretty proud.

We were all beginning to realize now that if this show was to be saved the navy was to do the saving. The navy with its ack-ack was keeping the planes high when they came over. The navy was shelling tanks and guns on shore. The navy was doing everything but actually march into Salerno itself. This combined American-British naval force was all under the command of Admiral Sir Andrew Cunningham, but here in the field of operations it was headed by our Admiral Hewitt. So closely did the British and American ships work together that it was impossible to tell where one left off and the other began. They all worked as a single unit under one head. If it hadn't been for these ships our men would have been driven off the beaches by now. Either that or so torn by casualties that they would have been an impotent, defenseless force.

Somehow the day passed and then the long night. We had eight calls to General Quarters that night. I took a sleeping pill and slept through three of them, but Van Alstyne couldn't do that. None of the crew could. Van was looking tired now. Nearly everyone except the indefatigable Sammy

Schulman was tired. Sammy was climbing up masts and gun turrets, getting pictures from all angles.

"I'll be mighty sore if I get knocked off," he said, quite seriously. "That would mean I've done all this work for nothing."

I was standing on the quarter deck at the head of the ladder the next morning. There was a small LCVI (landing-craft vehicle infantry) down at the foot of the ladder. The officer of the deck said the craft was going ashore with some messages from General Clark. It would return in a couple of hours. I decided to go along. I was getting mighty tired of being on an anchored ship; it was too much like impersonating a fish in a barrel. A trip to shore would at least break the monotony. I went down the ladder and hopped into the snub-nosed craft. It was a great relief to be moving. I took off my shirt and when the blunt nose of the boat hit the slight swells, the spray flew high and the sun tinted it with miniature rainbows. We weaved in and out of the anchored ships, heading for yellow beach only two miles away. It was a nice beach with fine white sand extending back from the water for perhaps sixty yards.

Men were unloading supplies from all kinds of craft. The unloading stopped when we heard the scream of aircraft flying very low, but it resumed when we saw that they were Spitfires—four of them. They were patroling up and down the beach at 1,000 feet and very lovely they looked. I slipped off my trousers and shoes and waded out into the clear, cool water. I lay there floating, and it was very peaceful. Beyond the sandy beach there was a large, white farmhouse with a red roof and, beside it, a white-washed granary. A mile back of the beach I could see a collection of houses which I knew to be the very aptly named town of Paestum. We had gotten in there now and, in truth, Paestum had been getting a pasting. Roman ruins don't seem very important when you're invading a country—except as cover against machine-gun fire.

Most of the men unloading were naked. Officers watched them carefully. They had to, lest men from one outfit grab supplies assigned to another outfit. Our army is great for that. Our lads would steal a battleship if they could get away with it. At night every jeep driver removes the magneto from his car. Otherwise his jeep would be gone. Our boys don't call it stealing—they call it "moonlight requisitioning."

I waded ashore and let the sun dry me. A jeep came along and an officer hopped out. He had cigarettes with him. The men who were unloading the barges gave a yell of joy as they scrambled for the cigarettes. He had perhaps a dozen cartons with him and each man got one package. I never saw men perk up as these youngsters on the beach did when those cigarettes arrived. When you're smoking a cigarette you get an illusion of normalcy, which helps.

"How has it been, soldier?" I asked one of the men.

"Pretty lousy," he said ruefully. "We've had two bad nights, but they dropped most of the bombs in the harbor. We've been watching them drop out there. Have they got your ship yet?"

I told him it hadn't been hit yet.

"Clarkie is on that, isn't he? I hope they don't get the old man. He's all right."

"If you guys could get set here on shore he'd have his headquarters here by now," I told him. Several of the others had gathered around.

"We're lucky we're still on the beach," one of them said. "Yesterday I woulda bet we'd be pushed off. I guess if it hadn't been for the navy we'd of been a lot of dead geese by now."

"Listen," another broke in. "How far have the Limeys got? Are they anywhere near yet?"

I shook my head. "They're a good hundred miles away. They weren't supposed to be on this part of the show anyhow. They were supposed to head for the Foggia plains on the other side of Italy. But I hear the plans have shifted and they're on the way to join you here."

"My God, I hope so," one of them said fervently. "We could use that Eighth Army."

"That's fine talk," I couldn't help but kid him. "Do you mean to say you big brave Yanks have to be taken care of by those Limeys you're always needling?"

They laughed a little and then one of them said, "Yeah, that was before we seen them fight. What the hell, a guy can be wrong, can't he? I'd love to look up right now and see that funny black hat of Monty's. Yeah man, nobody can ever make a crack to me about those Limeys. All I know is they can fight like hell."

I'd seen this happen again and again. Back in London there was very little friendliness between the British and American troops. They met in pubs and quarreled, and they met at dances and tried to grab each other's girls. The Americans (some of them) were boastful and the British resentful. Because they met only in pubs or at dances there was no firm ground on which to base any feeling of mutual respect. Then the idiots (American and British) who constantly told them that they must get along together and act like brothers only antagonized them further. But then came the North African campaign. Kassarine Pass especially showed our own troops that they didn't know everything, after all. It taught them that they were only amateurs in this game at which the British had worked for nearly four years. Then they saw the job done by Montgomery and his Eighth. They saw the RAF in action and saw the British Navy work. This was an England they hadn't seen in pubs and dance halls in London. These Limeys were tough as hell, they found out, and cruel when they had to be and yet, when it was all over, they laughed it off and refused to take bows. The performance of the Eighth in Sicily sealed this new feeling of respect and this was a typical manifestation of it.

I spent a couple of hours on the beach with the men. There were few signs of the shelling and bombing of the past forty-eight hours. A few landing barges were leaning drunkenly on their sides, but that was all. My barge was ready to pull out so I climbed aboard.

On the way back the three kids running the ship had a lot of fun. They played cowboys and Indians, using floating crates and boxes as Indians. "There's one," one of them would yell and the other two would pop at it with their Colts. They love those Colts because they never jam. They peppered every crate in the Bay of Salerno. The accuracy left much to be desired and then one of them, disgusted, sat behind the 20 mm. gun and started blasting away with that.

"There's a better target," I yelled to him. Two hundred yards in front of us was a submarine flying the Italian flag. It was heading for our command ship. The boy at the gun looked very wistful. He sighted the sub carefully. Twelve members of the crew were standing at attention on deck. They were immaculate in white uniforms and blue berets. The kid behind the gun wailed, "Oh, my God, what I could do to them!"

"It might cause some slight trouble if you shot them," I suggested mildly.

"Yeah, I guess you're right," he said regretfully.

We arrived back at our ship to find the Eyetie sub tied up to us. Its captain had come in to surrender. Our crew was leaning over the rail and the Italian-speaking members of our crew were having a lot of fun shouting down to the grinning men on the deck of the submarine. Later in the afternoon I climbed down a ladder to see what the sub was like. The best thing about being on the *Ancon* was the fact that Shapiro, Packard, Schulman and I really were allowed the run of the ship. We could do just about anything we wished. We were on and off the bridge all day and bouncing into Hewitt's cabin or General Clark's operations room at all hours. The ship had no secrets from us, and we felt rather proud that we were being trusted so implicitly. I was amazed to find the interior of the sub almost as clean as our own ship. The twenty-four-year-old captain smiled and welcomed me aboard in almost perfect English. A small brown dog barked joyously at his heels.

"You know," the captain said quite seriously, "I hadn't fired a torpedo for five weeks. Then I got the order not to fire on any American or British ships. An hour after I got that order, what happened? This big fat convoy passed within a mile of where I had surfaced. Oh, it was a great temptation."

"I'm glad you weren't trigger happy," I told him, "like so many of our kids."

The expression "trigger happy" was too much for him. I explained that our gunners in the heat of battle quite often banged away at any target in sight.

A grinning, white-coated Negro mess boy from our ship came down the narrow ladder with a huge tray. "With the captain's compliments, sir," he said, and placed the tray on the table. The sub captain blinked when he saw the huge Virginia ham. The small dog smelled the ham and started leaping toward it. The mess boy patted him, and the dog loved it.

"You want a dog?" the Eyetie sub captain asked the mess boy.

"Ahm a man who loves dawgs," the Negro said happily. "And, Captain, Ah means that dawgs loves me too."

"We have four puppies aboard," the captain said. "If you'd like one, take him."

He took us into the crew's sleeping quarters and there on

a blanket were four incredibly small brown-and-white puppies. The mess boy grabbed one and cradled it in his hand.

"Sir, from now on you is our mascot," he grinned. "And Lordy, Lordy, how we need a mascot! From now on your name is Sir."

"What kind of a name is that for a dog?" I asked.

"We call everyone Sir," the Negro boy laughed. "Why not call this hound dawg Sir, too? It's one name we won't forget."

We took the puppy back with us. The news in the operations room wasn't good. We had captured an airport at Montecavido near Salerno. A Spitfire had landed there and had no sooner stopped than an 88 from a German gun up in the hills had blasted it into eternity. We had laid two mesh strips on flat land back of Paestum to use as runways. It was all right for an emergency landing field, but that was all. Our air protection would still have to come from Sicily, 180 miles away. This whole operation was assuming the proportions of another Gallipoli. It was touch and go whether we'd be thrown out entirely. Our casualties were heavy because the Germans held the high ground and could pour down a withering fire at us.

That afternoon four tired but cheerful-looking figures climbed up the gangway. They were Captain Charles Andrews, Commander John Kramer, Lieutenant Douglas Fairbanks, Jr., and John Steinbeck. They had pulled off a real Dick Tracy stunt. Everything had gone according to plan—that is nearly everything. They had captured the island of Ventotene.

"They told us there would be Eyeties on the island but no Germans," Steinbeck laughed. "So six of us landed in a whale boat, not worrying much about opposition. We hit one beach and tossed our flashlights on it and shouted back and forth to each other that this was a bum place to land.

Then we went a couple of hundred yards to the right and found another place which wasn't so good. After four tries we found a good place, and went ashore and found a force of ninety-one Germans there. But what with all the noise we made and the light from our flashlights they thought we were a big force and they retreated to the town hall and barricaded themselves in. Well, the six of us couldn't really surround the place so we yelled for some help and, after a while, a few of the lads showed up and that was that."

"How did John Kramer behave?" I asked.

"He wasn't with us," Steinbeck grinned. "John took a PT boat and went out hunting. You know what he did? Hell, he sunk a 5,000-ton ammunition ship. There were a few E boats around too and they made a dash for John's PT boat, but John fooled them. Instead of running away he ran right toward the sinking ammo ship and they went on by him. So he got away. It was a lot of fun. How has it been here?" Steinbeck asked.

"It's been lovely here, oh, just lovely, John."

"We heard you'd been getting a pasting," he grinned.

"Stick around tonight, you'll see."

"The Skipper has other plans," John said. "He has his eye on another island. He wants to go after it tonight."

It was good to sit around just dishing with Andrews and Kramer and Douglas and John. Andrews is a fine naval officer, calm, experienced, objective. The others were like racehorses at the barrier. They couldn't wait to get going again.

"How do you like our navy, John?" I asked Steinbeck.

"Oh, it's a hell of a navy," Steinbeck said. "It's great to be with them, isn't it?"

I agreed. I was rapidly falling in love with our navy myself.

"I wish Jim and John McClain had been with us," Fairbanks said. "They would have loved it."

My brother Jim and John McClain were old friends of Fairbanks. Both were naval lieutenants.

"If Jim and John had been along," I said nonchalantly, "the skipper wouldn't have needed you and Kramer and those other guys."

We sat in the wardroom, drinking coffee, while Captain Andrews went into a huddle with Admiral Hewitt. Andrews came out, beaming. "We're off boys," he said. "Now let's see those maps."

Late that afternoon a group of prisoners came aboard. Some were from the island captured by Captain Andrews and his little force. Others had been captured on the beaches and had been brought to our ship for questioning. They stood on the gun deck waiting their turn, and it would be so nice to report that they looked poorly fed, dejected, relieved to be out of it, and completely convinced that Germany's cause was lost. I'd like to be able to say that, but it would be completely untrue. They were well-clothed, well-fed, smiling a bit patronizingly at us, completely confident and merely a bit downcast at what they considered their bad luck in being captured. We are not allowed to question prisoners without their consent. The Geneva Conference laid down that rule and it is strictly enforced.

I offered the six Germans cigarettes. They took them eagerly and gratefully. I explained that I was not an officer but a war correspondent and that they didn't have to talk to me or answer any questions if they didn't wish. They knew the rules, all right, but they didn't mind, they added. Where had I learned my German? one asked, smiling. When I told him I'd worked in Berlin for nearly a year and had gone back again for a shorter trip they laughed understandingly. Berlin German is the worst in the world and to them this explained my atrocious grammar, scanty vocabulary and horrible accent. They talked very freely and told me they didn't mind if I used what they said. I was careful to have them repeat that to Reynolds Packard and Sammy Schulman, who were standing by. I won't mention their names as that might embarrass them later on when they are exchanged.

They said some amazing things and their sincerity couldn't be doubted. One of them who had been captured on the island of Ventotene said that he and his fellow soldiers were amazed to see Americans. They had been told that there were no Americans in the Mediterranean theatre, that all had left after the Tunisian campaign.

"Who do you think captured Sicily?" I asked him.

"We heard that the Arabs under British officers had occupied Sicily," he answered. "But there was no fighting there, was there? Our troops found they had no use for Sicily and merely evacuated the place."

Their reason for not thinking any Americans were left in the Mediterranean theatre was that they had been told that the U boats formed a chain all the way from New York to Gibraltar and that no ships had been able to get past them. They believed this implicitly. Sammy Schulman, who really understood and talked German, was also convinced that these men were sincere and not putting on an act for our benefit. Two of them were stupid peasant types, quite incapable of any artifice or acting.

"Has New York been badly bombed?" one of them asked politely.

I told him that New York was still intact, and he smiled at me, unbelieving. When I added that I had only come from Moscow a few months before and that Moscow had never really been bombed either, they broke into incredulous smiles and two of them laughed outright.

"We know that Moscow is in ruins," one said seriously. "We have seen the moving pictures of it."

Perhaps clever Dr. Goebbels had shown pictures of Stalingrad and had labeled the pictures Moscow. The Russians had just begun their summer offensive, but these men hadn't heard of it and didn't believe it when I told them how many miles forward the Red Army had pushed. One of the men from the island had been a ground mechanic. I asked him what the Nazi pilots thought of our aircraft.

"Fair," he said carelessly. "You have no fighters to compare with our Focke-Wulf 190. We don't worry about your fighters at all except, perhaps, the Beaufighters, which are pretty good at night. Your Flying Fortresses are good, but they only carry 1,000 pounds of bombs. That isn't much."

Our Forts, of course, carry a great deal more than 1,000 pounds of bombs, but I couldn't convince my German pal of that. Most of them had a completely lopsided picture of the war. They had not heard of Italy's capitulation and did not believe it when I told them.

I asked if they hadn't seen the Eyetie submarine tied up to our starboard side. They shrugged their shoulders and said of course, they knew it was a submarine that we had captured or it was a British submarine flying an Eyetie flag. One of the men who had been captured on the beach talked for the first time. He was a tall, blond, good-looking Bavarian who had been in one of the tanks that the *Savannah* had blasted the day before. He was not quite as naive as the others about recent events, but he had been in Sicily.

"We were a little worried," he confessed, "when you landed the other morning. We thought it might be the Seventh Army. But when we saw that it was the Fifth we were much relieved."

"Why?"

He said, "We knew the Seventh was a tough army, like the Eighth, but the Fifth is a new, inexperienced army."

"You have a lot of respect for the Seventh?"

He nodded, "Yes," he said simply. "It is a good army. Just like the Eighth. But you haven't many divisions here."

"I don't know how many divisions we have," I told him. "But we have enough to hold the Mediterranean, I think."

He smiled deprecatingly. "Yes, you have won the battle of the Mediterranean, you and the British. We are beaten in the Mediterranean, but that isn't important. Wait until you try to invade Germany. Then you will see."

"I suppose the war will just begin for us then," I suggested.

"Yes, yes," he repeated. "The big war will start when you try to invade Germany. Sure, the war has just begun."

"I agree with you," I said quite honestly.

I had been talking to the prisoners on the quarter deck at the head of the gangway. At night some 300 soldiers slept here on cots and bed rolls. Now they were standing, held back by officers, looking at the German prisoners. A big sergeant beckoned to me, and I left the prisoners and walked over to him.

"I'd like to get at them. I'd like to get at them," the sergeant mumbled.

"You'll be ashore in a day or two and you'll have your chance," I said, and walked away. I wasn't disturbed though. This hatred was good; it was healthy. It meant that our men were finally realizing what they were fighting against. They were fighting against men who had murdered Poland and Czechoslovakia and Holland and Belgium and Norway; they were fighting men who, but for a lucky accident of geography, would have murdered us and our country long ago. To beat Germans you have to hate Germans. The conquered countries never hated fascism enough until it was too late. I have said this before and have been called a disciple of hate. Gentle preachers have reminded me that Christ taught no such philosophy of hatred. But I recall that when Christ arose in his righteous anger and flogged the money lenders from the temple, he didn't do it with honeyed phrases. There was honest hatred in his heart for the deceit and the lying he found in the temple and it found expression in the fury of the physical attack he made on the false priests. So many Americans think that it is all right to hate Japan, but it is unchristian to hate Germany. These people have never seen Coventry or Plymouth or London the morning after a raid; they have never seen armless and legless children living half lives in English hospitals; they have never seen the hideous, emaciated bodies of the starved you find in such cities as Vyazma and Kharkov after the Germans have left. When you've seen such sights you find it very easy to hate the Germans, and I don't mean any small clique of German leaders—I mean the 60,000,-000 or more Germans who are fighting this war.

The sergeant, of course, was utterly wrong in wishing to kill those prisoners. Actually we treat our prisoners exceptionally well. We live up to the spirit and the letter of the Geneva Conference. But I liked his spirit. It would make him a better fighter once he got ashore. I have, in the course of the past three years, talked to perhaps a hundred German prisoners. I have never, literally never, met one who was not a completely unregenerate Nazi, a fervent disciple of Hitler and a thorough believer in the eventual German victory. I have talked to British and American Intelligence officers whose sole job it was to question prisoners, and they said the same thing. It is seldom they told me that a prisoner has anything but supreme contempt and hatred for us and our democratic ideals.

One of the prisoners had been brought aboard with a bad body wound. A bullet had hit him in the back and had gone entirely through him—a wound that usually results in quick death. But our doctors on the beach had, to use the doctors' phrase, "sealed him up," and now he was down in our sick bay. The ship's doctor asked Sammy Schulman to do some translating for him. Each prisoner of war is asked to fill out a questionnaire. He wanted this wounded prisoner, who was resting easily now, to do that. I went down to the sick bay with Sammy. One of the questions asked was, "What is your religion?" I asked the doctor why he asked prisoners for that information.

"We treat our prisoners so well," he said, "that if they die we give them a burial service according to the rules of the church to which they belong. And we also furnish them with chaplains."

Sammy and I looked down at the wounded man. He, too, had been in one of the tanks that had been hit. He had escaped from his tank and was running when one of our men got him with a rifle bullet. Somehow, you wanted to feel sorry for him, lying there with deep lines furrowing his lean, hard face, but the coldness and malignant gleam in his eye kept your sympathy welled within you. He had just finished some chicken broth. He had been given the merciful injections of morphine, and a really fine doctor was constantly at his bedside. Yet, as he lay there silently, he somehow or other managed to convey his hatred and contempt for us. Sammy was very gentle in his questioning. He talked to him soothingly; he laid a package of cigarettes beside him. Sammy said he'd get him some chocolate if he wished it and, if he wanted brandy, the doctor had some. Sammy Schulman of New York City was as decent and as fine to this sullen, black-eyed Nazi as he would have been to a wounded American.

"You're a hell of a Jew, Sammy boy," I whispered to him. Sammy looked at me indignantly and said, "What the hell, the guy is wounded, isn't he?" Then Sammy told him about the questionnaire and asked him some questions. When he came to the question, "What is your religion?" the wounded man lifted his head a little and spit out, "Put down Nazism."

Then, sinking back, he rasped, *"Ich bin immer ein National Socialist. Heil, Hitler!"*

"Take it easy," Sammy said soothingly in German. "You'll be all right. Just relax—forget the war. You'll be well taken care of. I'll be back to see if you need anything."

We went out and climbed up on deck again. "He's a very tough guy, Sammy."

"He is," Sammy said, "but our guys are tough, too."

"This fellow knows what he is fighting for, all right. He isn't fighting for souvenirs."

"Our guys aren't fighting for souvenirs any more either," Sammy said.

Sammy and I stood at the rail. Once again General Quarters sounded, but by now we were all so weary that we ignored it. There was nothing we could do, except wear our life-belts and tin hats. The *Savannah*, the sun glinting on her gun barrels, was approaching us from aft. Evidently she was changing her anchorage. The cruisers did that occasionally, knowing that previous raiders had taken pictures and had the more valuable ships spotted.

"I wish we were on the *Savannah*," I told Sammy. "She, at least, was built to stand a beating. If we have many more near misses these plates of ours are sure to loosen up."

"Cy Peterman is on the *Savannah*," Sammy said. Peterman represents the *Philadelphia Inquirer*. He had been rather badly wounded in the Tunisian campaign, but was all right now.

The *Savannah* was abreast of us now, only about two hundred yards to starboard, and then it happened. There was no warning, no scream as the bomb plunged down. There was merely a sharp sheet of flame thrusting itself upwards from the forward No. 3 gun turret of the *Savannah*. We stood there frozen—unbelieving. The flame must have shot eighty feet into the air and then, as it receded, men who had been blown skyward fell with it, mingling with the flame and the orange smoke that turned to oily black as the flame died. The *Savannah* kept steaming slowly but her bow was low in the water. An orange ball of flame burst out of the turret and it seemed to dance there for a moment; and then the smoke billowed over it, hiding the forward part of the ship. This didn't seem real. It was a scene from a movie; something done with miniature boats in a miniature sea; those figures that had merged with the flame as it surged upwards weren't, couldn't be, men. I found myself gripping the rail so hard that my wrists ached. The *Savannah* steamed on and then turned across our bow. She turned and came past our port. I rushed to that side of the ship. The flames were licking upward from the gun turret like nervous fingers reaching and bending and reaching out again. I tried not to think of what was happening on that deck only two hundred yards away. The *Savannah* circled our stern and again slid past our port side. Again she was parallel to us and then another wall of flame and smoke burst from her a second before the explosion.

"Jesus, that's her magazine," a sailor muttered next to me. "That's exploded. The loading room got it . . ."

Perhaps a minute and a half had passed. Already I could see men with hoses playing water on the forward turrets. Sullivan brushed by me with three of his men. They stepped into a small craft that was standing by at the foot of the gangway. It hurried away. All sorts of small craft hurried to the side of the stricken cruiser. Some stopped to pick men from the water. The bow was quite low now. Seafires were buzzing overhead—two minutes late. Someone said it was a Dornier that had dropped that bomb, a Dornier with wings painted silver; he'd seen them flashing at about 12,000 feet just before the bomb dropped. Someone else said he had seen the bomb.

"But it didn't fall like bombs do," he said, bewildered. "I saw it all the way. It raced. It came down like a shell. It just didn't fall like they do. You could hardly see it."

"Maybe a rocket bomb," I suggested. I'd heard that the Germans were using rocket bombs. The advantage in this lay in the fact that the bomb gathered enough speed to make it armor piercing. Gravity plus the momentum of the rockets attached would give such a bomb the impact of a shell.

I looked for Sammy Schulman. He was there with his camera pointed toward the *Savannah*, but she was still steaming away from us—nearly half a mile away now.

"Did you get the explosion, Sammy?" I asked him.

"Yes," he said, without satisfaction. "I hope Cy is all right."

"Would he have been up forward, do you think? He might have been on the bridge. Or he might have been in the wardroom. Sammy, I know the *Savannah*. I've been on it in Algiers. The wardroom is forward just behind those gun turrets."

"I hope to God Cy is all right," Sammy said. "Was Herbert Matthews on it too?"

"No. Herbert was on a destroyer."

"Those poor guys," Sammy said. "Those poor guys."

Nobody on the deck looked natural. Until now we'd all kidded a lot about the near misses we'd had. Nobody said anything. Everyone, I think, felt useless, hopeless. We'd just seen a great many Americans killed—we had no way of knowing how many—and we were all stunned. In fiction, men would be looking skyward, shaking fists at the enemy planes and swearing. It wasn't like that at all. I walked aft. I sat there with the crew of our five-inch gun. The men were sitting behind their gun, not saying anything.

"Did you see it?" I asked, after a while.

"We saw it," one of them said. "But there were four

Spits or Seafires off the port side, and we were told to lay off. We might of got the son of a bitch, too," he said thoughtfully. "It must be something new they got. No Dornier I ever saw went that fast. It got clean away from the fighters. It was the only plane that got through. How the hell it made that direct hit, I don't know. You couldn't make a hit like that in practice."

"It must be a radio-controlled bomb," another said.

"I never heard of a radio-controlled bomb," I told him.

"Me either." He never dropped his eyes from the sky or lowered his hands from the gun. "But it could be. That hit wasn't natural. It was too good."

I went midship to the wardroom. Everyone was talking in subdued tones. Someone turned on the radio, and it was swing music, and everyone looked at the radio and the man who'd turned it on muttered, "Sorry," and turned it off again. The mess boys were fixing the tables, but they weren't grinning now. We'd all just attended a funeral of God knows how many men and everyone from Admiral Hewitt down to the youngest mess boy felt the same. Well, you don't feel natural at a funeral even if you don't know the dead man. After a while we stopped talking of the *Savannah* and rather elaborately began talking of other things. We answered each other mechanically, not really listening.

One of the air-force officers came from the operations room and sat with us. He looked tired. He and a few others had the job of directing the air show from the *Ancon* and he felt, of course, that they had failed.

"They might have got us with that one, Colonel," someone ventured to the air-force officer.

He nodded grimly. "They've been after us. We've been listening to their pilots talking back and forth. They aren't even bothering to code their conversation. They've got us spotted as the command ship and they're after us. Our masts

give us away. They'd like to get us. They'd like to get Hewitt
and Clark. They've got a good chance, too."

"That's nice to know," I said.

"Hell, it's the truth. The odd plane can always get through
any air defense and, if they're willing to take a loss, they
can send a bunch of them at us and some are bound to get
through. My God, a drink would do us all good now."

But there were no drinks. There was food, but no one
felt hungry. I went down to the cabin and shaved and took
a shower and tried to read a detective story. But I just
couldn't care who had murdered the millionaire, and so I gave
it up and finally fell asleep.

Van Alstyne woke me about six. "You can really sleep,
once you pop off," he said. "You slept through two General
Quarters."

"I wish I'd slept through that one this morning. I saw that
hit."

We went to the mess hall and the first person I saw was
Cy Peterman. It was good to see him alive. He wasn't feeling
very good. He had been in the wardroom with just one bulk-
head between him and the forward gun turrets. The blast
had knocked him a little silly, but he hadn't been hurt.

"I knew all those men," Cy said, as though he were talking
to himself.

"They were great. They never had a chance. That bomb
smashed right through that steel and exploded below. It didn't
kill anyone on the bridge. I don't know why. Captain Carey
is all right, thank God. He sent me over here with a British
Admiral we had on the *Savannah*. It looks like they'll save the
Savannah. It's down by the bow, but tonight they're going
to take it out to sea aways and, if it doesn't get hit, they'll
tow it to Malta. Or maybe it can get there under its own
steam. I don't know. . . . They were such good guys and
swell to me. They let me have the run of the ship."

Next morning Lionel Shapiro came to me with an idea he had. We had expected that within a day after the landing we would hold two or maybe three airfields. Arrangements had been made for press copy to be flown from those fields to Syracuse, Sicily. There were censors there and cables. Our stories could be sent from there. However, we didn't have those airfields yet, and Shapiro and Packard had been sending their copy ashore in the hope that it would be picked up by some fast PT boat and forwarded to Syracuse. Ken Clark had arranged that, but it was admittedly only a makeshift.

"Have you your story done?" Shapiro asked me.

"I've got two done, 4,000 words each. That's all *Collier's* can use on the whole operation," I told him. "But writing here, we're just writing to each other."

"You're about through then, as far as writing goes?" Shapiro asked.

"Sure, I've got all I can handle. Those stories are getting old down in my cabin."

"Well, now," Shapiro said, "Cy Peterman is in the same fix. Packard and I are going ashore and stay with the Fifth during the whole campaign, but I know you and Cy just wanted a few quick articles. I know how you can get to Syracuse pretty quickly with your copy and with mine. I heard that late this afternoon Montgomery's aide is coming here in one of those British sub chasers. He is coming to get a report from Clark to give Monty. Suppose you and Cy Peterman went back with him to Monty's headquarters with your stories and mine. Monty could get you to Syracuse somehow and you could file from there."

"It's an idea," I said. "I've had enough of this and, besides, I've got my story."

"I'll talk to the aide when he comes aboard. I know him," Shapiro said. "Incidentally, did you hear about Jack Belden? He got it—but bad. His leg was shattered, and he lay be-

tween our fire and theirs for five hours. That was yesterday.
They got him away though. He's on the way to Oran in a
destroyer."

What was it Jack Belden had said? "Here we go, trying
to beat the law of averages again." Jack hadn't beaten it this
time. I had—at least had up to now. The thought of Jack
wounded was a depressing one. I liked that guy. But sooner
or later, if you kept at it, you were bound to get hit.

"I bet Jack got a hell of a story," I said.

"Sure," Shapiro nodded. "But it's only a good story if you
get it on the cable."

A wave of homesickness hit me. It got into my throat and
my eyes and my consciousness. I wanted to go home and,
feeling as I did, it was about time I did. Seven months is a
long stretch to be away from home, especially if you felt
about your family as I did. It was tougher on the troops, I
knew. They couldn't suddenly decide they'd had enough and
head for home. Within limits, we correspondents could. And
I did have that cable in my pocket from *Collier's*.

Cy Peterman and I left that night. Packard had gone ashore,
but Sammy Schulman and Shapiro saw us off.

"For God's sake, don't lose my copy," Shapiro said. "And
get it off as soon as you can."

Schulman shook hands. "Remember I lent you a lighter a
few days ago?"

"You gave me a lighter a few days ago," I said, coldly.

"You only think I gave it to you. I lent it to you."

"Well, I need it, Sammy, and you have another one."

"So keep it." Then he added casually, "And listen, chum,
when you get back to New York give it to my wife, will
you? Tell her I'm swell."

"Sure, Sammy."

Cy and I walked down the gangway and stepped onto the
lean-looking sub chaser. It was the type of boat the British

[333]

call a motor launch. Monty's aide was a pleasant young chap and the captain of the boat was a tall, bearded youngster, Captain Friend. The *Ancon* loomed big above us. Schulman and Shapiro leaned over the rail and waved. We drew away from the *Ancon*. I had a moment's pang of disloyalty. I should have stayed, should have gone through the whole Italian campaign. Then I thought of home and blew a happy kiss to the ship. I'd had enough.

Syracuse, September, 1943

****

Chapter XVIII

THE CURTAIN RISES

CY AND I WERE too tired to sleep. We stood on the small bridge as our sleek hundred-footer slipped easily through the water. We kept looking back toward the Bay of Salerno, expecting any moment to see the long fingers of the tracer bullets search the night. It seemed too perfect a night for the Germans to ignore.

"I hope to God they don't hit the *Ancon*. I hope to God they don't hit the *Ancon*," I said to myself. Cy nodded and muttered something, and I realized I'd been talking or praying out loud.

We had dinner in the small wardroom with Monty's aide and Captain Friend. They gave us Spam and we pretended that it was a treat to us. Our army rations are the best in the world, but a steady diet of C rations does give you a bellyful of Spam. But we ate it, and the young captain actually produced beer—cold beer. It was almost unbelievably pleasant to know now that we were fifty miles from Salerno,

[335]

traveling south, and that we were very unlikely to run into anything disturbing. After dinner we went on deck again to look back, but no fireworks illumined the night. The fast ship purred along, not rolling or pitching. It seemed to skim over the surface of the water. There was a small dog on board. He was curious about everything.

"We've only had him two days," Friend explained. "He's an Eyetie dog we picked up. I don't think he's ever been on a ship before. He keeps looking for a tree."

We sat smoking—Peterman, Friend and I. Cy said lazily, "Do you know what you're sitting on?"

"I don't care what I'm sitting on," I told him sleepily.

"You're sitting on a depth charge," he said mildly. "But don't worry, it's only got 500 pounds of dynamite in it."

By now I was too sleepy to care. So was Cy. We went below and had the first undisturbed sleep in six days. Friend woke us at seven, just as we were coming into a picture-postcard harbor. This was Pizzo. The Eighth Army had landed here. Two LCIs, listing foolishly, showed that their landing had not been entirely unopposed.

Hills green with September foliage rose steeply behind the beach, and here and there red-thatched roofs covering white houses dotted the hillsides. The morning was clean and cool and peaceful. We had breakfast of sausage and a fried egg each. I hadn't had English sausage for some time.

"You know, when I was in London they used to make sausages out of bread crumbs," I said. "I see they've switched. They're using either sawdust or paper now."

"Aren't they bloody awful?" Friend said, looking admiringly at the sausage. "We can certainly do dreadful things to food, can't we?"

"You can," I told him.

"But those chaps on the *Ancon* were good to us. They gave me a carton of American cigarettes and a tin of coffee."

"A can of coffee," I corrected.

"In a tin or a can, it's still wonderful," he agreed amiably.

An hour later a jeep came for Cy and me. General Montgomery would be glad to see us. We tossed our musette bags and typewriters into the jeep and then tossed ourselves in behind them. Monty's headquarters were about four miles back of the coast, high in the hills. It was a beautiful drive over winding but excellent roads. I remembered travelers coming back from Italy full of praise for Mussolini. "The trains run on time and the roads are marvelous," they'd say. Dictators are great ones for making trains run on time and for building marvelous roads. About every mile we'd run into a gun that had been blasted by the fire of naval craft. It was very comforting to see big 88's lying on their backs, their gun barrels twisted grotesquely. It had taken accurate firing to get these guns on the hill roads, for now we were perhaps 800 feet above the harbor. We drove past some lovely villas and then the jeep turned into an olive grove. There were a dozen brown tents and three large trucks.

"This is the boss's headquarters," our driver said.

"Where?" I asked.

"Those trucks. He lives in them."

Peterman and I got out of the jeep (you really get "off" a jeep) and the door of one of the trucks opened and out hopped Monty's young aide. He took us to one of the other trucks, knocked at the door and Monty appeared. It was the first time I'd ever seen Montgomery, and I was surprised to find that he looked exactly as he did in pictures. So many generals don't. The sincere friendliness and warmth of General Eisenhower, for instance, is never really captured by the camera. General Spaatz too, mildest and most likable of men, looks like a martinet in pictures. But Monty looked exactly as one imagines he'd look. I'd heard a hundred stories (most undoubtedly apocryphal) about Monty. Winston

Churchill has said of him, "Impossible in defeat; intolerable in victory." Monty is a teetotaler, a vegetarian, and he doesn't smoke. Once he said to Churchill (according to the usual unreliable reports), "I don't drink, and I don't smoke. I get plenty of sleep, and I expect to live until I'm one hundred." Churchill snorted, "I drink and smoke and never get any sleep, and I expect to live to be two hundred."

Monty was dressed in shorts and a shirt open at the neck, and he wore his black beret. He greeted us cordially and suggested that we sit under the trees. It was pleasant sitting there, and peaceful, and the war seemed very far away. Nothing could have been less like the headquarters of perhaps the world's best tactical general. No members of his staff were around. No orderly or aides interrupted us. We sat there, and Monty said, "It's warm today. Let's have some lemonade. All right?"

Cy and I nodded, and then Montgomery, looking at us closely said, "How about a drop of gin in it? It'll do you both good."

Being asked by the famed teetotaler to have a drink was a shock. An orderly brought three tall glasses. He had put more than a drop of gin in our two glasses, but it tasted fine. We sat in comfortable chairs under a shady olive tree from which there hung a large birdcage. Four birds kept flitting about, singing happily.

"I bought these in Tunis," Monty laughed, noticing my glance at the birds. "They're bright little things and they sing well. They cost me a pound apiece, but it was money well spent. I take them along wherever I go."

We talked of the Sicilian campaign, and he expressed great admiration for General Omar Bradley. Bradley had been on his flank.

"He's a fine man and a fine general," Monty said, with animation. "Your generals are all fine. And, of course, General Eisenhower is magnificent. I made a little bet with him during the Sicilian show. I bet him I'd be in Catania within ten days of our bet. Well, I was there, so Eisenhower had to pay up. He had to give me a Flying Fortress. That's a great aircraft, but it almost killed me one day, so I gave it up. You know that short airfield at Palermo where you land down-hill? Well, they told us that a Fortress could land there all right, and we tried it. But we didn't have room enough to turn for our run and, if it hadn't been for some smart work on the part of Benson—he's my American pilot—things would have been very bad. So I gave the aircraft back to Eisenhower and asked him for something that landed a bit slower; something I could use on those short Sicilian airfields or on the small Italian airfields. He gave me a C-47, and I'm tickled to death with it. I just drive my jeep aboard and off we go. Are you from New York, by any chance?"

I told him that I was.

"I want to see New York after the war," he said thought-fully. "Wendell Willkie is a good friend of mine. He invited me to visit him after it's over. Said he'd show me New York."

"You really have to stay up late to see New York, sir," I told him. "But Willkie is the man to show you our town."

"Stay up late?" That alarmed him. "Oh, no. No, I never stay up late. The Salerno show is very difficult, isn't it?" He changed back to military matters without breaking his stride. "I wish I could get up there quickly to help Mark Clark. But it will take time. I'm giving my army two days of rest."

"Two days' rest," I exploded, thinking how sorely needed the Eighth was at Salerno.

"Yes," he said calmly. "I've been going hard lately; going fast, and my administration hasn't caught up with us." (By "administration" Montgomery meant supplies, communications, etc.) "Of course, the men don't call it a rest. Actually,

[339]

you know, I just stopped the advance to give them two days of training."

Peterman and I looked incredulous. We could think of no army in the world which needed "training" less than the Eighth. Veteran of three years of warfare, there couldn't be anything about fighting that the Eighth didn't know. Even our own men admitted that the Eighth was the best army in the world.

"The more you fight the more you have to train," Montgomery went on thoughtfully. "During these two days my officers will go over the mistakes we've made the past few weeks. The men won't make those mistakes again. Yes," he said, obviously relishing the phrase, "the more you fight the more you have to train. You see, a great army is an army that can fight anywhere, any time. When we finished fighting in North Africa, people thought that we were just specialists in desert warfare. Well, we were. The desert presents problems no other terrain presents. But when we hit Sicily we had a different terrain, and we had to adjust our fighting to that terrain. But a good army, a well-trained army, can do that without difficulty. A good army should be able to fight in the desert or in the Arctic. But to achieve that kind of efficiency you've got to train, train, train, constantly. Especially when you're fighting the Germans."

Montgomery's face was a study in concentration. When he talked it was as though he were thinking aloud, for he didn't address either Peterman or myself. He sat hunched forward, tracing patterns on the ground with his small swagger stick.

"They're great fighters, those Germans," he said slowly. "They're professionals. General Rommel is a fine General. That is, if you let him take the initiative. You can't let him do that, or he'll beat you. You've got to figure out what he is going to do—he usually does the orthodox thing—and then strike first; tip him off balance, as it were. I did that in Libya and Tripoli. You can't give him the initiative. Yes, the Germans are fine, professional soldiers. The Italians are not. They show that in the way they treat prisoners. The Germans treat prisoners well—as professional armies do. The Eyeties do not. In the matter of caring for their own wounded, the Germans are professional too. Seldom do we find German wounded when we advance. They've been taken away. And they bury their dead, too. That's a sign of a professional army. Lately, they've been burying their dead naked. This may mean they're short of clothing. In Sicily I had a rather bad time at one point and, after we had taken a hill, I wanted to know who we had been fighting. My men dug up a grave. They found six naked bodies in it. From the identification disks around their necks we discovered that they were Germans. All naked. They did that in Sicily, buried them six to a grave. . . . Yes, they're good, professional soldiers.

"Did you know," he smiled and his eyes twinkled, "I have two Italian divisions fighting for me now? They actually came over to me. Well, I didn't know what to do with them, so I suggested that they do police work behind us as we advanced. And another thing," he laughed, "I told them I could use some sappers. Yes, indeed, I could use some men to go ahead of us to clear out mines. Rather dangerous work. It'll be interesting to see how they work out."

Twice Peterman and I made a move to go; twice he waved us back into our seats. He was relaxed and enjoying his talk. Perhaps it was because he had such an obviously appreciative audience. He answered every question we asked and never once did he invoke that phrase so dreaded by us, "This is off the record." He had our glasses refilled and then he insisted on showing us through his trucks.

"I captured this one from General Messe in Tripoli," Montgomery laughed. "Quite comfortable, don't you agree?"

We did agree. The inside of the truck was lined with cedar

[341]

walls, and it held a large bed, a desk and a bathroom complete with everything including shower. The room (you could only think of it as a room) was immaculate, and you felt as though you were in one of these pre-war luxury trailers.

"Let me show you my guest room. I captured this one from old Electric Whiskers General Bergenzella," Montgomery said, as pleased as a kid showing off a new set of electric trains. The second truck was as neat and as comfortable as the first. This had a gleaming, white-tiled bathtub. There were two bunks, electric lights, and pictures hanging on the walls. Muslin curtains framed the two small windows of the truck.

"The King liked this. So did Wendell Willkie, when he stayed with me. Have you seen this?"

Montgomery pulled his famous Australian hat out of a closet. On it was pinned the insignia of every outfit in his army. There must have been forty regimental badges pinned on the hat. Some were Australian, some New Zealand, some South African and some English. The third truck of his mobile headquarters contained nothing but maps. Maps of past campaigns and then the map he was using at the moment.

"I captured two airports yesterday," he said casually, pointing to the map of Southern Italy. "They may come in handy, but none of these airfields we have here are all-weather airfields. They're like the Sicilian fields—no concrete runways. When the rains come, they'll be nothing but mud. I'm afraid we can't give Tedder and Tooey Spaatz much help until we capture some all-weather airfields for them. We may get some at Foggia. I'll be there in a week or so."

We came out into the bright sun again. It was almost noon. A cool breeze from the sea took the bite out of the sun. A command car had driven up and was waiting for us. Monty walked to the car with us.

"I've been listening to the BBC the last few days," he said.

"They seem very optimistic. I suppose people at home think that now we've invaded Italy the war is about over. Do they feel that way in your country?"

"I imagine so. We're optimistic by nature."

"Oh, if they only knew the truth! You chaps should tell them," he said earnestly. "Invading Italy only means that the war has finally begun. The other campaigns were preliminary actions. Libya, Tripoli, North Africa, and even Sicily. But now we have landed on the enemy mainland. Now we are really at grips with him. Yes, this means that the war has finally begun. Yes," he repeated, "it has just begun."

We shook hands and climbed into the command car. "This man will take you to Reggio. That's just across from Messina. A ferry runs across the Straits every hour. Go to the naval base at Messina and they'll take care of you. You want to reach Syracuse, don't you?"

"We want to get wherever we can find censors and cables," Peterman said. "Syracuse, or Malta or Palermo or Algiers."

"Well, I can get you as far as Reggio anyhow," Montgomery grinned. "It's a pleasant drive, and I've had the men put some food in your car. By the way," he said very casually, almost bashfully, "I read in some American magazine— do you have a magazine called *Time* or *Life*, or something like that? You do? Well, I read that girls in New York are wearing hats modeled after my beret. Is that true?"

We laughed and said it was undoubtedly true and he stood there as we drove away, a slight figure, who should have looked rather absurd in his shorts and his jaunty black beret— but who somehow didn't.

Peterman and I looked at each other.

"What do you think of him?" I asked.

"I think he was bit by a fox when he was young," Cy said. "No fool—he. He knows the answers."

[343]

I agreed. "I'm glad he's on our side. How about those notes?"

"I got pages of them," Cy said gleefully. "And he never said 'off the record' once."

"You've got the first exclusive newspaper interview he ever gave, as far as I know."

"Sure," Cy said gloomily, "and not a censor or a cable office within 300 miles."

Time after time our progress was halted by huge convoys of supplies coming the other way. These were run in typically efficient Montgomery manner. There were soldiers acting as traffic cops all the way from Pizzo to Reggio. They wore distinguishing armbands, and they waved the trucks on, urging them to travel faster. This was Montgomery's "administration" catching up with him. We must have passed at least 3,000 trucks, amphibious "ducks," field kitchens, tanks, heavy guns—all traveling fast. Never once did we see a vehicle pulled off the roadside for repairs. They all ran smoothly, without any jamming or crowding—this was the Eighth Army. We went through Tropes and Nicotera and finally reached Scilla on the Italian side of the Straits of Messina. We stopped and looked over toward Sicily.

"These Eyeties don't even know how to spell," Peterman said. "When I went to school this place was spelled S-c-y-l-l-a. And where there is a Scylla there must be a Charybdis."

"That rock over there isn't Gibraltar," I told him, pointing.

It was Charybdis, all right, but we saw no beautiful mermaid enticing passing mariners, but maybe Ovid was only kidding us about the whole thing. The Straits were calm and the sun glistened on the smooth water. We went on to Reggio. For days our big guns across in Sicily had lambasted the city. Reggio was virtually deserted. We drove to the dock and, with the luck we'd been having, weren't surprised to find a ferry just ready to leave. It was a big LCI, and it crossed over to Messina in half an hour. Seen from a distance, Messina was lovely. When we entered the harbor, a circular basin open only on the north, its small opening protected by a boom, Messina was something else again.

"This place looks as though an earthquake hit it," I said to Cy.

"It did," my scholarly colleague said. "Back in 1908, and it killed 50,000 people."

Messina was born to misery. It was destroyed first by the Carthaginians in 400 B.C. Ever since then it has been getting kicked around, if not by Octavian or the Saracens or Charles I of Anjou, it was the plague or obstreperous behavior on the part of its neighbor, an unruly character named Mount Aetna. But Messina didn't know what a beating was until Tooey Spaatz and his Fortresses came along. Messina had the misfortune to be a definite military objective. It controlled the Straits of Messina; it was the last stronghold in Sicily defended by the Germans. It had to be destroyed and, when Spaatz and his merry men set out to destroy a city, they don't miss. Messina looked like something a child had built with toy blocks and had then carelessly knocked over. You felt like averting your eyes when you saw Messina.

The commander of the port was an alert-looking British captain. He received us affably. He smiled as though secretly amused when neither Cy nor I wanted to talk of Salerno. All we wanted was to get to a cable office. Syracuse was the nearest. That was an overnight jaunt by sea, but it so happened that there was a gunboat leaving within half an hour for Augusta, only thirty miles from Syracuse. If we didn't mind being crowded? We didn't mind, so we soon found ourselves on a rather dingy and very old gunboat. It was a nice night and a pleasant trip, even though we had to sleep on the floor of the wardroom. At dawn we found ourselves entering the harbor of Augusta. Augusta, too, looked lopsided. There were six Eyetie submarines lying in the harbor. They had come in a few days before. They still flew the Italian flag. There was an RAF mess just off the pier and we went to it and dove into sausage and eggs and hot, well-brewed tea. The boss man gave us a jeep and a driver to take us to Syracuse. We were having fantastic luck on transport. The luck held until we reached the headquarters of Press Relations. The combined British and American staff were all old friends and it was pleasant enough, but Lieutenant Colonel Max Boyd, in charge, laughed when I told him I had about 8,000 words to send to *Collier's.*

"Our facilities are pretty limited," he said. "We can only send about that many words a day and we have to take care of stories coming from Salerno and from the Eighth Army. Why not go back to Algiers? I can get you on a plane first thing in the morning."

I decided to do that, while Cy decided to go to Malta to see if he could salvage some of his gear from the *Savannah,* which had been towed there during the night. Meanwhile we had a bright afternoon and a nice-looking beach, so we took advantage of both. Max Boyd somehow wangled me a high priority on a plane next morning and, within four hours, I was in Algiers, my stories were filed, and I was on my way home. Of course, it wasn't quite that simple. For the moment the air route was jammed, so I decided to travel by boat. Our PRO men said that plenty of boats were leaving Oran. I might catch a fast one that traveled without escort and which made the trip in nine or ten days. I'd rather travel by boat than plane any time, so I jumped at that idea. I found that I had become allergic to airplanes—even friendly ones. Then, too, I was still slightly deaf from that five-inch gun on the *Ancon.* I also had a bit of a hangover from my various attacks of dysentery. A boat ride would mean a good rest, and I'd arrive in New York feeling good. Off to Oran I went.

I was in for a shock. No ships were due to leave for at least two or three weeks, and they would be slow-moving boats in convoy. The naval authorities were fine, though. They had a few places on the American Export flying boats which left from a base in the Casablanca region. I had been accredited to the navy in the Salerno show, hadn't I? That's right, I said, I had. Well, then there was no difficulty. The navy would give me traveling orders. I would represent the navy. When you're in the war zone red tape is virtually unknown. Before leaving Oran I went to see Jack Belden, who was in the military hospital. His leg was in a huge cast and it was stuck out above him in one of those pulley arrangements. Belden was furious. He'd have to stay there for months, he said, until all those smashed bone fragments knitted.

"The hell of it is, that I feel all right," Jack said gloomily. "Everything is all right about me but my leg."

"Did you hear from your office on that story you wrote?"

Jack nodded. "I got a nice cable. I guess they liked the story."

"Liked it!" I yelled. "Listen, you dope—you wrote the best story to come out of the war so far. It was so good that the censors in Algiers hated to cut it. Even though you had some lines in it that should have been cut. So they sent the story along to GHQ asking if those lines could remain. They say it went right up to Ike, and he thought it was so good that he okayed it. That's what we hear around PRO in Algiers."

"That's nice. I wonder if Ike really did read it?" In his admiration and liking for General Eisenhower, Belden was like the rest of us. If I refer to the Commander in Chief as "Ike" it is only because that was the custom among ourselves. I needn't add that he was always "Sir" to us when we met him at press conferences. It is a habit with us to use nicknames or first names in discussing the mighty. Just as Eisenhower was

[347]

always Ike, so was General Sir Harold Alexander always Alex; Montgomery was never anything but Monty while General Doolittle was Jimmy and General Spaatz invariably Tooey. Some of the generals we had known since our London days, and we had become really friendly with them. We knew men like General Terry Allen, General Robert Mc-Clure, General Roosevelt and a few others well enough to address them familiarly, but for the most part we felt the same constraint and discipline and used the same address to the high-ranking officers that any captain would use. Technically, we had the rank of captain. This was in case we were captured. Then we would be given the treatment called for by our rank. Incidentally, we would also be given the pay of an army captain.

The flight from Oran to the air base in West Africa was a nasty one. We flew to Gibraltar first, and landing there is not exactly my idea of good, clean fun. The ceiling was low and we were never more than 400 feet above the waters of the Mediterranean. Someone said casually, "there it is," and to the left of us, seemingly some four or five feet off our wing tip, was the big Rock. A thin white shroud of fog was wrapped around its top. We had to make two tries before we landed—a common occurrence at Gibraltar. The concrete runway is right in the shadow of the Rock and the huge hunk of limestone pitted with caves does strange things to the wind currents. Sometimes pilots find themselves "landing" a hundred feet above the runway; sometimes (and this often spells disaster) fifty feet below it. Many planes taking off from Gib's runway have gone right into the water as a down draught took control. Pilots hate landing or taking off from the Rock. But we made it, refueled and then left for the base. This was a naval air base in charge of Captain William Turner, a cheerful, regular navy man who knew his job thoroughly. He had organized a pleasant officers' club and offered me its hospitality. I'd be off in two or three days, he said.

"You're lucky," he added. "This is about the last trip that will be made via the northern route. You go directly to Foynes, spend a day there, and then you're off for New York. A nice, quick, two-day trip. But I see your passport is expired. I'll send you to Casa where we have a Consul."

I'd actually forgotten that sometimes passports were still being used. I hadn't been asked to show mine since leaving Russia. When you travel on army planes in uniform the formalities are negligible. Both our army and navy are scrupulously meticulous in investigating you before you become an accredited correspondent, but once you are accredited you are trusted completely and accepted by the armed forces as one of them. The next morning Captain Turner had a car and driver waiting for me, and I headed for Casablanca to have my passport brought up to date. I'd never been to Casa before. It was immaculately clean, a rarity in African cities.

"Is there really a Rick's Café here?" I asked the sailor who was driving me.

"Naw," he said in disgust. "Soon as we got here we all went looking for it, but it was a phony. There's no Rick's Café in Casa." Rick's Café was the scene of Humphrey Bogart's adventures in the picture *Casablanca*. It didn't take long to have my passport taken care of, and then I had two hours to kill before my driver was ready to leave. I thought I might go sightseeing in the native quarter, but then I passed Red Cross headquarters and saw they were showing a picture called *Action in the North Atlantic*. I noticed that two of my favorite actors were in it, Bogart and Sam Levene. I wavered and was lost. I'd much rather see a good movie than a good city any time. I spent two hours living through a couple of tough convoy trips with Bogart, Sam and the others.

Then I headed back to Captain Turner. I was really ashamed to say I'd spent the afternoon at the movies instead of taking the opportunity to look over one of the most interesting cities in Africa. Al Jolson and Harry Akst, the song writer, had arrived. Jolson was hoarse from a long stretch of singing at camps in Sicily and North Africa, and he had a bad cold, but he insisted upon giving a show for the base. It was a good show, and afterwards, Harry Akst, a great man on those keys, sat around with the men for hours playing anything they asked for.

"They asked for every song you ever heard of," Harry moaned later, "except 'Dinah.'" Harry had written Dinah.

I've been home for a month now and for the first time in seven months I'm completely bewildered. It was a shock to pick up the papers and read columns of criticism of our war effort. Everything I saw in the war zone led me to believe that our matériel was the best in the world; that a military miracle had been achieved in the rapid training of our troops; that our war effort was being handled with a minimum of red tape, lost effort and inefficiency. I knew that neither General Marshall nor General Eisenhower could wave magic wands and have the ships arrive in the Mediterranean right on time, loaded with just what we needed for combat. I felt that somebody back home must be doing a wonderful job of organization and administration to effect this result. I knew that when an American soldier set foot on an enemy beach he had the best equipment possible. He had everything that human ingenuity could give him to protect himself and to minimize his danger. He even had two ampoules of morphine and a package of sulfa powder in his pocket. His emergency rations were the best ever devised, and they even included something which, to the GI, is more important than food—cigarettes and matches. Somebody back home must have been responsible for all this. The army couldn't do it alone. Yet, from the papers, one would think that Washington was a madhouse, inhabited by certified lunatics, crooks or shady politicians. It was disheartening, because when you first come home you're so filled with pride at the great job America has done and is doing that you feel like waving a flag. You get so impatient with the snide, petty criticism of our leaders that you end up by diving into the sport pages. You read the most senseless, absurd speeches by some of our duly elected members of Congress, and you shudder and wonder why they don't inform themselves about conditions before they spout at great length and always within the framework of their preconceived political convictions. When you return you are laboring under the apparently absurd delusion that we are at war with Japan and Germany. Reading some newspapers, you might be pardoned for thinking that we are at war with Britain and with the President of the United States.

I arrived home and immediately went to a quiet resort for a week to catch my breath and to get accustomed to the fact that when you are awakened at night by the sound of an airplane engine you don't have to freeze with terror or look for a slit trench. It takes some time to realize that any plane you hear back home is a friendly one. I tolerated the lovely country resort for a week. Elderly gentlemen dressed each night for dinner and then dozed off in comfortable chairs in the hotel lobby. I felt that every now and then one of them would wake up and stop a passing bellboy to ask, "Is Roosevelt dead yet?" When the bellboy said "No," the elderly, black-tied gentleman would look disappointed and then go back to sleep.

At the resort a man asked me where I lived. I told him I lived in New York City. "How awful!" he said, looking at me sympathetically. "All you see there are Jews."

[351]

"I'm used to being with Jews," I told him. "Where I've been lately the place is full of them."

"Where have you been?" he asked.

"I've been with the First Division in Sicily," I said. "Full of Jews. It'll please you to know a hell of a lot of them were killed."

He looked at me and blinked, not understanding, and I walked away because I was a little afraid that I might get sick or slug him.

This was the America I returned to. Our men abroad deserve something better than a country which is still stupid with reaction and prejudice. There are no Democrats, no Republicans at the front. There are no Protestants, no Catholics, no Jews at the front. There are men in uniform who, at the very best, are giving up a year or two of their lives to serve a country they believe in. To paraphrase Tolstoy again, those maggots who continually gnaw at the healthy body of America perhaps can do no permanent harm, but we would be fools to allow them to go too far.

I know of no one in America (except the parents and wives and children of the dead) who has as yet been called upon to make any real sacrifice. We suffer some minor inconveniences, but actually the war hasn't touched us yet. It hasn't touched us as it has touched the people of Britain or Russia. I am sure that if we were called upon to make the sacrifices they have made we, as a people, would be quite equal to our destiny. Whether that time will ever come, I don't know. I doubt it very much. But if the time does come it may find us unprepared, mentally. It is a shock to anyone returning from the front to hear people talk and write of the German Army with contempt. Our people, for some strange reason, fear and hate the Japs but dismiss the Germans casually. It is merely a matter of mopping up now, they tell you. You can't discuss the war for half an hour without hearing someone say, "Oh,

Germany will crack up any minute now. I remember back in 1918 . . ." Maybe Germany will crack suddenly from within. I hope so. I know that neither the American nor British G-2 have any concrete information which would provide evidence to that effect. I do know that within the past few months Germany has put into combat the Focke-Wulf 200, a magnificent heavy aircraft, so well armed that nothing we have can as yet cope with it on equal terms. Pilots on anti-submarine patrol off the coasts of Portugal and Africa have told me that this plane scares them, so that they shy off whenever they can, instead of risking combat. I know the German submarines were inactive for some months and, while credulous wishful thinkers chortled, "The submarine menace is ended," our naval men warned, "The chances are they've been called in to be fitted with new weapons." That proved to be the case. I know that no fighter plane in the world (with the possible exception of the Spitfire 9) can compare with the German Focke-Fulf 190. Our pilots have told me this.

I know that the Germans have a bomb, rocket-propelled, that has our research men going gray. This was the bomb that hit the *Savannah*; the one that sank the battleship *Roma*.

Our combat generals think the German Army is as strong as ever. They may be wrong but, after all, their opinion, based on experience, seems worth considering. They don't think that we can lose this war, but they don't see yet how we can win it. Neither do I. Once we really take Italy and have air bases in Northern Italy the real job of invading Germany will come. The great air invasion of the past few months has been the prelude. I can't forget what General Montgomery said, "The war has finally begun." I think he is right. The preliminaries are over. The actors have learned their lines. The dress rehearsal has been held. The orchestra has played the overture. The play is about to begin. The curtain rises.

New York, December, 1943